HX
313.5
R54
1990

Rigby, T. H. (Thomas
Henry), 1925-

The changing Soviet
system.

$49.95

DATE			

THE CHANGING SOVIET SYSTEM

For Richard and Kate

The Changing Soviet System

Mono-organisational Socialism from its
Origins to Gorbachev's Restructuring

T.H. Rigby

Edward Elgar

Published by
Edward Elgar Publishing Limited
Gower House
Croft Road
Aldershot
Hants GU11 3HR
England

Edward Elgar Publishing Company
Old Post Road
Brookfield
Vermont 05036
USA

British Library Cataloguing in Publication Data
Rigby, T.H. (Thomas Henry), 1925–
   The changing Soviet system : mono-
   organisational socialism from its origins to
   Gorbachev's restructuring.
   1. Soviet Union. Politics, history
   I. Title
   320.947

ISBN 1–85278–304–4

Printed in Great Britain by
Billing & Sons Ltd, Worcester

Contents

Acknowledgements

The material collected in this volume reflects my research and reflections, over a period of nearly forty years, on the origins, nature and evolution of the Soviet socio-political order. It owes much to the assistance provided by a large variety of institutions and colleagues in several countries. To mention them separately would amount to a veritable catalogue of Soviet studies since the 1940s, but I cannot forego this opportunity to express my profound gratitude to all who have helped me with their encouragement, advice, example, criticism or professional services. Some special debts are recorded in the Introduction. Everything here was written at the Australian National University, and I wish to record my appreciation of the privilege of working for half a lifetime in this unique institution.

I owe the idea of this collection and its companion volume *Political Elites in the USSR* to Edward Elgar, and he and Julie Leppard have been unfailingly helpful, sagacious and efficient at all stages of its production. My special thanks are due to Brigitte Coles and Christine Treadwell, who transmuted my ball-point scrawl into impeccable camera-ready copy.

Six of the nine chapters here have been published previously. Full details are given at the beginning of the chapters concerned, and I should like to express my appreciation here to the original publishers for their agreement to my including them in this volume: to *World Politics* for Chapter 3; to W.W. Norton & Co. Inc., for Chapter 4; to Praeger Publishers for Chapter 5; to *Comparative Politics* for Chapter 6; to the Macmillan Press Ltd for Chapter 7; and to *Survey* for Chapter 8.

T.H. Rigby

Canberra, February 1990

vii

1 Introduction

The purpose of this volume is to make more readily available a number of essays on the origins, nature and development of the Soviet socio-political system, which I have published in various places over the past three decades, and to offer an interpretation of the changes that system has undergone since the election of Mikhail Gorbachev as General Secretary.

In this chapter I shall introduce the main concepts and themes considered in the book and say something about *their* origins and development. Mindful of how tedious the ageing scholar in autobiographical mode can be, I shall be sparing with the reminiscences, but the history of Western ideas about the Soviet Union is of no little intellectual and practical interest, particularly in a period of major change in that country, so a few paragraphs relevant to my own modest involvement may be in order.

The Path to a Concept

Had pre-history or anthropology been subjects available at Melbourne University at the end of the Second World War I may never have made the Soviet Union the focus of my life's work. Since they were not, I found myself studying Russian, largely because that was the most exotic language being taught, and political science, to which I was seduced by Percy Partridge's lectures. Still, these choices were, perhaps, not entirely fortuitous. A thoughtful lad brought up in a working class neighbourhood during the 1930s and with three years of army service behind him was unlikely to be entirely indifferent to the USSR, and I certainly was not. On the strength of reading Hewlett Johnson's *The Socialist Sixth of the World* and a little quiet persuasion after an Army Education lecture, I had applied to join the Australian Communist Party, and managed to attend two clandestine cell meetings in the Morotai bush before leaving for home. It was enough, however: our 'leader' displayed the same dreary dogmatism encountered in the religious enthusiasts with whom I had disputed in my high school years; put on my guard, I proceeded, once home, to read all I could find both 'for' and 'against', and the available literature even at that time afforded signs enough that something terrible had gone wrong on the way to Utopia. So, when the local party branch finally sent my membership card, I promptly returned it, with a letter of earnest pomposity appropriate to my 21 years.

Still, my curiosity was well and truly kindled, to be copiously fuelled by the noisy student debates between our communists, who had taken over the University's most influential political club, and their varied critics, and perhaps even more, by my studies of Russian literature and Soviet politics and history. Some of the ideas that figure large in later chapters of this volume began to form during these undergraduate years, and with my MA thesis, entitled 'The Soviet View on Southeast Asia', I took my first untutored steps in 'Sovietological' research.

My heaviest intellectual debts during these apprenticeship years were to Karl Marx and Max Weber, although I could never claim to be a real disciple of either. From Marx I learned first and foremost the importance of basic processes and relationships of socio-economic activity as determinants of social structure. But I had serious misgivings almost from the beginning about his stress on forms of property, largely because I could not see how this could be accommodated to any plausible account of the social distribution of power and privilege in the USSR. Here the ideas of Trotsky and certain of his followers proved stimulating (particularly Trotsky's *The Revolution Betrayed* and James Burnham's *The Managerial Revolution*) although not entirely convincing.

It was at this point, in my final (third) undergraduate year, that I was introduced to Weber[1] and soon found myself captivated by his typological analysis of the forms of domination (*Herrschaft*) and authority. True, there emerged what seemed to me certain conceptual inconsistencies, but in struggling with these I became aware that behind Weber's typology of authority, which was tied to forms of legitimation, one could glimpse the vague outlines of a typology of more fundamental elements of social structure, which I was to term 'modes of coordination'. This, in turn, offered a way of describing and classifying societies which, it seemed to me, allowed a more adequate characterisation and socio-historical 'placing' of Soviet society than those attempted in terms of Marxist categories.

That was in 1949, and it was to be 14 years before I returned to these matters. Throughout this period, whether engaged on my MA and PhD theses (the latter in London on 'The Selection of Leading Personnel in the Soviet State and Communist Party' under the non-intrusive supervision of W.A. Robson and Hugh Seton-Watson), working in the Research Department of the UK Foreign Office and the British Embassy in Moscow (where I was fortunate to serve with E.E. Orchard, the most knowledgeable – though non-publishing – British specialist on Soviet politics), collaborating with Leonard Schapiro on his book *The Communist Party of the Soviet Union*, teaching at the Canberra University College, or researching as a visiting scholar at Columbia University's Russian Institute, I was concerned above all to build up my empirical knowledge of Soviet society and its political system. Then in 1963, having joined the Australian National University's Research School of Social Sciences, I took part in a study group on Weber convened by Percy Partridge, and began to work seriously again on those theoretical questions I have just outlined. From this there emerged two papers, 'Traditional, Market and Organizational Societies and the USSR', *World Politics*, 1964, (reproduced as Chapter 3 of this book), and 'Max Weber's Typology of Authority: A Difficulty and Some Suggestions' (*The Australian and New Zealand Journal of Sociology*, 1966; its central argument is outlined below in Chapter 7, pp.175–76).

Having arrived at my first ontogenetical sketch of the Soviet socio-political system as what I was eventually to term 'mono-organisational socialism', the focal concept of this book, I can conscientiously spare the reader further reminiscences, and proceed directly to an outline of that concept in its mature form.

Mono-organisational Socialism in the USSR

I was tempted to call this book *The Soviet Enterprise*, a pun that encapsulates both the genesis and the sociology of the system. On the one hand, when Lenin's Bolsheviks took power in 1917 they were launching an enterprise of breathtaking consequence: to transform human society from top to bottom, destroying capitalism and building communism on its ruins. On the other hand, what came out of their efforts was an enterprise in the sense in which Alfred G. Meyer once wrote of 'USSR Incorporated'.[2] Meyer did not intend this merely as a heuristic analogy, as have those who have written similarly of 'Japan Incorporated'.[3] He meant that Soviet society, unlike that of Japan or any other capitalist country, even a 'totalitarian' one like Nazi Germany, was wholly run by a congeries of official hierarchies, each of them enjoying a monopoly in a given field of activity, and bound together and integrated by the hierarchy of the Communist Party apparatus, into a single centralised organisational structure, much as if all legally operating entities in the society had been taken over and were being run by a single giant firm. Other writers, too, have stressed this aspect of Soviet society, notably Allen Kassof and Maria Hirszowicz who have written respectively of the 'administered society' and the 'bureaucratic Leviathan',[4] and most specialists, perhaps, would see this as a feature unique to systems of the Soviet type, although not all would see it as their central, defining feature. I shall be arguing its centrality in what follows.

The pun is thus intended to enlighten, not to amuse. It is of fundamental importance to understand that Soviet society is an 'enterprise' in both these meanings of the term, if one is to make sense of how that society has developed and how it operates. At the same time, while surely not foreordained by some inexorable logic or historical necessity, the two aspects were in fact welded together into the foundations of the new Soviet order from its beginnings, and it is not difficult to see elements in the pre-history of this order which made this outcome – to put it no more strongly – a distinct possibility.

The realities of Soviet society today seem remote indeed from the ideal of socialism and communism (then scarcely distinguished) espoused by Marx and his early followers, namely a society of freely cooperating individuals with no state officialdom to command and coerce them. Yet Marxists believed from the start that achieving their ideal would require them to organise and lead a party that could mobilise the working class to overthrow their oppressors, and that they would have to make use of the state machine to create the new social order, even if there proved to be disagreement as to how much 'the proletariat' could make use of the 'bourgeois' state for this purpose, and although the 'proletarian state' was to begin 'withering away' as the new order entrenched itself. There was, moreover, a Saint-Simonian strand to Marxist socialism which was inspired less by the dream of a society without compulsion than by a yen for a rationally managed order to replace the 'chaos' of capitalism.

Perhaps, therefore, it is not to be wondered at that certain perceptive observers did not have to await the evidence afforded by post-revolutionary Russia to discern in the pre-revolutionary socialist movement the roots of a new form of bureaucratic despotism and a new exploitative society. 'Socialism', Max Weber foretold, 'would require a still higher degree of formal bureaucratisation than capitalism';[5] as Gerth and Mills have commented, 'the state would indeed become total, and Weber, hating bureaucracy as a shackle upon the liberal individual, felt that socialism would thus lead to a further serfdom'.[6] In the case of Robert Michels, a similar pessimism was reinforced by the expectation that the omnicompetent bureaucracy of the socialist state would be run by an uncontrollable oligarchy.[7] Perhaps most prescient of all was J.W. Machajski, who came to see in Marxist socialism a movement to overthrow capitalism in the interests not of the proletariat, but of the 'intellectual workers', who would become a new ruling class-based on a form of knowledge capital.[8]

If some of Lenin's contemporaries thus descried in Marxist socialism the potential for bureaucratic despotism, few would have been surprised that it was precisely Lenin's wing of revolutionary Marxism that actualised this potential. For Bolshevism was widely seen, by Russian and foreign observers alike, as manifesting in extreme form those elements in Marxism most apt to engender such a caricature of the socialist ideal: the elevation of the party organisation over the ordinary worker and citizen, the stress on discipline and hierarchy, the rejection of any legal or moral inhibitions on the actions of a revolutionary leadership, and so on. In the next chapter I shall be examining the experience of pre-revolutionary Bolshevism with this issue in mind, and later in the present chapter I shall review some of the arguments for an alternative explanation of the emergence of a mono-organisational society in the USSR, namely that the trend towards such a society was already present in pre-revolutionary Russia, so that Bolshevism figures more as a catalyst than as a prime cause. Before going on to that, however, it is time to offer a first outline of my view of Soviet society as mono-organisational socialism, so it will be clearer just what it is whose origins we are seeking to identify.

Distilling and in some measure refining the fuller accounts offered in later chapters, I would now list its defining characteristics as follows.

1. All spheres of social activity are directed and managed (not just controlled) by formal, hierarchical organisations set up by the political authorities for this purpose.

2. One organisation, that of the Communist Party, is entrusted with integrating all the others into a single organisational whole, and does so primarily by appropriating and exercising on their behalf the key prerogatives of any autonomous organisation, namely determination of their goals, structures and leadership.

3. Tradition and exchange nevertheless continue to play a significant, if subsidiary, part in governing social activity, operating both openly within prescribed structures and mechanisms, and clandestinely within the 'informal organisation' of the official hierarchies.

4. Formal position within the centralised and integrated complex of official organisations (rather than, for example, wealth, birth or popularity) is the chief determinant of power, status and material reward.

5. Politics, in the sense of competition to influence decisions and their implementation, is mostly structured around the formal and informal organisation of the official hierarchies and is in large part concealed from public view, although there is often a controlled airing of alternatives in selected areas of economic and social policy.

6. The system and its demands are legitimated primarily by the goal of building a fully communist society and by the Marxist–Leninist world view in which this goal is embedded, these being protected from overt criticism and competition by close control over public communication and association backed by massive coercive machinery.

There are a number of important aspects of the Soviet mono-organisational system which are not specified in this list of defining characteristics, as I do not regard them as essential to it. These include the structure of supreme power, the constitutional order, forms of property and various subsidiary modes of legitimation, which will be considered in later chapters.

Here a couple of remarks about terminology should be inserted. I have used the term 'organisations' rather than 'bureaucracies' not on the sometimes argued grounds that they diverge too far from Weber's ideal type (see Chapter 7). It seems perfectly sensible to refer to the Soviet managerial, party, police etc. 'bureaucracies', provided this is simply taken to mean the hierarchies of appointive, salaried officials who run these organisations. But there is far more to such organisations than their bureaucracies, just as there is far more to a capitalist firm than its management or more to a church than its clergy. By the same token, while it seems apt to describe the Soviet system as a 'bureaucracy', in the sense that it is run by those staffing its official organisations, this on its own is a misleadingly incomplete characterisation of the system.

Next, it will be clear now that the prefix mono- is used here simply in one of its dictionary meanings, namely 'single'. It indicates that this is not just a society made up of formal organisations, but a society structured and operating substantially as a *single* organisation. This needs emphasis, for as the term mono-organisational has gained currency it has sometimes been taken to mean something quite different, as a revival, perhaps, of the image of a 'monolithic society', a unity of rocklike solidarity unmarked by a single crack or fissure, which was coined by Stalin's propagandists and later turned against them by Western critics.[9] In fact this 'monolithic' image, always misleading, quickly lost after Stalin's death whatever poetic validity it may have had earlier.[10] I fear some colleagues may even suspect me of inventing the mono-organisational concept simply to dress up in new clothes the unfashionable 'totalitarian model', despite all the ink I have spilt criticising the latter – partly because there *is* no agreed model of totalitarianism, partly because of the political abuse and popular misunderstandings associated with it, but mostly because it fails to catch what is essential and distinctive to Soviet-type systems (see Chapter 6). Such a critical conflating of 'totalitarian', 'bureaucratic' and 'mono-organisational' images of the USSR sometimes rests on the demonstrably erroneous assumption that they all ignore the conflictual, pluralistic aspect of Soviet politics and picture the centralised determination of grass-roots behaviour as near perfect. Moreover, one sometimes encounters a certain parochialism that can conceive of political activity only in terms appropriate to the peculiar realities of modern bourgeois market societies.

What makes it so difficult to arrive at a common understanding of the Soviet system, and at the same time so important to do so, is that it is a radically new social order, one moreover that has manifested a considerable durability and a capacity for impressive achievements in important fields of endeavour, while inspiring or imposing variants of itself which now embrace over a third of humanity. How we characterise this new species of human society will depend on how deeply we perceive its novelty to extend. If what strikes us most is the vast expansion of political control over social activity we may characterise it according to some concept of 'totalitarianism'. If we focus on its class structure understood in terms of property relationships we are likely to characterise it as some form of 'socialism' – 'real', or 'developed', or 'deformed', or 'state', or 'bureaucratic' socialism, etc. And so on.

It is my contention that the novelty of this form of society is so profound that we can only characterise it adequately by reference to the most fundamental elements of social life, namely the modes of combining individual action, that is the mechanisms for defining, assigning and coordinating social roles. All human societies known to us employ a variety of such 'role mechanisms', as I shall call them (in earlier expositions I wrote of 'modes of coordination'), but a variety reducible to three basic mechanisms found in numerous guises and combinations. Roles may be defined, assigned and coordinated, firstly, by *custom*, that is in ways evolved by past generations and reproduced without deliberate change by each new one. Secondly, roles may be defined, assigned and coordinated in a process of *exchange* between individuals and groups (in earlier expositions: 'contract'). Exchange, unlike custom, requires an exercise of will and rational calculation on the part of both interacting participants, although not necessarily of equal weight. And thirdly, roles may be defined, assigned and coordinated by *command*, that is by an exercise of will and rational calculation by one side only, while the other side is required only to obey, that is to confine the exercise of its will and rational calculation to performing the tasks assigned it.

No human society is built wholly on the basis of one or other of these role mechanisms. Even the simplest food-gathering community, for example, employs exchange and command alongside the predominant mechanism of custom. Custom and command both play a large part in the heavily exchange-oriented societies of modern capitalism. And, as already indicated, both custom and exchange are very much in evidence in Soviet mono-organisational society, despite the predominance of the command mechanism. But it is equally plain that one mechanism *will* often predominate. One may distinguish structures of social action resting mainly on custom ('traditional structures'), structures resting mainly on exchange ('markets'), and structures resting mainly on command ('formal hierarchical organisations' – 'organisations' for short). Moreover, as already implied, such structures may be seen as predominant in societies taken as a whole, so that one may speak of traditional, market and organisational societies, and there is a clear evolutionary trend from the first to the other two.

In 'Western' industrialised societies large-scale organisations have come to predominate in more and more fields of life, but at the same time social interactions both at the organisational and at the individual level have made use of ever more varied and complex structures of exchange. It would be appropriate, therefore, to label them 'market-organisational societies'. These market-organisational societies also make extensive use of voluntary 'associations', structures which manifest an often complex blend of exchange and command mechanisms. A similar blend is characteristic of the political structures and processes of market-organisational societies.

Mono-organisational societies of the Soviet type are the product, first, of a deliberate effort to eliminate or marginalise traditional and market structures, second, of the absorption of all areas of activity by designated organisations, third, of the conversion of *de jure* associations into *de facto* hierarchical organisations, and fourth, of the subordination of the whole to one organisation, namely the Communist Party, entrusted with the conscious, overall coordination of all social activity.

The close and complex relationship which evidently exists between technology and social structure should not lead us into a crude technological determinism, for there are plenty of historical instances of communities with a similar range and level of technological knowledge but with very different social arrangements. For some decades both market-organisational and mono-organisational societies demonstrated that they could operate effectively with very similar technologies. The word 'effectively', to be sure, begs many questions, for each had its well recognised strengths and weaknesses, but both seemed capable of providing the main requirements of a viable and effective social system: internal order, protection against external attack, meeting the basic physiological and psychic needs of the population, and maintenance of its key structures and processes. Few of us, of course, would regard elementary effectiveness and viability as the sole criteria, or even the chief criteria, for judging the worth of a society, nor is there any guarantee that they will persist as the internal and external environments change under the influence of technological, demographic and other developments. Despite the impressive innovatory and adaptive capacity demonstrated by Western market-organisational societies even in their so-called 'late capitalist' phase there are reasons enough to question its effectiveness and viability in the long run. In the case of mono-organisational socialism, however, doubts as to its effectiveness and viability, already widespread by the early 1980s, provoked Gorbachev's efforts at 'restructuring' the system in its homeland, and assumed compelling force with its collapse throughout Eastern Europe. Could any *perestroika* (restructuring) now restore its viability and effectiveness, or would it inevitably bring the demise of mono-organisational socialism? This is the question we explore in the final chapter of this book.

Tsarist Russia: Seedbed of the Mono-organisational Society?

The matter of continuities and discontinuities between pre- and post-revolutionary Russian society is one that would require a different kind of book to examine properly. However, since it is touched on in a general way in several chapters of this book, it seems appropriate to offer at this point some systematic, if necessarily tentative, remarks on the question: can the mono-organisational system of the USSR be seen as simply a new variant or logical continuation of the socio-political order of Tsarist Russia? While a plain unqualified 'yes' would strike most readers as preposterous, a resounding 'no' is likely to leave them dissatisfied. Most of us, in other words, would probably think there is something in the notion. But how much? And what precisely?

There have been many past societies whose rulers have claimed and in varying degrees exercised the right to dispose freely of the lives and possessions of all their subjects, and to direct economic and other activities throughout the land through hierarchies of appointive officials. One thinks first and foremost of the numerous 'oriental despotisms' or 'hydraulic societies' from ancient Egypt through Imperial China to pre-Columbian America.[11] Such societies resembled the mono-organisational societies of the twentieth-century more in intent than achievement, if only because the available technologies of communication and transport were inadequate for the systematic centralised management of all social processes, and these still depended heavily on a variety of traditional and market mechanisms.

As for Muscovite Russia, it seems realistic to regard it, with Wittfogel, as an oriental despotism *manqué*. As Richard Pipes has pointed out, Russia's geographical conditions ruled out the establishment of such relatively fast and efficient communication networks as were essential to the systems maintained by a Persian king or Chinese emperor, and her rulers had to settle for keeping their local agents in a state of dependence while allowing them a relatively free hand in exploiting 'their' territories so long as they met their basic obligations in money and men.[12]

The 'service state' which emerged from Peter the Great's reforms also proved a far smaller step towards the Soviet system of today than has sometimes been suggested. On paper the scope and direction of these reforms seem ominous: they divided the whole population into four categories whose rights (including property rights) were dependent on meeting prescribed obligations to the state; all social groups and institutions, including the Church, were placed either directly or indirectly under the authority of the Emperor and his servants; and the central bureaucracy was expanded and rationalised and its 'reach' extended more deeply and effectively into the provinces. In practice, of course, Peter's reforms changed far less than was intended, and it was not long before counter-reforms began to undermine their logic. Of crucial importance here was the 'liberation' of the gentry in 1762 from the obligation to serve the state and the confirmation and extension of their rights under Catherine the Great's 1785 'Charter of the Nobility'.

Contradictory tendencies are evident in the evolution of Russian society during the final century and a half of the monarchy. While the role of custom gradually receded, it was not only the command hierarchies of the state that extended their scope and power; so, too, did the mechanisms of market exchange and institutions facilitating the autonomous cooperation and interaction of citizens in various spheres of activity. Thus on the one hand the state bureaucracy steadily expanded, established a firm base at provincial and district level, radically improved its communications, and moved into new fields such as education and transport; the state took a leading role in promoting industrialisation and was the chief consumer of Russian manufactures; and an elaborate censorship machinery and pervasive political police with punitive powers independent of the courts were established. On the other hand, however, capitalist banks, joint-stock companies and stock exchanges were allowed to establish themselves; law was progressively disengaged from administration and an autonomous judiciary established; an independent-minded 'intelligentsia' emerged within the educated strata, and the regime gradually habituated itself to the existence of independent publications, theatres and associations, which, while always constrained by the censorship and political police, built up in Russia a flourishing and fertile market in ideas; and a degree of competitive public participation in political life was permitted at the provincial level from the 1860s and at the national level after the 1905 Revolution.

Seen in retrospect, not one, but two, new potential societies seem to have been growing within the womb of the society of late Imperial Russia: a new and unique mono-organisational society, and a market-organisational society similar to those of the capitalist West. Each was taking institutional shape around distinct élite groups: on the one hand a career officialdom whose leading figures shared effectively in the autocratic power of the Emperor and which staffed a state machine deeply penetrating most fields of social life, and on the other the industrial, commercial and professional 'middle class' dominant in the Duma, the city and provincial councils and in most voluntary associations.

The former certainly had the upper hand as long as the monarchy lasted, and it is not difficult to imagine circumstances in which the bureaucratic autocracy might have taken such a firm hold on economic and cultural life in Russia as to push it well along the mono-organisational road. Nevertheless, looking at all the changes in the half-century before the First World War, one could easily conclude that the dominant trend lay in the opposite direction. And certainly, despite the police clamp-down and the curbing of the Duma after 1907, Russia has never (except between the March and October Revolutions) enjoyed such freedom of expression, movement and association as in the last years of the monarchy, while the capitalist market economy continued to burgeon and Stolypin's agricultural reforms were beginning to liberate the peasantry from the shackles of the rural communes. Was Russia, then, not limping along behind Europe's other autocratic empires in Germany and Austria-Hungary towards the inexorable goal of a liberal–democratic capitalist–market society?

And this may well have been where she would have ended up had it not been for the trauma of involvement in the First World War and the revolution it engendered. Indeed after the overthrow of Tsarism it seemed at first as if the race between the embryo mono-organisational society and the embryo market-organisational society had been decisively won by the latter. War and revolution, however, make a vicious pair of midwives, and the squawking infant was smothered in its cradle.

The changeling begotten by Lenin that took its place grew lustily and its mono-organisational features were soon plain to see. In some two decades it became the world's first full-grown if immature mono-organisational society. The outcome seems paradoxical. Tsarist officialdom, the chief vehicle of the mono-organisational tendencies in pre-revolutionary Russia, surely had no more implacable enemies than Lenin and his Bolsheviks! Was it not Lenin's aim to sweep away the existing state machine, to replace it with one purged of career officials and based on the soviets and other 'mass organisations', and ultimately to eliminate the state altogether? The key to the paradox is, of course, the common aversion of Tsarist officialdom and Lenin's Bolsheviks to the ideal of a society free of conscious, centralised control and direction and operating largely through the spontaneous interaction of autonomous individuals and groups. Lenin saw his task as to place Russia under new *management*. 'Russia', he wrote shortly before the Bolshevik seizure of power, 'was run (*upravlyali*) after the 1905 Revolution by 130,000 landowners...and it is alleged that 240,000 members of the party of Bolsheviks will be unable to run Russia'.[13] It was this mentality that conjured up a new bureaucratic autocracy to replace the old, but one whose itch to control and direct was immeasurably greater than its predecessor's, since it aimed at nothing less than the total remaking of Russia's socio-economic order and the beliefs, attitudes and behaviour of its inhabitants. It was thus a far superior vehicle for the transition to a fully-fledged mono-organisational society than had been the Tsarist bureaucracy and its masters.

This analysis suggests, first, that tendencies towards a mono-organisational order were indeed apparent in the old Russia; second, that it was by no means historically preordained that they should triumph; and third, that the links between these tendencies and the Soviet mono-organisational system of today were for the most part indirect ones. This last point deserves some elaboration. Patterns of thought and behaviour inherited from Russia's pre-revolutionary past have played an important part in moulding the Soviet socio-political order, and it is worth trying to identify them and to enquire into the mechanisms of transition. At this point, however, let us just consider some of the most salient characteristics of the mentality and operation of Tsarist autocracy and officialdom as a basis for later comparison.

First, the top executive bodies and positions in the state were filled with civil servants rather than, for example, with men experienced in party politics, the practice of law or journalism, or men of trust and authority solely by virtue of their noble status, links to the court, or standing in their local communities. And since high-level, lateral recruitment to the bureaucracy was unusual, these were men who had spent virtually the whole of their adult lives climbing the ladder of state service. The exceptions, if they can be called that, were career army officers who had been transferred at a relatively high level – for example, as provincial governors, from the military to the civil departments.[14]   It is true, as Max Weber recognised, that any bureaucractic order necessarily has an extra-bureaucratic element at the top, and in Russia this took the form of the Emperor himself and his court. All the later Romanov monarchs took very seriously their responsibilities as divinely ordained autocratic rulers and there is no doubt that their quirks and preferences, and sometimes also the unofficial influence of members of the imperial family and others in the court circles, had a major effect on the personnel and operations of government. However, it was the high-level career officials occupying the key offices of state who were not only the chief executors of the Emperor's will, but also, on the whole, the major influences in molding it.

This leads to the second point: political power at the topmost level was a weakly institutionalised blend of personal and oligarchical elements. In theory, even under the 1906 Constitution, the Emperor enjoyed unlimited personal authority, but in practice a substantial group of high officials shared in the policy-making process, in part by virtue of their formal offices and standing within such collective bodies as the Senate, the State Council (*Gosudarstvennyi sovet*), the Committee of Ministers (*Komitet ministrov*) and later the Council of Ministers (*Sovet ministrov*), with their fluid and vaguely defined powers and functions, and in part through their informal links and relationships.[15]

Thirdly, the politics that mattered most in Imperial Russia was 'bureaucratic politics', fought out on two intersecting dimensions: that of jurisdictional and policy conflict between different formal divisions of the government machine – for example, between the development-oriented Finance Ministry and the conservative Interior Ministry (*Ministerstvo vnutrennykh del* - MVD) – and that of competition between informal cliques, most of them clientelist groups based on prior service together.[16]

Fourthly, those (including Lenin), who have identified Imperial Russian officialdom (*chinovniki*) with the landowning class (*pomeshchiki*) or the 'nobility' (*dvorianstvo* – also translated 'gentry') were gravely misled. To be sure, the system that grew up in Muscovite times and that was carried to its logical extreme by Peter the Great made the inheritance of noble status and the possession of land with its associated servile workforce equally conditional upon civil or military service at the Tsar's pleasure. Only nobles could own serfs and noble status could be achieved automatically by promotion to a certain rank (*chin*) in the state service. However, the three elements began to separate in the second half of the eighteenth century and their unravelling accelerated throughout the nineteenth. Achieving high rank in the bureaucracy required a long apprenticeship in dusty offices, and ever fewer scions of wealthy aristocratic families found this congenial.[17] Meanwhile, following the emancipation of the serfs in 1861, the gentry rapidly lost their economic dominance – by the end of the imperial era two-thirds of the cultivated land and most of the livestock were in the hands of the peasantry.[18] It is true that men of noble birth still predominated at the highest levels of the bureaucracy, but the majority of these were the sons, grandsons or great grandsons of officials automatically ennobled through promotion and were largely or wholly dependent for their livelihood on their official salaries.[19] By the final years of serfdom something like half the gentry evidently owned no serfs.[20] Ownership of estates, houses or dachas was greater among the upper ranks, but even here it declined rapidly in the second half of the century. Between 1853 and 1902 the proportion in the second highest class of officials who possessed no real property increased from 3 per cent to 43 per cent, and in the fourth highest class 36 per cent to 67 per cent, while the proportion owning large estates went down from 55 to 9 per cent in the case of the second class and from 9 to 3 per cent in that of the fourth.[21] Even at the apex of the service, the august band of ministers, directorate heads and their assistants, barely one-third in the late Tsarist era owned rural estates.[22] If one can speak of a 'ruling class' in pre-revolutionary Russia, it was a class defined by appointive office-holding rather than in terms of property or inherited status.

Fifthly, despite the very significant legal reforms of the 1860s and the establishment of quasi-parliamentary institutions after 1905, the old Russia lived to the end under a government of men rather than a government of laws. If this was anchored, on both the theoretical and the practical levels, in the boundless prerogative of the Emperor, it was also deeply entrenched in the political culture of Russia's officialdom and of the nation at large – a political culture ultimately rooted in the Byzantine inheritance and the long years of Mongol rule. As Hans Rogger has reminded us, it was the historian Karamzin who asked Alexander I in 1811 why he bothered to write laws, adding that it is men that govern, not documents. Fifty wise and conscientious provincial governers would be far more use than all the councils and regulations. And seventy years later Alexander III was advised by his *emanuensis* Pobedonostsev, 'Institutions are of no importance. Everything depends on individuals'.[23] It is this mentality that marked Russia off from the contemporary bureaucratic empires of Germany and Austria-Hungary, where the principle that the actions of representatives of the state, from top to bottom, should be bound by law, was well entrenched in both belief and practice. There were thoughtful Russian officials throughout the nineteenth century who realised that their country, too, must follow the path of the *Rechtsstaat* if it wished to flourish and offer a prosperous and civilized life to its citizens. A few years before the Revolution the reforming conservative Chairman of the Council of Ministers P.A. Stolypin wrote, 'The fatherland, transformed by the will of the monarch ... must become a government of laws'.[24] The full poignancy of this statement can be appreciated if we recall that it was made two generations after the adoption of Alexander II's legal reforms, and several years after the establishment of the Duma, the quasi-parlimentary powers of which Stolypin himself had been instrumental in curbing, and shortly before he fell victim to an act of lawlessness involving both the revolutionary underground and the secret police.

This elevation of the qualities and will of individual officials over law and institutions found varied expression in pre-revolutionary Russia. One was the decree of 14 August 1881 which empowered provincial governors or the Interior Ministry (MVD) to suspend the operation of the laws in a given area and so freely undertake arrests, banishments, closing of publications, bannings of meetings etc. A senior police official was later to confess that this caused the fate of the 'entire population of Russia to become dependent on the personal opinions of the functionaries of the political police'.[25] Again, the Council of Ministers established after the 1905 Revolution looked like a big step towards the institutionalisation of government, but it was expressly forbidden to consider a range of matters, including foreign affairs and defence, except by special permission of the Emperor.[26] Meanwhile, elective city and provincial councils now existed, but the MVD and provincial governors enjoyed the power to veto their choice of key officials, remove them, or substitute minority candidates. The elections of 217 mayors and the board members of 318 city councils were annulled between 1900 and 1914, while up to 1909 fully 81 elected chairman of provincial *zemstva* were vetoed.[27] Thus free elections were accepted by the authorities only insofar as they brought the 'right' people to office. On the other hand state officials could often commit legal and disciplinary offences with impunity so long as they enjoyed the confidence of their superiors, for the latter's consent was required before charges against them could be pressed in the courts.

The behaviour patterns outlined above offer by no means a rounded picture of the socio-political order of late Imperial Russia, for I have been focusing just on the world of state officialdom; that is, on that part of pre-revolutionary society within which the tendencies towards a mono-organisational system were concentrated. How far these patterns were to be replicated in the mature mono-organisational society of the USSR is a matter to be explored later.

Plan of this Book

All the material presented here bears directly or indirectly on the concept of the Soviet system as one of mono-organisational socialism. Whatever continuities we may see between this system and the pre-revolutionary socio-political order of Russia, it was evidently not directly engendered by the latter, but rather by Lenin and his Bolshevik followers. It is to these, therefore, that we turn in Chapter 2, which was written for this volume in order to fill a gap in my earlier accounts of the Soviet system, especially in the first, 1964, account included here as Chapter 3. This account failed to give sufficient weight to the role of ideas, their relationship to pre- and post-revolutionary organisational structures and processes, to the way power is exercised and the way it is legitimated. Chapter 2, while it does not purport to break new ground in our knowledge of Lenin's Bolshevism, seeks to highlight those aspects that gave it the *potential* to engender the mono-organisational system, without, I hope, exaggerating them or suggesting that they made later developments inevitable.

A second defect of this 1964 account is betrayed by its title, which speaks merely of *organisational* societies. Although I already conceived of such societies as constituting in some real sense a *single* organisation, I had not, as yet, gone far in exploring the implications of this. Chapters 4 and 7 reflect, I believe, a better conceptualisation of this key aspect of the system. My present position, summarised earlier in this chapter, incorporates two further innovations. The first is the inclusion of 'socialism' in my definition of the Soviet mono-organisational system, which is intended as an acknowledgement of both the legitimating and the enstructuring importance of socialist ideas in the evolution of the system. The other is a somewhat sharper picture of the integrating role of the party.

In Chapter 4 I offer an analysis of how Lenin's Bolshevism evolved into fully-fledged mono-organisational socialism under Stalin, seeking to bring out the interplay between historical, organisational, ideological and personal factors. It also seeks to identify those aspects of the Soviet system of the Stalin era that were essential to mono-organisational socialism and those that reflected the specific conditions of his personal tyranny.

Chapter 7 focuses on a core element of the mono-organisational system through all its phases down to the 1980s, namely the nexus between the legitimating goal of communism, the structure of power, and the predominant operating mechanisms of Soviet society. The position argued here has provoked considerable interest and some controversy, particularly around the use made of the distinction between formal–legal rationality and goal rationality. While the issues involved are too complex to be rehearsed here, the reader should be warned that, although there is room here for genuine theoretical disagreement, there is also some danger, on too quick a reading, of simply misinterpreting what is being argued. I do not contend, for example, that under mono-organisational socialism mass compliance with the demands of the regime has rested primarily on a common commitment to the goal of communism, let alone that the pursuit of that goal has been the real rationale of those demands. This chapter also offers a review of the exceedingly disparate literature on political legitimation as it relates to communist systems.

Despite the distinctiveness of mono-organisational socialism, valuable insights into important aspects of its operation can be obtained from studies of large-scale public and private organisations in Western societies. The influence of this literature is reflected in this volume, but more substantially and explicitly in two other book chapters for which there has been insufficient space to include here.[28]

I turn now to three chapters which do not directly address the concept of mono-organisational socialism, but which complement it in various ways. In Chapter 6, originally a review article, I discuss a number of alternative ways of conceptualising Soviet-type systems, focusing especially on the once (still?) dominant totalitarianism, and briefly asserting the advantages of the mono-organisational concept.[29]

Chapter 5, 'The Embourgeoisement of the Soviet Union and the Proletarianization of Communist China', is very much the intellectual outlier of this book, and indeed something of a curiosity in Western Sovietology: an attempt to employ Marxist concepts (albeit rather idiosyncratically) to analyse broad trends in communist societies. It was originally written in 1960, a very bad season for Marxism among English-speaking social scientists, and five years before the launching of Mao's Great Proletarian Cultural Revolution, so it can claim a certain prescience. It was also before the 'Liberman proposals' opened up the prospect of intensified 'embourgeoisement' in the Soviet Union, a prospect to be dimmed by the bureaucratic reaction that set in after the fall of Khrushchev, but revived with a vengeance in the mid-1980s. What I did not foresee was the eventual collapse of Mao's 'proletarianisation' and China's subsequent (if perhaps temporary) outrunning of the Soviet Union in the opposite direction.

The chapter order is governed primarily by a rough historical logic, but I thought it useful to precede the final chapter, which brings the story up to the present day, with another broad historical chapter (Chapter 8) suggestive of the deeper significance of the crisis of mono-organisational socialism and the efforts of the Gorbachev regime to resolve it. It deals with the preoccupation of Russian rulers, from Muscovite times on, with external and internal threats to security, and the consequent hypertrophy of the state, isolation and stagnation, interrupted when the latter reaches the point of dangerously threatening security by successive 'revolutions from above'. The article, written over 20 years ago, poses at the end the question whether the Soviet Union was not on the eve of changes which 'could affect the patterns not just of the past half-century, but of the past half-millenium'. It is a measure of the structural rigidity of the Brezhnev era that this passage has such a contemporary ring. In Chapter 9 I analyse the changes in the Soviet socio-political order since 1985, seeking to establish how far these have led to a reformed version of the mono-organisational system and how far to a break with the fundamentals of that system. And beyond that, what chance is there that this is at last the revolution from above to end all revolutions from above?

Notes and References

1 In the two recently published English translations of selections of his writings, namely Max Weber, *The Theory of Social and Economic Organisation*, translated by A.M. Henderson and Talcott Parsons, ed. with an introduction by Talcott Parsons (The Free Press of Glencoe, New York), 1947, and *From Max Weber: Essays in Sociology*, translated, edited and with an Introduction by H.H. Gerth and C. Wright Mills, (Kegan Paul, London), 1948.

2 Alfred G. Meyer, 'USSR Incorporated', *Slavic Review*, October 1961.

3 See James C. Abegglen, ed., *Business Strategies for Japan*, (Sophia, Tokyo), 1970, Chapter 4, and Namiki Nobuyoshi, '"Japan, Inc.":

Reality or Facade', in Hyoe Murakami and Johannes Hirschmeier, eds, *Politics and Economics in Contemporary Japan*, (Japan Culture Institute, Tokyo), 1979, pp.111–26.

4 See Allen Kassof, 'The Administered Society', *World Politics*, vol.XVI, no.4 (July 1964), and Maria Hirszowicz, *The Bureaucratic Leviathan. A Study in the Sociology of Communism*, (Martin Robertson, Oxford), 1980.

5 Max Weber, *Economy and Society. An Outline of Interpretative Sociology*, ed. Guenther Roth and Claus Wittich (University of California Press, Berkeley), 1978, vol.1, p.225.

6 Gerth and Mills, pp.49–50.

7 See Robert Michels, *Political Parties*, trans. Eden and Cedar Paul, (Dover Publications, New York), 1959, Chapter IV.

8 A. Vol'sky (J.W. Machajski), *Umstvennyi rabochii* (Inter-language Literary Associates, New York), 1968. His work, alas, remains unavailable in English.

9 Such a misunderstanding might have been avoided had I used the Latin prefix *uni-* rather than the Greek *mono-*, thereby incidentally mollifying the linguistic purist, 'organisational' being itself of Latin derivation.

10 See T.H. Rigby, 'The Deconcentration of Power in the USSR – 1953–1964, in J.D.B. Miller and T.H. Rigby, *The Disintegrating Monolith. Pluralist Trends in the Communist World*, (The Australian National University, Canberra), 1965, pp.17–45.

11 Cf. Karl A. Wittfogel, *Oriental Despotism. A Comparative Study of Total Power*, (Yale University Press, New Haven), 1957.

12 See Richard Pipes, *Russia under the Old Regime*, (Penguin Books, Harmondsworth), 1977, p.20–2.

13 V.I. Lenin, *'Uderzhat li bol'sheviki gosudarstvennuyu vlast'?'*, *Polnoe sobranie sochinenii*, 5th ed., vol.34, (Moscow), 1962, p.313.

14 The most extensively studied branch of the Tsarist bureaucracy is the key Ministry of Internal Affairs. On careers see especially Daniel T. Orlovsky, 'The Limits of Reform', *The Ministry of Internal Affairs in Imperial Russia, 1802-1881* (Harvard University Press, Cambridge, Mass.), 1981, Chapter 4. See also P.A. Zaionchkovsky, *Pravitel'stvennyi apparat samoderzhavnoi Rossii v XIX B*, (Mysl', Moscow), 1978.

15 See P.A. Zaionchkovsky, *Rossiiskoe samoderzhavie v kontse XIX stoletiya*, (Mysl', Moscow), 1970.

16 Ibid, Orlovsky, op.cit. See also Alexander Ular, *Russia from Within*, (Heinemann, London), 1905.

17 Pipes, *Russia under the Old Regime*, p.189.

18 Pipes 190ff., Hans Rogger, *Russia in the Age of Modernisation and Revolution*, (Longman, London and New York), 1983, pp.89–90.

19 See Orlovsky, p.108–9. By the turn of the century about three-fifths of the gentry owed their noble status either to their own official achievements (rank or honours attained in the civil or military service), or such achievements by their mostly recent forebears. See A.P. Korelin, *Dvoryanstvo v poreformennoi Rossii, 1861-1904 g.g.*, (Nauka, Moscow), 1979, pp.32–3. According to Korelin (p.94) in 1897 71.5 per cent of officials of classes I–IV of the civil service had gentry status and 37.9 per cent of those in classes V–VIII. As Dominic Lieven has recently shown, however, the nexus between high office, ancient lineage and ownership of large estates remained strong at the august level of the State Council. See his *Russia's Rulers under the Old Regime*, (Yale University Press, New Haven and London), 1989, Chapter 2.

20 Zaionchkovsky, *Pravitel'svennyi apparat*, p.43. This seems a fair interpretation of the rather obscure official figures cited.

21 Ibid., pp.97–8.

22 Korelin, p.100.

23 See Rogger, p.40.

24 *Istoricheskii arkhiv*, no.4 (1959), p.153, quoted Rogger, p.224.

25 Cited Pipes, p.307.

26 Rogger, p.40.

27 Ibid., pp.60–2.

28 'Politics in the Mono-organizational Society', in Andrew C. Janos, ed., *Authoritarian Politics in Communist Europe. Uniformity and Diversity in One-Party States*, (University of California Institute of International Relations, Berkeley), 1976, pp.31–80, and 'A Conceptual Approach to Authority, Power and Policy in the Soviet Union', Chapter 2 in T.H. Rigby, Archie Brown and Peter Reddaway, eds, *Authority, Power and Policy in the USSR*, (Macmillan, London), 1980. The latter also offers an earlier version of the view of political legitimation in the USSR presented here in Chapter 6.) Also

relevant is my article 'Bureaucratic Politics: An Introduction', *Public Administration*, (Sydney), vol.XXXII, no.1 (March 1973), pp.1–20.

29 See also my article 'New Trends in the Study of Soviet Politics', *Politics*, (Sydney), vol.V, no.1 (May 1970), pp.1–17.

2 A Dictatorship for Communism

The single-party dictatorship in the Soviet Union, and the whole socio-political order to which it has given rise, were established for the sole purpose of creating a 'communist' society. In what sense this exalted, if tragically misconceived, purpose continues to *maintain* the system we shall consider later. That it was what motivated Lenin and his followers in *setting up* the system, however, there can be no doubt. Nor has it ceased to serve as the ultimate intellectual and moral justification for its continued existence. 'The supreme goal of the Soviet state', we read in the preamble to the present (1977) Constitution of the USSR, 'is the building of a classless communist society'. And it is for *this* reason that the Communist Party is accorded (in article 6) the role of 'leading and directing force of Soviet society and the nucleus of its political system, of all state organisations and all public (*obshchestvennye*) organisations'. 'The Communist Party', the article continues, 'armed with Marxism–Leninism, determines the general perspectives of the development of society and the course of domestic and foreign policy of the USSR, directs the great constructive work of the soviet people, and imparts a planned, systematic and theoretically substantiated character to their struggle for the victory of communism'.

It is the elevation of 'the building of communism' as the sovereign goal of all social activity and the sole absolute value in Soviet society, and the consequent relativisation of all other goals and values, that gave rise to, and continued for decades to legitimate, the suppression

23

of all opposition to the Communist Party and its ideology, the centralisation of power within the party itself, and the subordination of all organisations and institutions to party control and direction. In this chapter we are concerned with the pre-revolutionary roots of this system, in the goals, ideas and organisational character of Lenin's Bolshevism.

In the Beginning was the Word

Lenin and his Bolshevik followers took power in 1917 not for the sake of power, not merely for the sake of their proclaimed policies of 'bread, peace and land', and certainly not for the sake of their native Russia, but because they carried in their heads the vision of a totally new society and aimed to translate that vision into reality. Whether they would acknowledge the Soviet society of today as an approximation to that vision may be open to doubt, but this is not at issue here. The point is that the drive to actualise their vision engendered a more profound transformation of Russia than any act of revolutionary will had ever before wrought in a great nation, and that the result was a historically novel form of human society. The *logos* of that vision must therefore form the starting point of our analysis.

That Lenin and his followers possessed the will and convictions necessary to essay a root-and-branch reshaping of Russian society they owed in large part to their commitment to certain key tenets of Marxism. The essential determining characteristic of any society they saw in its class structure, classes being defined in terms of forms of property and the associated 'relations of production' between owners and workers: slave-owners and slaves, feudal landlords and serfs, capitalists and wage-workers. These relations were inherently exploitative and antagonistic, and they formed the 'material' base on which the whole legal, political and cultural life of a given society were erected. Class struggles were the engine of history – struggles between exploiting and exploited classes within an ongoing social system, and struggles for dominance between rising and declining exploiting classes, culminating in the revolutionary transformation of society under a new ruling class. Thus the 'bourgeois revolutions' in England in the mid-seventeenth century and in France in the late eighteenth were decisive phases in the transfer of power from the feudal landowning class to the capitalist bourgeoisie and the attendant transmutation of the legal and political order and of the dominant culture and values.

Living as he did under capitalism, Marx devoted his greatest attention to the study of capitalist society, its origins, development and the conditions for its revolutionary transformation. So, incidentally, have most of his intellectual disciples, and indeed it has often been suggested that it is in the analysis of capitalist societies that his theories acquire their greatest plausibility.

Capitalism, for the Marxist Revolutionary, was both supreme friend and supreme enemy. On the one hand, it dissolved all time-hallowed authorities and illusions and engendered a previously unimaginable explosion in productive capacity, while at the same time progressively reducing the overwhelming majority of the population to the condition of wage-earning 'proletarians', a quintessentially revolutionary class because they 'have nothing to lose but their chains' and are habituated by the conditions of factory labour to patterns of organised activity which can be turned against their oppressors. On the other hand, capitalism is the *ultimate* variant of exploitative class society, for no new property-based form of production–relations emerges and grows within it, and thus its overthrow will be spearheaded not by a new exploiting class but for the first time in history by an exploited class, namely the proletariat. The latter, in destroying capitalism, will thereby remove the material basis for all antagonistic class relations, and open the way to socialism (or communism – Marx himself did not consistently distinguish them) in which ultimately the whole coercive legal and political order will dissolve and the principle 'from each according to his abilities, to each according to his needs' will prevail.

Hence the Marxist's 'dialectical' approach to capitalism. As a progressive, modernising order which prepares the ground for socialism it is to be welcomed, and indeed in its earlier stages the Marxist revolutionary should often support it against its enemies and foster its growth; but as the one force then standing between humanity and the non-exploitative, 'truly human' order of socialism, it is to be opposed and in due course destroyed.

This egregiously schematic outline is not intended as an introduction to Marxist theory, which the reader should seek elsewhere,[1] but rather as an indication of those central tenets which informed the thought and action of Lenin and his followers when they took power in 1917. They believed themselves to be launching the proletarian revolution, the crucial act in a project of supreme historical importance, which promised nothing less than the salvation of humanity from age-old oppression, ignorance and alienation. They believed their actions were guided by a uniquely scientific understanding of history and of contemporary society.

Those actions were not to be inhibited by considerations of law, morality or religion, which, as Marx wrote of his proletarians, they regarded as 'so many bourgeois prejudices, behind which lurk in ambush just as many bourgeois interests'.[2] And by the same token, the whole existing economic system, all political institutions, the whole pattern of organised life in Russia, its culture and its customs – since all were seen as supports for the hated system of class oppression now being overthrown – likewise became the proper objects of revolutionary assault.

Their Marxist convictions therefore tell us much about why the Bolsheviks seized power and what they sought to do with it. But they do not suffice fully to explain their actions. For Marxism as a political movement had already separated into a number of streams, and we have to ask what *kind* of Marxists the Bolsheviks were, what was distinctive about them as a political organisation, and in what ways their Russian setting influenced their outlook and modes of behaviour.

Russia's Revolutionary Intelligentsia

As Marxism spread in Russia in the 1880s it took root in minds that had already absorbed, in varying mixes, traditions of political thought and action accumulated by several generations of their countrymen. Russia's Marxists, of course, were not all ethnic Russians: many were Poles, Jews or members of other ethnic minorities of the multi-national empire. They all inhabited, however, both the political world of late Tsarist Russia and, perhaps even more pertinently, the mental world of the Russian intelligentsia.

That mental world, it has often been pointed out, reflected the dualism in Russian life and culture engendered by selective Westernisation under Peter the Great and his successors. The Russian élite, in acquiring Western tastes and education, were not only progressively more estranged from the masses of their fellow-countrymen, but were imbued with standards of comparison by which their own country could not but fail miserably. The majority of the privileged, of course, were little, if at all, troubled by this, but there were already some, even before the eighteenth century was out, who suffered deeply from an awareness both of their nation's backwardness and of the gulf separating them from ordinary Russian people.

In subsequent generations several distinct strands of thought and action were to emerge from this. There were those who sought to change the political and social system from within. They had some notable successes, especially following Russia's defeats in the Crimean and Russo-Japanese Wars, when their arguments drew strength from the danger of total political collapse. More typical were the experiences of such moderate in-system reformers as Speransky in the early nineteenth century, Loris-Melikov in the late nineteenth, and Stolypin in the early twentieth, who were brought to a stop one way or another before they could effect much change. In general, of course, the political order was hostile to the independent and critical thought that stemmed ultimately from Western influences, and it is not surprising, therefore, that independent and critical thought was for its part generally hostile to the political order. Pushkin alluded to this when he said that 'only a revolutionary head can love Russia'. The very concept of the 'intelligentsia', a term invented in Russia in the 1860s and later borrowed by other languages, embodied this element of aversion and alienation from the ambient realities, an element that might in practice range from ineffectual disdain to an active, fiery hatred.[3]

The aristocratic army officers who staged the abortive Decembrist revolt in 1825 were both the first and the last movement of the revolutionary intelligentsia drawn wholly from within the élite. As education spread, the 'conscience-stricken noblemen' were increasingly diluted by *intelligenty* drawn from the families of poorer gentry and officials, priests, merchants and artisans, often moved as much by the resentments peculiar to the social or ethnic outsider as by 'mere' selfless idealism. In the middle decades of the nineteenth century the genuine revolutionaries formed only a tiny fragment of the intelligentsia, and the political police had little difficulty in tracking them down and dealing with them. However, habits of clandestine organisation were learned and transmitted, while the police themselves helped create ever new revolutionaries by their heavy-handed repression of all independent activity, even the most innocent discussion circle, a process that continued into the twentieth century.

Unlike the earliest revolutionary organisations, Russia's revolutionary Marxists aimed to transform the socio-political order not *simply* through organising a violent seizure of power but by mobilizing for this purpose the mass action of a whole social class. In this, we should note, they were preceded by the revolutionary populists (the *narodniki* – from *narod*– 'the people'), except that these sought to mobilise the peasantry, while the Marxists of course focused on the proletariat. There existed, to be sure, also a terrorist strand within populism, which went right back to Bakunin, Marx's chief critic in the First International, but it was only when the efforts of hundreds of young idealists to take enlightenment to the villages (the 'going to the people' of the 1870s) met with indifference and worse, that significant numbers of them turned in desperation to terrorism. Radical political populism, in the form of the Socialist Revolutionary Party (the SRs), remained in the early twentieth century the chief rival of revolutionary Marxism on the left of the political spectrum.

Russian Marxism was from the first a movement within the intelligentsia, displaying the same range of action-orientation as was found in the intelligentsia generally – from passive intellectual adherence to propaganda to legal or semi-legal social action and on to conspiratorial political organisation. Both the leadership and the core following of its revolutionary wing continued to be drawn predominantly from the intelligentsia right up to 1917 – and beyond. Their direct continuity with earlier streams of the revolutionary intelligentsia was epitomised by the intellectual and political career of the 'father of Russian social democracy' G.V. Plekhanov, who started his political life as a revolutionary populist. A no less striking illustration is provided by the young Lenin. According to one possibly apocryphal account, on the eve of the execution of his brother Alexander for participating in a conspiracy to assassinate the Tsar, Lenin is said to have walked up and down in his room repeating 'No! That is not the way!'. Whether literally true or not, this story brings out the essential fact that the disagreement between the two brothers was not about the revolutionary goal but about the political means. The seventeen-year-old Lenin's sense of carrying forward the vision and mission of his non-Marxist predecessors among the Russian radical intelligentsia was no youthful aberration, as was shown by his adoption, a decade and a half later, of the title of Chernyshevsky's revolutionary novel of the 1860s for the most influential of his political pamphlets, *What is to be Done?*.

Notwithstanding the often bitter conflicts between populism and Marxism for the minds and hearts of the radical intelligentsia, the two had much in common: rejection of religion, hatred for the Tsarist system, belief in socialism as a cooperative, harmonious, egalitarian society, elevation of the good of the cause as the overriding moral value, and a disdain for capitalism and liberal constitutionalism. Indeed by the time Marxism began to make ground in Russia these basic components of its outlook had been entrenched in a substantial section of the intelligentsia for a whole generation. Thus there is justice in the claims of the Soviet Communist Party to be the spiritual heirs not only of Marx and

Engels, but also of Herzen and Chernyshevsky, Pisarev and Lavrov. But it was not only in the sphere of ideas that the ground was well prepared for revolutionary Marxism. For the techniques and habits of conspiratorial organisation, which went back to the early years of the century, had been developed and refined by populist radicals and given theoretical underpinning by such pre-Marxist revolutionaries as Pestel and Tkachov.

Despite all this common ground, however, and despite the fact that many populists were greatly influenced by Marxism, two major issues separated Russia's Marxists and populists, namely the future of the peasant commune (the *obshchina*) and the future of capitalism in Russia. Throughout the centuries of serfdom, peasant-used land was in the hands not of individual households but of the village community as a whole, the commune, personified by a council of male heads of households, which from time to time reassigned the use of land according to need, organised various farm operations performed by the villagers in common, and exercised certain disciplinary powers over the community. The emancipation of the serfs in 1861 not only preserved the commune but added to its functions. The populists, whatever their disagreements over the proper path to socialism, were united in seeing the *obshchina*, purged of the distorting legacy of serfdom and autocracy, as the foundation of the new classless society. The vigorous survival of the peasant commune into the industrial era was a precious and unique privilege of Russia which would enable it to accomplish the transition to socialism without passing through the dehumanising torments of capitalism. Although Marx himself conceded this possibility, *provided* the proletarian revolution first triumphed in the industrialised West and that capitalism had meanwhile not made too much headway in Russia,[4] it was hotly contested by Russian Marxists, who insisted that socialism in their country, too, could only emerge 'from the womb' of large-scale industrial capitalism. In the process, they believed, the commune would inevitably decay. And by the 1890s, with industrialisation proceeding at a cracking pace, they were able to claim that the special conditions under which Marx envisaged a possible separate 'Russian path to socialism' were now gone forever.

By the turn of the century Marxism was well established as one of the major streams of thought and action within the radical intelligentsia of Russia. It displayed a similar spectrum of political engagement to its populist rival, lacking only the latter's terrorist wing. There were the misleadingly nicknamed 'legal Marxists', who largely (but not entirely) abjured clandestine political activity and for whom Marxism was valued primarily as a scientific demonstration of the historical necessity for a liberal capitalist order in Russia. Most of them later moved away from Marxism and several became convinced Christians. There were the 'economists', who believed that under Russia's 'backward' conditions the cause of socialism could best be served by pursuing the economic aims and aspirations of the workers, largely leaving to the liberal bourgeoisie the political task of accomplishing the 'bourgeois revolution'. And then there were the 'orthodox' social democrats, for whom the political struggle against the Tsarist order was paramount, since the bourgeois revolution was the prime precondition for a successful transition to socialism, and the Russian bourgeoisie was too weak to overthrow the autocracy without the support of the 'proletariat'. Because prior to 1906 there was no such thing as *legal* political opposition in the Russian Empire, politically active Marxism inevitably meant *revolutionary* Marxism, whose adherents took over the conspiratorial patterns and techniques pioneered by past generations of Russian Revolutionaries, often spending long years in prison, banishment to remote corners of Siberia, or in West European exile.

Revolutionary Marxism in Russia thus took shape in the bitter struggles with populism, 'legal Marxism' and 'economism' on the one hand, and with the Tsarist authorities on the other. Its very self-definition as 'social democracy' bears witness to the supreme importance of the great German Social Democratic Party, the pride and joy of the Second International, as inspiration and model. Nearly all its leaders, and none more than Plekhanov and Lenin, proclaimed themselves in unqualified agreement with the 'orthodox' German social democracy of August Bebel and Karl Kautsky. The establishment in 1898 if a 'Russian Social Democratic Party' by a nine-person 'congress' was a monument to this, embellished by the adoption of a letter 'to German Social Democracy' commemorating the fiftieth anniversary of the 1848 Revolution, which was hailed as an inspiration to the Russian proletariat in their daunting task of overthrowing absolutism in Russia too.[5] The element of farce here is heightened when one considers that at this time there were already several dozen Social Democrats sitting in the German parliament, whereas Russia did not even have a parliament. Any temptation to scorn, however, is soon dispelled when we recall the situation in the two countries just two decades later.

The Marxist revolutionaries over whom the new party and its ephemeral Central Committee claimed to exercise leadership consisted of scores of tiny groups widely scattered through the cities of central Russia and the Ukraine, Poland, Latvia and Transcaucasia, many of them loosely linked into local 'unions of struggle', and others constituting an autonomous 'General Union of Jewish Workers of Russia and Poland' (the 'Bund'). Partly under the impact of the 1891 famine and the strikes of 1895 such clandestine groups had multiplied, and their activities had evolved from mere study and discussion, to 'propaganda' classes secretly conducted among local factory workers, and finally to 'agitation'; that is, involving themselves in local workers' grievances, assisting them with advice, printing and distribution of leaflets, etc., and seeking to influence and direct them in strikes and other confrontations with employers and the authorities.

This growing involvement with the Russian industrial workers of the 1890s, a largely first-generation 'proletariat' whose poverty, powerlessness, disorientation and often atrocious working and living conditions seemed to confirm Marx's stereotype of half a century earlier, could not but strengthen the young activists of the social democratic 'underground' in their Marxist convictions and their commitment to revolution. Some groups succeeded in gathering around them considerable numbers of worker adherents, a few of whom were to throw themselves heart and soul into the social democratic movement. However, it cannot be said that they achieved much influence over the day-to-day struggles of the workers, and relations between the 'intellectuals' (largely students) who ran the groups and their worker adherents were often marred by mutual incomprehension, cross-purposes and ill-feeling. Moreover, efforts to pursue effective lines of activity were constantly being frustrated by the ever-present police surveillance, punctuated with spates of arrests, and the attendant obsession with security. The dénouement came in the months following the foundation 'congress' of the Social Democratic Party, when several hundred underground activists around the country were arrested, including all but one of the congress delegates.[6]

The 1898 'Congress' did not, therefore, mark the beginning of the Russian Social Democratic Party as an organised entity. It remained a collection of largely isolated and often ephemeral groups united only by a common core of belief and a shared revolutionary goal and tradition. A central focus was in some measure provided by the émigré luminaries of Russian social democracy grouped around Plekhanov and Axelrod, who not only presented a standard of orthodox belief but also published journals and leaflets which were smuggled to the underground activists at home. But the latter were often painfully aware of the remoteness of these great minds from the daily realities with which they themselves had to deal. Moreover it was precisely in the years around the turn of the century, when the underground was reeling from the effects of the post-congress arrests, that the conflicts between the orthodox and the 'economists' among the emigre leaders came to a head, intensified by the dispute over Bernstein's 'revisionism' in the German Social Democratic Party, and the embattled undergrounders were presented not only with contradictory messages but also with the unedifying spectacle of personal and factional squabbles dressed up as conflicts of principle.[7] Clearly, something new was needed if the dreams of a nationwide party of revolutionary Marxists was ever to become a reality.

The Theory and Practice of Leninism

Lest the idea of dealing with this much researched and much disputed topic in the space of a few pages be seen as absurdly pretentious or arrogantly dismissive, the limited objectives of what follows should be made clear. It is not part of the purpose of this book to add to the extensive and invaluable work of other scholars on the development of Lenin's thought[8] or on the emergence and evolution of Bolshevism as the Leninist wing of the Russian Social Democratic Workers' Party (RSDWP).[9] But it was, after all, Lenin and his Bolshevik followers who were destined to become Russia's revolutionary word made flesh, and we must therefore remind ourselves of certain basic elements in Lenin's thinking and in the attitudes and practices that became entrenched among his adherents, if we are to understand the direction they were to give to the development of the new society ushered in by their seizure of power.

Vladimir Ilyich Ulyanov, known to history by his 'party' name of Lenin, was in his early thirties when he emerged as a central figure in the development of Russian Revolutionary Marxism in the first years of the century. Up to that time his attitudes and activities had marked him as the archetypal 'orthodox', Plekhanovite Social Democrat, remarkable only for his driving energy and polemical flair. There was nothing unusual for a revolutionary intellectual about his upbringing in the family of a dedicated educationalist who had acquired gentry status with promotion to the appropriate rank in the civil service, in his youthful introduction to revolutionary ideas, his early populism before conversion to Marxism, his expulsion from Kazan University for political activism (he was later to take his law degree as an external student from St Petersburg University), his subsequent involvement in the organisation of clandestine groups, or his arrest and banishment to Siberia at the end of 1895. Certainly he had already made his mark in the party before the turn of the century, by virtue of his successes as an aggressive polemicist (primarily against the populists and later the 'legal Marxists'), an organiser (collaborating with Yulii Osipovich Martov in the establishment of the underground St Petersburg Union of Struggle for the Emancipation of the Working Class) and a scholar (notably for his book *The Development of Capitalism in Russia*, written in Siberian exile). But, despite some deviations from Plekhanov's views on matters of detail, Lenin's party reputation in all these areas derived in no small measure precisely from his effectiveness as a protagonist of orthodox positions.

In fact, some of the most fundamental elements of 'Leninism', which were later to be widely condemned as a denial of both socialism and democracy, were well grounded in Plekhanov's doctrines on how Marxism should be applied to Russian conditions. This was true of his contention that the working class could not attain to a fully socialist consciousness solely through the experience of its own day-to-day struggles, but that this must be brought to it by the intelligentsia through the medium of an organised social democratic movement, and that the proletariat, its class consciousness so aroused, should exercise 'hegemony' in the 'bourgeois–revolution', that is, the overthrow of the Tsarist order.[10] To be sure, important theoretical differences did later emerge, especially when Lenin became convinced that it was not the bourgeoisie, but the peasantry, which was the natural junior ally of the proletariat in the revolutionary struggle. But it was not so much the theoretical disagreements as the practical conclusions that Lenin drew from *shared* theoretical positions, that were to drive a wedge between him and his followers on the one hand, and the rest of 'orthodox' social democracy on the other.

This, however, was still in the future, and in the meantime they had collaborated on a bold and substantially successful venture: that of reviving the shattered social democratic underground and giving it a central focus and a measure of cohesion through the medium of an authoritative newspaper, published abroad and distributed in Russia by a clandestine network of agents. The idea was Lenin's, and on his release from Siberian exile he won enthusiastic support for it first from his former comrades in the St Petersburg League of Struggle, Martov and Potresov, and then, journeying to Geneva, from the émigré leaders, Plekhanov and Alexrod. The newspaper, which they named *Iskra* ('The Spark'), was conceived not only as an organ of propaganda (informing and enlightening the activists) and agitation (stimulating and guiding worker actions against employers and the authorities), but also, most importantly, of *organisation*, for the scattered and isolated groups would now be marching to the same tune and be linked together and to a single centre through the *Iskra* distribution network.

The venture was well-timed. The years 1900–1903 brought a wave of social and political unrest, with widespread large-scale strikes and demonstrations, and the associated revival of political activism was not confined to the Marxists, but extended also to the peasant-oriented populists and to the liberals from whose ranks were founded respectively the Socialist Revolutionary Party (the SRs) and the Constitutional Democratic Party (the Cadets), both destined to be leading competitors with revolutionary Marxism up to 1917 and beyond. A revival of organised social democracy at this period would therefore doubtless have occurred even without *Iskra*. The latter, however, gave a big push to the scale and the direction of the revival, and it was vital in the preparation for the Second Congress of the RSDRP in 1903, although the 43 Congress participants were not limited to 'Iskraites' but represented a broad spectrum of Russian social democracy including the 'economists' and 'legal marxists'.

With this success, however, came further division. For by now it was plain that Lenin's ideas on how the party should be organised, if it were to perform effectively its 'vanguard' role vis-à-vis the proletariat and its 'hegemonic' role in the struggle against the Tsarist order, were at odds with important aspects of the social democratic tradition. These ideas, which informed his whole approach to the *Iskra* operation, were articulated in a number of his writings at this time, most clearly and systematically in the 1902 pamphlet *What is to be Done?*. Lenin argued that while the working-class movement as a whole could properly embrace a variety of organisations and activities, both legal and illegal, under Russian conditions the *party*, which would have the task of giving them overall leadership and coordination, must take the form of a highly selective, clandestine, centralised and disciplined organisation of full-time activists. 'The only serious organisational principle for the actual workers of our movement', he wrote, 'should be the strictest secrecy, the strictest selection of members, and the training of professional revolutionaries.'[11] Such a formula obviously excluded actual workers from the 'workers' party, and Lenin underlined this by arguing that while the party should not be confined to intellectuals, but should seek to recruit and train working-class revolutionaries and, once these were ready for party membership, they should normally become both fully employed and fully supported by the party.[12] It also meant that democracy, in the sense of open discussion and the election of leaders, was out of the question; instead you would have something of far greater value, namely 'complete, comradely mutual confidence among revolutionaries', who possess 'a lively sense of their *responsibility* [emphasis Lenin's], knowing as they do from experience that an organisation of real revolutionaries will stop at nothing to rid itself of an unworthy member'.[13] Lenin stressed that the party should be organised from the top down rather than from the bottom up. In his 1904 pamphlet, *One Step Forward, Two Steps Back*, he conceded that in this sense it was 'bureaucratic',[14] but his favourite analogy was that of an army. It was a 'militant vanguard', destined to become the 'regular troops' of the revolution.[15]

These ideas, and the practices they encouraged within the local underground groups and committees, were obnoxious to many social democrats, because they tended to turn the 'proletarian' party into an élite corps separate from, and superordinated over, the working proletarians, and to pour scorn on the democratic element in the international social democratic tradition. Some went further and saw here a modern-day Jacobinism, or a reversion to the ideas of Tkachov or even Blanqui, in that the prospects for successful revolution were made to depend primarily on the machinations of a band of conspirators rather than the class struggle.

The issue came to a head in the course of the Second Congress, which extended over nearly three weeks, starting in Brussels and finishing in London. Lenin now found himself opposed not only by 'economist' delegates and other critics of *Iskra*, but also by several of his *Iskra* collaborators, notably his old comrade Martov (but not yet by Plekhanov, though he, too, was soon to split with Lenin and to denounce his views and methods as a perversion of Marxism).[16] The crucial confrontation erupted in the discussion of article 1 of the party rules, which defined who was entitled to join. Lenin's draft envisaged a membership limited to those prepared to undertake 'personal participation in one of the party organisations' – that is, to full-time activists – while Martov's alternative extended it to 'everyone who accepts the party programme, supports the party by material means and affords it regular personal assistance under the guidance of one of its organisations'. The latter won a slight majority of votes. However, the issue had polarised the delegates into supporters and opponents of Lenin, the former predominating after a walk-out by the delegates of the Jewish Bund and the 'economists' and so gaining a small majority in the Central Committee and Party Council. They were therefore dubbed the *bol'sheviki*, the 'majority people' from the word *bol'she* (more), while their opponents were called the *men'sheviki*, the 'minority people', from *men'she* (less). The cleavage turned out to be permanent, and the names stuck, giving a distinct psychological advantage to Lenin and his supporters.

The kaleidoscopic history of Lenin's Bolshevism during the last fourteen years of the Tsarist order cannot be considered here in any detail. The shifts and turns of its face and fate reflected both the sharp changes occurring in Russian society and politics, and the course of the sectarian struggles inside the revolutionary movement itself. The wave of demonstrations, mutinies and peasant violence known as the 1905 Revolution brought an enormous influx of members into all the revolutionary and radical parties, while the consequent establishment of an elective parliamentary assembly (the Duma) and other liberalising measures such as the legalisation of trade unions opened up broad possibilities of 'above ground' political activity. The Bolsheviks were scarcely less energetic than their Menshevik rivals in exploiting these. This combination of legal with underground activities persisted despite the police clamp-down from 1907 on and the associated contraction in the social democratic ranks from a peak of about 150,000 to some 10,000 by 1910.[17] The resumption of rapid industrial growth and with it the upsurge of worker militancy in the years preceding the First World War led the Bolsheviks to devote much of their energies to the activities of the trade unions and other 'economic' organisations of the workers. Throughout this period both Bolsheviks and Mensheviks had members sitting in the Duma, and from 1912 the Bolsheviks also published a legal newspaper in Russia, *Pravda*.

Lenin himself spent practically the whole of these years abroad (based in Geneva or Paris and during the war in Cracow), engaged in constant struggles to gain control of the social democratic movement and to mould it to his purposes, struggles involving the convening of conferences and counter-conferences, the setting-up and takeover of committees and counter-committees, the forming and shifting of alliances and the recruitment and discarding of collaborators. The issues were important and genuine enough: whether to stand members for the Duma, and later whether to keep them there; whether to persist with underground activities or to concentrate on what could now be done legally; how to relate to the workers 'spontaneous' struggle; whether Marxism should be understood and propagated as a new religion (the controversy over 'god-building'); the proper strategy and tactics of socialists towards the national aspirations of Russia's subject peoples; whether to make common cause with the middle-class liberals or the land-hungry peasants; and after 1914 whether or not to support Russia's war effort.

These were not simply Bolshevik versus Menshevik issues, for the RSDWP also embraced the Jewish Bund and the Polish and Lettish socialists, as well as smaller groups within the Russian party proper, notably those around Plekhanov and Trotsky. The cleavages, moreover, sometimes cut across these main divisions; for example on the question of whether or not to keep socialist deputies in the Duma Lenin found himself aligned with the Mensheviks against many of his own adherents.[18] Yet however important the policy issues were and however genuine and passionate Lenin's commitment to particular positions, what most distinguished his comportment in all these disputes was his thorough blending of issue and power: the power of his faction and his power within that faction. It is pointless to argue over whether Lenin was obsessed with power for its own sake. What is clear is that when he was convinced (as he usually was) that he knew what was right, he regarded it as pusillanimous and irresponsible not to fight for that right with all his mind and energy, and without scrupling over methods. Opposition was not to be compromised with, it was to be defeated.

It was perhaps inevitable, therefore, that having despaired of gaining effective dominance of the RSDWP as a whole, he would eventually move – as he did at the Prague Conference of 1912 – to place his own followers under an entirely separate executive responsive to his will and judgement, claiming to speak on behalf of the whole party and collaborating with other groups of social democrats only on his own terms.

Nevertheless right up to 1917 Lenin's aspiration to weld his supporters into a centralised, disciplined, hierarchically structured organisation bore only modest fruits. To start with, most of the time there was no regularly functioning executive body inside Russia, and although Lenin sought to keep in touch from Geneva with the scattered Bolshevik committees through the medium of smuggled and coded correspondence conducted mostly by his wife Krupskaya, the slowness and unreliability of such communications rendered it impossible to direct their activities in any concrete way. Second, revolutionary social democrats inside Russia were often bemused and repelled by the bitter factional disputes among the émigré notables, and although most of them had sooner or later to identify themselves as either Bolshevik or Menshevik, they often continued to cooperate inside the one committee. The Prague Conference in 1912 accelerated the process of separation, but even in 1917 there were quite a few local organisations that simply called themselves 'social democratic', thus disavowing any unequivocal and exclusive subordination to either the Bolshevik or Menshevik central executives.

Another major factor was the changing character of the grass-roots party membership. In the euphoria of 1905 the original core of revolutionary intellectuals was swamped by vast numbers of mostly working-class recruits, and then as the police got the upper hand again after 1907 there was a disastrous fall-off in membership, many local organisations being reduced to a handful of members and some disappearing altogether. Those who held on were largely workers; the educated activists had suffered disproportionately from the constant waves of arrests, some had emigrated, and many had dropped out of the revolutionary movement, moved either by disillusionment or by the new opportunities for living a normal life while serving progressive causes within the law.[19] The so-called 'flight of the intellectuals' seriously damaged the effectiveness of local committees by depriving them of the skills which the educated revolutionary could contribute to the basic party tasks of organisation, propaganda and agitation: also an educated revolutionary was often able to devote his full-time to the cause by virtue of his private income or the help of well-to-do family or friends.[20] Lenin's ideal of the party as an organisation of professional revolutionaries was obviously unachievable under these circumstances, and he was realistic enough to acknowledge this, thereby scandalising some of his supporters. At this period he came to see virtue in the necessity of relying predominantly on a new breed of revolutionary activists employed in the factories, educated almost entirely by the party but thoroughly attuned to the mood and needs of the rank-and-file worker.[21] This change in the social composition of the party was not confined to its rank-and-file membership. David Lane's analysis of the biographies of over a thousand social democrats active in Russia in the period 1898–1907 showed that among all those identified as Bolsheviks 44 per cent had a higher education, 23 per cent secondary, and 9 per cent primary (with 24 per cent unknown), and among rank-and-file Bolsheviks 16 per cent had higher education, 19 per cent secondary and 21 per cent primary (44 per cent unknown).[22] What data he was able to obtain on the social origin of rank-and-file communists at this period suggest that only about half of them came from working-class or peasant families and the other half came from the gentry or middle class.[23] No comparable analysis for the period after 1907 is available, but all reports make clear that the rank-and-file membership became virtually confined to working men of lower-class origin and very little formal education, while among the local leadership the proportion of educated Bolsheviks of upper- or middle-class background declined rapidly. Only 5 per cent of the delegates to the Second RSDWP Congress in 1903 were workers; the proportion leaped to 25 per cent at the Fourth Congress in 1906 and to 40 per cent at the Fifth Congress in the following year. At the Bolshevik-only Prague Conference of 1912, fully 64 per cent of the delegates, who were mostly leaders of local committees inside Russia, were identified as workers.[24]

The substantial proletarianisation of the party's membership in the decade before the revolution was accompanied by some less obvious changes. Always a party of young men, it became even more so during this period. The median age of Lane's sample of local Bolshevik leaders active between 1898 and 1907 was 26, and four-fifths of his rank-and-file Bolsheviks were under 30.[25] Delegates to RSDWP Congresses between 1903 and 1906 averaged between 30.1 and 31.7. The average went down to 27.7 at the Fifth Congress in 1907 and to 26.1 at the Prague Conference. By the latter date there were many local leaders in their early twenties and rank-and-file members in their teens.[26] From the earliest days a number of women occupied prominent positions in the party, largely in secretarial roles, and this continued after 1907. The majority of Bolsheviks, however, were always men, and although no reliable general statistics are available the indications are that the 'flight of the intelligentsia' reduced the proportion of women in the local organisations still further. There were 19 women at the Fifth Congress in 1907, most of them Bolsheviks, but none at all at the Prague Conference five years later.[27]

If Lenin was forced by circumstances to qualify his ideal of the party as an organisation of professional revolutionaries, he was likewise constrained to compromise on his military–bureaucratic concept of its internal relationships. It would be a mistake to absolutise Bolshevik–Menshevik differences on this aspect. In particular, all saw a role for the Central Committee in the 'allocation of forces' (the assignment of leading activists to particular organisations) and recognised the need to temper election with cooptation.[28] All, too, accepted the principle of 'democratic centralism', which provided that, so far as practicable under prevailing political circumstances, there was to be broad discussion at all levels before decisions were taken, usually by simple majority vote, but once decisions were reached all were to obey them without further argument and the decisions of higher echelons were to prevail over those of lower ones.[29] Within this ostensible consensus, however, there was room for wide differences of emphasis and interpretation, associated with sharply contrasting patterns of behaviour.

Lenin's position, as we have seen, stood at one extreme, and is perhaps most succinctly and graphically summed up in his 'Letter to a Comrade on our Organisational Tasks', circulated in hectographed form before the Second Congress, and subsequently published in Geneva as a pamphlet. The party should be like an orchestra, he argued, with the centre as conductor; to do that effectively, it had to know precisely 'who is playing what fiddle and where he's playing it, where what instruments have been and are being studied, who is playing a false note and where and why, and who should be transferred to correct the dissonance, and how and where to, etc.'.[30] He deplored the 'inappropriate and immoderate application of the elective principle' and stressed the Central Committee's responsibility for 'the allocation of forces, the appointment of persons and groups'.[31] Similarly in the relationships between the local committees and their subordinate district bodies, 'The composition of the district group should be determined by the committee, that is, the committee *appoints* one or two of its members (or even non-members) as delegates for such-and-such a district and authorizes these delegates *to put together the district group,* all members of which should again be confirmed, so to speak, in their appointments' (emphasis in the original).[32] And finally the district groups and subcommittees form the base-level groups in the same way.[33] The bureaucratic character of this model is obvious, and is perhaps made more explicit than intended by a passage in which Lenin refers to the party's 'members and its functionaries (*dolzhnostnye litsa*)'.[34] It is bureaucratic, in its insistence on hierarchy, on the upward flow of information and the downward flow of authority, on a clear division of labour and responsibilities, and on the importance of relevant training and experience. It is not bureaucratic, however, in the sense of being rule-bound. On the contrary, it denies that an insistence on rules will bring order into the work of the party; this can only be achieved by keeping the centre informed of all that is going on.[35]

There is no evidence that Lenin ever came to reject this bureaucratic–military model as mistaken. Experience was to show, however, that it was only partly realisable, and Lenin had to settle for something far short of the ideal. We have already noted the role in this of the conditions prevailing after the 1905 Revolution, but there were two more basic obstacles. The first was the efficiency of the Okhrana in crippling the main component in the model, its illegal organisation, by identifying, tracking down, and arresting key committee members and the agents and couriers sent by the émigré and Russian-based centres, by constant surveillance and harassment, intercepting communications, and so on. As mentioned earlier, Lenin's constant efforts to establish a Central Committee inside Russia exercising effective direction of the local committees enjoyed only modest and spasmodic success. There were attempts to make up for this in part through the medium of regional (*oblastnye*) committees, each responsible for the party organisations in a group of provinces (*gubernii*). These, however, were rendered ineffective by the police, who regularly rounded up their key figures. Ironically, considering Lenin's passionate insistence on the necessity of retaining the clandestine party apparatus, it was largely through such legal channels as the Bolshevik Duma fraction and the open party newspaper *Pravda* that such coordination and guidance as existed was achieved. But if Lenin's party never evolved a clear hierarchy of command through which the centre monitored and directed day-to-day operations around the country, this is not to say that it had no organisational cohesion at all. The leadership determined current goals, priorities and standards and it had considerable success in conveying these, through its legal and illegal publications, through open and secret correspondence, and by occasional specific instructions and postings of personnel, to the local leaders, activists and ordinary members. The latter – and this is what being a Bolshevik involved – sought on the whole to conform their activities to those goals, priorities and standards, in the light of their specific circumstances, combining their efforts in whatever ways seemed effective, without much concern for formal roles or rights. The Bolshevik organisation thus took on qualities which Burns and Stalker have identified as typical of what they call organic management systems, in which

> individuals have to perform their special tasks in the light of their knowledge of the tasks of the firm as a whole. Jobs lose much of their formal definition in terms of methods, duties and powers, which have to be redefined continually by interaction with others participating in a task. Interaction runs laterally as much as vertically. Communication between people of different ranks tends to resemble lateral consultation rather than vertical command. Omniscience can no longer be imputed to the head of the concern.[36]

The other main factor frustrating Lenin's efforts to build a party organisation on the bureaucratic–military model was the widespread attachment to democratic attitudes and practices among the rank-and-file membership. These, as we have noted, were present from the inception of the Russian social democratic movement, were indeed indispensible to the recognition of the RSDWP by the fraternal parties of the Second International, and Lenin had perforce to acknowledge the principle of *democratic centralism*, whatever his private reservations. Police harassment, of course, drastically impeded democratic procedures like local conferences, party elections and the involvement of wider circles of members in decisions. Nevertheless the assumption that such procedures *should* be followed as far as possible was widespread. Paradoxically, they would perhaps have been accorded less respect if police efforts had been less effective and Lenin had been able to run a tighter ship. Meanwhile the opportunity and need after 1905 for the Bolsheviks to become involved in the activities of such legal working-class organisations as the trade unions, insurance funds and cooperatives, all of which were formally structured along democratic lines, tended to reinforce the sense that such procedures were normal and legitimate among socialists.[37] Democracy, then, was not a mere sham in pre-revolutionary Bolshevism. In however qualified a form and degree, it became entrenched as a genuine and important element in the pattern of thought and behaviour of Lenin's followers. Both the genuineness and the qualifications in practice are exemplified by the way party officials and committee members were commonly chosen, namely by a blend of election and cooptation. This blend, obviously a far cry from Lenin's purely top-down model as advocated in such earlier writings as his 'Letter to a Comrade', cited above, was given official endorsement by the Cracow conference of leading Bolsheviks in January 1913.[38]

The genuine democratic element in pre-revolutionary Bolshevik attitudes and practices has tended to be passed over and the contrasts in this respect between Bolsheviks and Mensheviks are often exaggerated. We should, however, beware of over-correcting. If the blend of democratic and military–bureaucratic elements in the organisation and behaviour of the varied components that made up the RSDWP can be seen as a continuum, the Bolsheviks certainly stood at one extreme of that continuum. Moreover, while there came to be many issues dividing Lenin's followers from other social democrats, it was his top-down approach to organisation that provoked the split in the first place and it remained a permanent and potent source of division. There were all sorts of reasons why a young convert to social democracy could gravitate to one or other faction, but if he gave a high priority to intra-party democracy he would be unlikely to opt for the Bolsheviks. And if some degree of attachment to democracy was widespread among the Bolshevik rank-and-file, it was not characteristic of the hard men that tended to come to the fore in the underground organisations: men like Vyacheslav Skryabin (Molotov), Iosif Dzhugashvili (Stalin), Andrei Bubnov and Grigori Ordzhonikidze. These were the sort of men Lenin increasingly relied on after 1912 to run his organisation, and his chief lieutenant from 1909 on, Grigory Radomysl'sky (Zinoviev), was cast very much in the same mould.

Towards the Proletarian Dictatorship

Had Tsar Nicholas II and his advisors not embroiled Russia in the First World War Lenin's Bolsheviks might never have merited more than a footnote in today's history books. Indeed, if Imperial Russia's spectacular economic growth, the shift from the commune into family farms, the mass education programme, rudimentary parliamentarism and substantial civil rights had continued uninterrupted for another fifteen or twenty years there were reasonable chances of her achieving a more or less peaceful transition to a modern bourgeois order by the middle of the century. Even, however, if this evolutionary development had been cut short later by some other trauma, and some kind of revolutionary change had ensued, it is unlikely that Lenin would have been in a position, if still alive and active, to play any major role in it. Meanwhile, the combination of substantial legal possibilities for useful political activity with constant and effective police repression of the illegal apparatus might well in time have domesticated the Russian social democratic movement, Bolsheviks included, to the existing order, as had already happened in Germany.

It is worth pondering briefly on such 'might have beens', for it is difficult to exaggerate the impact of the war on Lenin's fortunes and thus on the whole future evolution of Russia. One incidental effect of its outbreak was to cut short serious efforts by the International Socialist Bureau to force unity on the Russian social democrats, efforts which might have further isolated Lenin and accelerated the trend to 'domestication'. What, however, was of more fateful consequence was that Lenin immediately perceived and then consistently pursued with his usual single-minded zeal the possibility that the war between states could be turned into a war between classes. As early as January 1913 he had written that 'war between Austria and Russia would be a very useful thing for the revolution in all of Eastern Europe'.[39] And now, with the socialist leaders in Western Europe betraying the repeated anti-war resolutions of the

Second International and rushing to support their nations' war efforts, Lenin proclaimed the defeat of Tsarism as the 'least evil' and called on genuinely internationalist socialists in all the belligerent states to support a programme of fraternisation in the trenches, political strikes and ultimately of civil war. Outside Russia few heeded his call, but at home his words were to fall on more fertile soil.

The social democratic members of Russia's Duma, in glaring contrast to most socialist parliamentarians elsewhere, refused to support the war, and the bulk of party activists, Bolshevik and Menshevik alike, followed suit. However, whereas the Bolsheviks were consistent and unequivocal in their opposition to the war – and in November 1914 their Duma deputies were all arrested, along with Lenin's chief agent inside Russia, Kamenev, for attending an anti-war conference – the Menshevik leaders spoke with many voices. At one extreme stood Plekhanov, who did indeed call for support of Russia's war against the central powers; at the other were Martov and his colleagues in the Menshevik Secretariat in exile, who shared Lenin's wholehearted condemnation of the war and belief in revolution as the only ultimate solution, while however rejecting his emphasis on Russia's defeat as the 'least evil' (that is, the most desirable outcome); and in between there was every gradation of qualified opposition to the war effort and qualified support for it. The result was that for the great many Russian social democrats who felt support for the regime's war measures to be contrary to the workers' interests and inconsistent with Marxism, Lenin seemed to be offering the only determined and consistent leadership. The war thus gave another wrench to the kaleidoscope of social democratic factionalism, both among the émigrés and inside Russia, and among leaders, activists and rank-and-file members; many who had previously opposed Lenin now identified themselves as Bolsheviks, or, like Trotsky, moved into closer alignment with him. (In 1917 Trotsky and his small band of supporters were to cast aside their reservations and become fully-fledged Bolsheviks.) This realignment did not occur overnight. Many worker socialists were caught up in the great surge of patriotism that followed the outbreak of war. But as economic conditions deteriorated and the casuality lists lengthened, the tide of support turned towards those who had been the toughest opponents of the war effort.

Many have noted the irony that after a century of conspiring, agitating and suffering for the overthrow of the Tsarist regime, Russia's revolutionaries of all hues were caught by surprise when in March 1917 it actually happened, and played no direct part in it.

Their role was nevertheless vital in having eaten away at the legitimacy of the old order and in now providing political alternatives for the construction of a new one. What was not so apparent at first, but was soon to emerge all too starkly, was that it was alternatives in the plural that were on offer, and they were not all mutually reconcilable. There were, first, the alternative political parties, principally the liberal Octobrists and Cadets, the populist Socialist Revolutionaries (SRs) and the social democrats – still divided basically into Mensheviks and Bolsheviks. All at first seemed agreed on turning Russia into a democracy, and on convening a Constituent Assembly to decide on the details, but they were deeply divided both by the interests to which they appealed and by their ultimate goals. Second there were the alternative institutions: on the one hand there was the Provisional Government, claiming authority from the Duma and dominated at first by the liberals (later the balance was to shift towards the SRs and Mensheviks), and on the other the councils (soviets) of workers' and soldiers' deputies chosen at mass meetings in factories and barracks, first and foremost the Petrograd Soviet, and dominated by the Mensheviks, Bolsheviks and SRs.

By the middle of the year the Bolsheviks had emerged as the alternative of alternatives, the irreconcilable of irreconcilables, and again the crucial issue was the war. It was the war, whose deprivations and carnage had both aroused the Petrograd masses to open revolt and deterred the soldiers of the garrison from suppressing them, that paved the way to revolution, as Lenin had hoped. But instead of taking immediate steps to stop the war, the heirs to imperial power, liberals and socialists alike, now caught the vision of a democratic Russia allied with the democracies of the West triumphing over the German and Austrian autocracies and thus ensuring the whole of Europe a democratic – and perhaps a socialist – future. This near-consensus implied substantial cooperation between the Provisional Government and the soviets, and there were at first even prominent Bolshevik leaders who were prepared to go along with it. A few weeks later Lenin put a dramatic end to that, immediately on his arrival in Petrograd from Switzerland, made possible by the cooperation of the German authorities. His position was again simple, consistent and unequivocal: the war remained an imperialist war; and peace could only come when power passed from the bourgeoisie into the hands of the proletariat and poorest peasants; there should therefore be no cooperation with the Provisional Government, which should be replaced by a republic of workers' and peasants' deputies, ushering in radical social changes; it was on the basis of this platform that the Bolsheviks should now set about working for a majority in the soviets.[40]

This bold and brutally uncompromising programme, which amounted to a call for a Bolshevik-led seizure of power through the medium of the soviets, caught many of Lenin's supporters flat-footed, but it undoubtedly chimed in with the mood of many rank-and-file party members and ordinary workers, and within three weeks he had gained endorsement for it at a special conference of 152 Bolshevik delegates from around the country (the 'April Conference'). It was a programme based on a penetrating assessment of the emergent political opportunities in the wake of the February–March Revolution, viewed through a conceptual prism comprised of both old and new elements in Lenin's thinking. Of key importance here were the concepts of 'imperialism' as the ultimate stage of capitalism; of the revolutionary alliance of the proletariat and the poorer peasantry; and of the soviets as the state form of the proletarian dictatorship. Each of these deserves a somewhat closer look.

Lenin's pamphlet *Imperialism, the Highest Stage of Capitalism*, written in early 1916, rested for its economic analysis on the works of J.A. Hobson *Imperialism* (1902) and Rudolf Hilferding *Finanzkapital* (1910), and in its exposition of the revolutionary implications drew heavily on the wartime writings of his young collaborator Nikolai Bukharin. The advanced capitalist states were now dominated by oligarchies of finance capitalists competing among themselves for control of territories for the extraction of raw materials and especially the export of capital. Hence the inevitability of wars between the imperialist powers for the redistribution of markets and of wars of national liberation in the colonies. The world was being transformed into a single, dynamic imperialist system in which the grievances of proletarians against capitalists were intermeshed with national grievances and peasant and local bourgeois grievances against feudal survivals and the domination of foreign capital in the colonial and less developed countries. A revolution leading ultimately to the collapse of the whole international system could be initiated at any point, but was now less likely in the 'metropoles' than on the periphery, where the sufferings of the masses were greatest and the combination of grievances most explosive.[41]

This doctrine gave powerful theoretical underpinning to a number of tactical lines which Lenin had been pursuing for many years. Most obviously it justified the telescoping of the bourgeois and the proletarian revolutions in 'backward' Russia in advance of – and hopefully leading to – the overthrow of capitalism in the West.

Secondly it confirmed Lenin's advocacy of the right of self-determination – including the right of secession – of subject nationalities, and first and foremost of Russia's national minorities, whose resentments and aspirations he wished to harness to his revolutionary cause. And, thirdly, it provided new and powerful arguments for the contention which, along with his concept of the party, divided Lenin more than any other issue from his fellow radicals in the RSDRP, namely that the peasantry should be the chief ally of the Russian proletariat not only in the bourgeois revolution but in taking the first steps towards socialism.

In Marxist terms the situation in the villages was marked by both 'feudal' and 'bourgeois' contradictions. On the one hand the emancipation of the serfs had left the gentry in possession of substantial holdings of farmland, now worked by hired labour, which the peasants thought should belong by right to the village community. On the other hand social differences were emerging among the peasants themselves, sometimes generating bitter resentments, especially vis-à-vis those enterprising families which had withdrawn from the *obshchina* and consolidated their strips into prosperous farms. The Bolsheviks sought to mobilise all these grievances in support of their cause. Thus, while they appealed first and foremost to the poorest elements among the peasantry and to the rural proletariat of farm labourers, they also urged the villagers as a whole to seize and split up among themselves the gentry land. Although they provided this policy with the socialist figleaf of 'nationalisation of all land' (the peasants were just to have the use of it), this was in essence the old populist programme of a 'black repartition' (*chernyi peredel*) which they were now with justice accused of 'stealing' from the SRs. Not only this, but since the latter, along with the Mensheviks and the Cadets, were committed to postponing all such radical measures till they could be decided by a Constituent Assembly, the Bolsheviks were now able to entice away a good deal of their peasant support by telling the villagers simply to help themselves without further ado.[42]

This same marriage of Marxist analysis and pragmatism displayed here in Lenin's tactics towards the peasantry is evident too in his approach to the soviets. As we have seen, Lenin was at first much taken with the potential of the soviets, once brought under effective Bolshevik leadership, to serve as the constituent units of 'a republic of soviets of workers', farm-labourers' and peasants' deputies throughout the country, from top to bottom'. What attracted Lenin in the soviets was not only that they provided an alternative basis of power and sphere of political action to the

Provisional Government and 'bourgeois' state generally, but their structure and mode of operation. For in his eyes they displayed precisely those features which Marx had celebrated in the Paris Commune and which he himself was to make so much of later in the year in his pamphlet *The State and Revolution*, namely that they contained in the same elected persons both 'legislative' and 'executive' functions. In other words they made their own rules, took their own decisions, and then carried them out themselves, with the voluntary help of the 'masses', and without the mediation of professional politicians or bureaucrats. These, Lenin stressed, were the essential characteristics of the future socialist state, for the 'bourgeois' state machine, contrary to the views of Kautsky and other leaders of the Second International, could not serve the proletariat as an instrument for the transition to socialism, but must be utterly smashed and swept away, to be replaced by a new state order modelled on the Commune.

Many writers have remarked on the uncharacteristic Utopianism of Lenin's 'commune' image of the future socialist state which he propagated during 1917. As Kolakowski puts it, 'it had about as much to do with the state that was soon to come into existence as Thomas More's fantasies had with the England of Henry VIII'.[43] Yet, while few would argue that Lenin only *pretended* to believe in his Utopia when he was writing about it, it proved no obstacle to his pragmatism whatsoever. When in the middle months of 1917 he despaired of establishing Bolshevik control of the soviets, he discarded the slogan 'all power to the soviets!' and declared that the party must seize power directly, independent of and if necessary *against* the soviets. By September–October, however, the Bolsheviks were gaining ground in the soviets by leaps and bounds, and the original formula was revived.

In the event, the outward forms of the 'soviet' regime established by the November 7th coup were to owe much to the commune model; its inner character, however, conformed rather to that other major concept expounded in *The State and Revolution*, namely 'the dictatorship of the proletariat', which Lenin likewise derived from Marx. 'Between capitalist and communist society', wrote the master in 1875 in his *Critique of the Gotha Programme*, 'lies the period of the revolutionary transformation of the one into the other. There corresponds to this also a political transition period in which the state can be nothing but the revolutionary dictatorship of the proletariat....'[44] Having recorded this reflection, Marx scarcely gave it a further thought. For Lenin, however, who saw his task as precisely that of achieving such a 'revolutionary transformation', it was to become the fulcrum of his thought and action, and he was always quite clear and frank about its essential meaning. 'Dictatorship', he had written as far back as 1906, 'means unlimited power based on force, and not on law'.[45] Such was the power he sought through the overthrow of the Provisional Government, soviets or no soviets, and despite the fact that the party scarcely gets a mention in *The State and Revolution*, there is no doubt who was intended to exercise that power: his party, since it was the 'vanguard of the proletariat', and in practice it was his party's 'most authoritative, influential and experienced members, who are elected to the most responsible positions, and are called leaders'.[46] In devising his party's strategy and tactics for the crucial struggle of 1917, no less than in devising his strategy and tactics for the intra-party struggles of the previous two decades, Lenin devoted enormous thought and passion to establishing and expounding their theoretical grounds. But in 1917, no less than in the past, his ultimate litmus test for correct theory, for correct strategy, and for correct tactics, was the test of power: did it make for a greater or lesser concentration of power in his and his followers' hands? The difference was that it was now not just dominance over a minor political party that was at stake, but absolute power over a mighty state controlling a sixth of the earth's surface.

But what of this party that was destined to exercise the world's first 'proletarian dictatorship'? In what shape was it to assume this supreme historic task? As we have seen, following the enormous expansion engendered by the 1905 Revolution, the RSDWP was by 1909–10 reduced by disillusionment and repression to a mere remnant. Between then and the outbreak of the First WorldWar the revival of working-class militancy brought many new recruits to the party, though the 'flight of the intellectuals' continued, and the Bolsheviks asserted a greater (though still incomplete) organisational separateness from the rest of the RSDWP. The initial impact of the war was disastrous. The rank-and-file of the revolutionary parties were not immune to the general upsurge of patriotism. Their activists were largely young men of military age, and many were conscripted, while those that remained were systematically rounded up by the police Within a year, however, the mood of the masses was beginning to sour. Strikes broke out and in the course of 1916 became more and more widespread. Revulsion against the war and desperation over rapidly worsening conditions drove many workers and others into the radical parties, and in particular into the ranks of the Bolsheviks, who were now rewarded for their uncompromising anti-war stand.[47] The estimate of the total number of Bolsheviks on the eve of the February Revolution most widely cited by soviet party historians is 23,600.[48] About three-fifths of them are said to have been workers, a mere 8 per cent peasants, and the remaining third were drawn from urban middle class groups (white-collar workers, professionals, students, etc.).[49]

The collapse of the old order, removing as it did all restrictions on the activities of the radical parties while engendering intense competition between them to maximise their support, brought a headlong growth of Bolshevik membership, which seems to have at least doubled in the few weeks leading up to the April Conference. Membership statistics for the months that followed are understandably confused and contradictory, but there were probably something of the order of a quarter million Bolsheviks in the party's ranks by the time of the seizure of power.[50] The proportion of workers seems to have remained stable at close to 60 per cent, but there were some significant changes in the composition of the non-worker membership. Peasants, most of them peasants in uniform, are said to have increased to about 15 per cent. There is abundant evidence, on the other hand, that the 'intelligentsia' (professionals and others with advanced education, including students) were still shunning the Bolsheviks, and they made up an ever smaller percentage in the local organisations. By contrast, the party was attracting considerable numbers of office-workers and others in lower-grade white-collar occupations, who evidently supplied something like 30 per cent of all recruits during 1917.[51]

The great expansion of the Bolshevik and other left-wing parties in 1917 was just one manifestation of that explosion of mass political activism which found simultaneous expression in the mushrooming factory and soldiers' committees, in the trade unions, and the soviets. Indeed the key task that faced the Bolsheviks was to remain attuned to this mass activism, to penetrate and ultimately control it organisationally, and to harness it to the party's purposes. It was now that the experience, acquired by local Bolshevik committees in the pre-war years, of involvement in the workers' struggles through factory-based cells and agitational activities focused on specific grievances, came into its own. That experience, however, was now spread very thin, for there was a desperate shortage of veteran activists to staff the scores of new and resuscitated party committees around the country and the thousands of party groups formed within the factories and mass organisations. It is true that many case-hardened undergrounders were now returning from prison and Siberian exile, while many other old Bolsheviks who had dropped out of political activity now rallied with renewed hope and vigour to the party's cause. Nevertheless at the grass-roots the handful of experienced members were obliged to rely mainly on newly recruited activists who had demonstrated the right attitudes and qualities in the daily rough-and-tumble of the soviets, factory committees, and trade unions.

The key positions at the centre and in the local committees were monopolised throughout 1917 by party veterans, and for the most part veterans of the underground rather than the emigration. The 264 voting and non-voting delegates to the Bolshevik Congress (called the Sixth) convened in August were asked to fill in questionnaires on their background and pre-revolutionary and current political activity. Two-thirds of them (171) did so, and analysis of these tells us much about the commanding heights of the party in the lead-up to the seizure of power.[52] On average they had been in the party for ten years, and only one in 17 had less than three years', service. Most of them were strikingly youthful veterans, however. Their average age was 29, the youngest being 18 and the oldest (Lenin) 47. Only 16 per cent had been politically active outside Russia, half of these for two years or less. The vast majority, then, had acquired their party experience in the underground struggle at home, and for their pains almost two-thirds of them had done time in prison and a third in internal exile. By their basic occupation 40 per cent were blue-collar workers, 13 per cent white-collar workers, and 32 per cent intellectuals (writers, teachers, lawyers, doctors, etc.). The rest had no definite occupation. A third had enjoyed higher education and another quarter had gone to secondary school. Only six per cent of this party leadership cadre were women. Ethnic Russians made up 54 per cent, Jews 17 per cent, Latvians 10 per cent, Poles 5 per cent, Ukrainians and Georgians 4 per cent each, and six other nationalities were represented. These young revolutionaries, then, displayed a wide diversity of ethnic and social background, education and skills, as no doubt they did in personal character; overshadowing this diversity, however, was the common experience of total commitment to the revolutionary cause, with all its sacrifices and dangers, its comradeship and shared enemies, sorrows and exhilaration.

By this time Lenin's Bolsheviks had taken organisational shape as a multi-tiered, nationwide hierarchy, running down from the Central Committee and its Secretariat through regional, city and district committees to the workplace cells. Yet nothing could be more misleading than to imagine them as a disciplined revolutionary army deployed in battle through a firm line of command.[53] Its 'General Staff' consisted of secretaries Yakov Sverdlov and Elena Stasova with some half-dozen assistants. Although they were said to have despatched some 1,700 letters to subordinate organisations between March and October, examination of those that have survived shows very few to have had the character of clear, concrete directives.[54] Moreover the Secretariat had neither the information nor the effective powers to exercise the Central Committee's responsibilities for 'assigning party forces'. Even when it did attempt repostings those concerned more often than not declined to comply and there was no way of calling them to heel.[55]   On occasion major local committees and even the Central Bureau of Military Organisations departed from Central Committee policies on important issues.[56] Nevertheless there is probably justice in the argument that, whatever the Bolsheviks' organisational deficiencies, Lenin had instilled in them a far greater sense of the *importance* of organisation and discipline than that of their socialist rivals, and this helped them to operate with greater cohesion, flexibility and dispatch. It showed up, for example, in the relative effectiveness of their caucasing inside the soviets and other mass organisations. Without this they would probably never have been able to win control of the Second Congress of Soviets or to mobilise their supporters to actually take power in Petrograd and around the country. However, no less crucial to their success than the organisational edge they had over their competitors was the platform of policies they offered the masses in competing for their support.

There was probably as much democracy as there was centralism in the operation of the Bolshevik party during 1917. This dichotomy, however, scarcely catches its flavour. More helpful is the 'organic' model of organisation which we have already employed to characterise pre-war Bolshevism.   This was no 'mechanistic' organisation feeding detailed information up the line and detailed instructions down the line. The centre attempted no more than to set basic goals ('win control of the soviets, seize power' etc.), to supply the slogans around which the party was to mobilize mass support ('bread', 'peace', 'land'), and to frame broad guidelines on tactics. The rest was up to the local committees. And the latter operated with a very high level of rank-and-file participation. Decision-making was often akin to 'brainstorming', and often turbulent. The division of labour was fluid and informal: members turned their hand to whatever they could best contribute to the job in train. This was vividly reflected in the responses of Sixth Congress delegates to the question of what party roles they performed (committee members, organisers, propagandists, agitators, treasurers, printery managers etc.). A mere quarter of them named one role only, while a quarter named four or more. And on top of these were their roles in non-party organisations – in the soviets, trade unions, city dumas, *zemstva*, factory committees, etc. – often in more than one of them.[57]

A similar pattern prevailed at the apex of the pyramid. The Central Committee, consisting after the Sixth Congress of 21 voting and 8 alternate members,[58] considered and decided most important tactical and organisational issues. Its meetings were frequent but irregular, averaging one a week. Attendance varied widely. At first there was a distinction between 'plenary' and 'narrow' meetings, but the latter, which eleven designated members were entitled to attend, faded out of existence early in September. Later meetings consisted of anything from eight to eighteen members and alternates. There were usually some five or six agenda items, sometimes hotly contested, and decided by simple majority vote. Current party tasks and key roles in soviet and other bodies were allocated and reallocated as circumstances changed.

This, then, was the revolutionary party that took power in Petrograd on 7 November 1917 (October 24th in the old calendar) and proclaimed the establishment of a Russian Worker and Peasant Soviet Republic. The drama of events that led to this victory has been so often recounted that here we need sketch in only the barest outline.[59] The key factors were the progressive disintegration of the army on the Eastern Front, beginning with the February Revolution and accelerating with the debacle of Kerensky's offensive in June; the radical mood of the troops garrisoning Petrograd and their determination not to be sent to the front; the failure of the Provisional Government to solve the problem of food supplies to the cities, which had precipitated the February rising; the assumption by the peasants in and out of uniform that the downfall of the monarchy meant the collapse of all aspects of the old order and in particular the gentry's authority and ownership of land; the disorganisation of industry and the associated attempts by workers' factory committees to assume control over management; the consequent resurgence and growing intensity of mass discontent and anger, now directed against the Provisional Government; the fact that the Bolsheviks were the only major party not represented in the Government and therefore free to give a lead to radical opposition, through their agitation and propaganda, and the organisation of demonstrations, protest meetings, strikes and workers' committees; and finally their more effective organisation and their possession in Lenin of a leader of unrivalled singlemindedness, drive and authority over his followers.

Although initially enjoying only modest support, the Bolsheviks succeeded by vigorous exploitation of these factors in rapidly building up their numbers and influence in the soviets, soldiers' committees, factory committees and trade unions.[60] The extent and alarming implications of that influence were made manifest in early July by the mass armed demonstration of tens of thousands of Petrograd workers and soldiers demanding the transfer of state power to the soviets. Although the Bolshevik leadership evidently did not organise this, they attempted to place themselves at its head, thereby affording the Provisional Government ample reason to move against them when the *Putsch* collapsed, with the support of the Menshevik and Socialist Revolutionary leaders of the Central Executive Committee of the Congress of Soviets. Several Bolshevik leaders were arrested, but Lenin and Zinoviev managed to go into hiding in Finland. It was now that the slogan 'all power to the soviets' was replaced by 'all power to the working class, led by the Bolshevik party'.

This defeat did little to stem the tide of support for the Bolsheviks; indeed the July days further accelerated it by dramatising that the Bolsheviks were the sole militant spokesmen for the masses' deepest-held grievances. They were able to hold their Sixth Congress semi-openly and to elect their new Central Committee. More and more local soviets passed into their hands and with them more potential delegates to the All-Russian Congress of Soviets. Nor – although for a time they had to operate semi-clandestinely – was the Government in a position to eliminate the Bolshevik Military Organisation with its links to sympathetic units in the Petrograd garrison, or the Bolshevik-dominated armed detachments of workers – the Red Guards. Then at the end of August came the government crisis that shifted the balance of forces decisively in the Bolsheviks' favour. Prime Minister Kerensky, influenced by rumours of an impending Bolshevik coup, entered into discussions with Commander-in-Chief Kornilov on the imposition of martial law in Petrograd, but then evidently decided that the latter was planning to depose him; in the resulting confrontation the Government called on all 'democratic' forces, including the Bolsheviks, to save the revolution from military dictatorship, and this legitimated the Bolsheviks' access to weapons and their influence among the troops garrisoning Petrograd.

By early September the Bolsheviks had won a majority in both the Petrograd and Moscow Soviets, and within a week Lenin was writing to the Central Committee from his hiding-place in Finland, 'the Bolsheviks can and must take state power into their own hands'.

Some of his leading comrades were by this time attracted by the possibility of a peaceful transition to a multi-party soviet government, and his initial pleas met with an embarrassed silence. A new Congress of Soviets was indeed in the offing, but Lenin derided the idea of waiting in the hope it would contain a Bolshevik majority. Even more vehemently was he opposed to awaiting the Constituent Assembly elections, as he recognised that his party would be heavily outnumbered in this more fully representative body. In the days and weeks that followed he bombarded the Central Committee with missives of ever more passionate urgency, and finally at a meeting on 10 October, which he attended in disguise, he secured a majority vote for insurrection. Ostensibly as a precaution against a right-wing coup, a Military Revolutionary Committee (MRC) was set up under the Petrograd Soviet which was now headed by Trotsky. On 25 October (7 November) soldiers were directed by the MRC to occupy key transport and communication facilities and government buildings. They encountered no serious resistance, hardly any troops now being prepared to defend the Provisional Government. By the small hours of the following morning, after an assault on the Imperial Winter Palace where the Provisional Government was in session, its ministers were taken into custody, although Kerensky managed to slip away. Russia's brief false dawn of 'bourgeois' democracy was at an end.

By a mixture of good luck and design, the Bolshevik coup coincided with the convening of the Second Congress of Soviets. Elected predominantly from urban areas and military units where the Bolsheviks were unusually strong, the Congress contained some 300 Bolsheviks among the 670 delegates. After a stormy exchange the Mensheviks and the Right SRs walked out in protest against the armed rising. The rump of Bolsheviks and Left SRs, who had supported the rising, now endorsed its result. 'The Congress takes power into its hands', they resolved. 'All power in the localities passes to soviets of workers', soldiers' and peasants' deputies, whose duty it is to establish genuine revolutionary order.' They elected a Central Executive Committee and an all-Bolshevik government styled the 'Council of Peoples Commissars', and headed by Lenin.

Lenin had now achieved the goal which had consumed him since his arrival in Petrograd seven months earlier: he and his Bolshevik followers had taken power in the Russian capital. In the weeks and months that followed they were to extend that power over most of European Russia. That they could claim with some plausibility to exercise it in the name of the soviets was undoubtedly of great help in maintaining and consolidating their authority. Yet it is abundantly clear that for Lenin this was of secondary importance: it was not *soviet* power that mattered, but *Bolshevik* power. On this key question he differed radically not only from the majority of socialists, but even from many of his own supporters, who took the slogan 'all power to the soviets' seriously and assumed that that power should be shared by all the major parties represented in the soviets.

There were, then, good grounds for seeing in the Bolshevik seizure of power the triumph of Jacobinism, the establishment of a revolutionary dictatorship by a self-chosen political élite, a tradition with deep roots in the Russian revolutionary intelligentsia going right back to the Decembrists.[61] Yet there was more to it than a mere Blanquist coup by a handful of conspirators, despite contemporary and later accusations to this effect. Sensitive to the charge, Lenin put his rebuttal to the Central Committee in a letter written in mid-September.

> To be successful, insurrection must rely not upon conspiracy and not upon a party, but upon the advanced class. Insurrection must rely upon *a revolutionary upsurge of the people.* That is the second point. Insurrection must rely upon such a *crucial moment* in the history of the growing revolution when the activity of the advanced ranks of the people is at its height, and when the vacillations in the ranks of the enemy and *in the ranks of the weak, half-hearted and irresolute friends of the revolution* are strongest. This is the third point and these three conditions for raising the question of insurrection distinguish Marxism from Blanquism. (Emphasis in the original.)[62]

He went on to argue, and surely he was right, that these conditions were not present in July but now they were. Insurrection, therefore, now reduced itself to 'an art', and not to treat it as such would be 'a betrayal of Marxism and a betrayal of the revolution'.

The 'advanced class' referred to here was of course the proletariat, and the 'revolution' was the proletarian revolution. The purpose of the insurrection was to establish the 'dictatorship of the proletariat', his central concern in *The State and Revolution*, written at much the same time as this letter. Nor was the October coup envisaged as simply a proletarian revolution *for Russia.*, although nourished by the hopes, hates and experience of generations of the Russian revolutionary intelligentsia. 'We are out to rebuild the world', wrote Lenin in April, in 'The Tasks of the Proletariat in Our Revolution'.[63] And in his opening speech at the party conference two weeks later, he had said:

Comrades, we are assembled here, as the first conference of the proletarian party, in conditions of the Russian Revolution and a developing world revolution as well....

In the nineteenth century Marx and Engels, observing the proletarian movement in various countries and analysing the possible prospects for a social revolution, repeatedly asserted that the roles would, in general, be distributed among these countries in proportion to, and in accordance with their historically conditioned national features....

The great honour of beginning the revolution has fallen to the Russian proletariat. But the Russian proletariat must not forget that its movement and revolution are only part of a world revolutionary proletarian movement, which in Germany, for example, is gaining momentum with every passing day. Only from this angle can we define our tasks.[64]

The proletarian revolution in Russia, then, would open the way to the building of a communist society not only in Russia itself, but in the whole world. It was for this lofty goal that he led the Bolshevik party into establishing their 'proletarian dictatorship' in Petrograd seven months later.

Notes and References

1 References to the general literature on Marxism may be supererogatory, but particularly apt for our present purposes are Leszek Kolakowski, *Main Currents of Marxism. Its Origins, Growth and Dissolution*, translated from the Polish by P.S. Falla, 3 vols., (Oxford University Press, Oxford, New York, etc.), 1978; references here are to the 1981 paperback edition. For a brief introduction, see Alfred G. Meyer, *Marxism. The Unity of Theory and Practice*, (Harvard Unity Press, Cambridge, Mass.), 1954.

2 Marx and Engels, 'The Communist Manifesto', cited here from Frederic C. Bender, *Karl Marx: Essential Writings*, (Harper Torchbooks, New York, London, etc.), 1972, p.252.

3 Perhaps the best brief introduction to the intelligentsia is still John Maynard, *Russia in Flux. Before October*, (Gollancz, London), 1941, Chapter 7.

4 See Kolakowski, vol.2, pp.323–4.

5　See *Pervyi s"ezd RSDRP. Mart 1898 goda. Dokumenty i materialy,* (Gospolizdat, Moscow, 1958) pp.101–2 (text), p.322 (n.46). The initials RSDRP stood for the Russian Social Democratic *Workers'* Party. The word 'workers', absent in early documents of the Congress, first appeared in its 'Manifesto' composed by the 'legal Marxist' Struve. See ibid., pp.xvi, 82. The term for 'Russian' was *rossiiskaia*, not *russkaia*, indicating that it pertained to the territory of the Russian state, not just the ethnically Russian nation.

6　For an excellent brief account of the local social democratic organisations during this period, see J.L.H. Keep, *The Rise of Social Democracy in Russia,* (Clarendon Press, Oxford), 1963, pp.39–54.

7　See Keep, pp.54–66.

8　See Kolakowski, vol.2.

9　Ibid.; also Leonard Schapiro, *The Communist Party of the Soviet Union,* (Methuen, London), 1963, Part One.

10　See G.V. Plekhanov, *Sochineniia,* 2nd edn., (Moscow, 1923-27), vol.II, p.84, Kolakowski, vol.2, pp.333–4, and Samuel H. Baron, *Plekhanov. The Father of Russian Marxism,* (Routledge and Kegan Paul, London), 1963, pp.103–10.

11　*What is to be Done?,* V.I. Lenin, *Selected Works in Three Volumes,* (Foreign Languages Publishing House, Moscow, translation of 1960 Russian edn., n.d.), vol.1, p.241.

12　Ibid., pp.227–9.

13　Ibid., p.241.

14　Lenin, *Collected Works,* second (English) edn., vol.7, (Progress Publishers, Moscow), 1965, p.405, note.

15　The *locus classicus* is again his *What is to be Done?* See Lenin, *Selected Works,* vol.1, pp.216–9, 268–9.

16　See Baron, Chapter 13.

17　Robert Service, *The Bolshevik Party in Revolution 1917–1923. A Study in Organisational Change,* (Macmillan, London), 1979, p.30.

18　On the disputes within the RSDWP during these years see Schapiro, Chapters III–VIII.

19　Dropping out at this stage did not necessarily mean being lost permanently to the Bolshevik cause. Many threw themselves into the fray again in 1917 after many years of doing little or no work for the party; amongst them were some half dozen old Bolsheviks who nevertheless enjoyed Lenin's confidence sufficiently to be coopted to his government. See T.H. Rigby, *Lenin's Government. Sovnarkom 1917–1922*, (Cambridge University Press, Cambridge), 1979, pp.146–7.

20 See Ralph Carter Elwood, *Russian Social Democracy in the Underground. A Study of the RSDRP in the Ukraine, 1907–1914.* (Van Gorcum, Assen), 1974, pp.60–4.

21 See Lenin, *PSS*, vol.19, p.411.

22 David Lane, *The Roots of Russian Communism. A Social and Historical Study of Social Democracy 1898–1907*, (Martin Robertson, London), 1975, p.47. Percentages rounded to the nearest digit.

23 Ibid., p.49.

24 The Prague Conference was attended by far fewer delegates than the earlier congresses and was therefore not entirely comparable. However other figures are available that indicate an even heavier Bolshevik reliance on working-class members to run the local organisations during this period. See Elwood, pp.65–6.

25 Lane, *The Roots of Russian Communism*, pp.36–7.

26 Elwood, p.68.

27 See Elwood, pp.66–7.

28 In the prolonged and lengthy debates on the Organisational Rules of the RSDWP at the Second Congress these points were incorporated into the Rules without being questioned in principle by a single delegate. See *Vtoroi s"ezd RSDRP. Iiul'-Avgust 1903 goda. Protokoly*, (Gosudarstvennoe izdatel'stvo politicheskoi literatury, Moscow), 1959, pp.300–12, 426.

29 Cf. Elwood, pp.88–9.

30 Lenin, *PSS*, vol.7, p.22.

31 Ibid., pp.7–8.

32 Ibid., p.13.

33 Ibid., p.24.

34 Ibid., p.19.

35 Ibid., p.24.

36 Tom Burns and G.M. Stalker, *The Management of Innovation*, (Tavistock Publications, London), 1961, p.6.

37 On party structures and practices between 1907 and 1914 the most valuable account will be found in Elwood, especially Chapter III.

38 See *KPSS v rezoliutsiiakh*, vol.1, (Politizdat, Moscow), 1970, p.360.

39 In a letter to Gorky cited by John S. Reshetar, Jr., *A Concise History of the Communist Party of the Soviet Union*, (Praeger, New York), 1960, p.106.

40 This programme was first systematically outlined in his article 'The Tasks of the Proletariat in the Present Revolution', published in *Pravda* on 7 April 1917 (old style). See *PSS* vol.31, pp.149–86.

41 Lenin, 'Imperialism, the Highest Stage of Capitalism', *Selected Works*, vol.1, pp.707–815; cf. Kolakowski, vol.2, pp.297–304, 491–7.

42 See Graeme J. Gill, *Peasants and Government in the Russian Revolution*, (Macmillan, London), 1979.

43 Kolakowski, vol.2, p.500.

44 Karl Marx and Friedrich Engels, *Selected Works* (Gospolitizdat, Moscow), 1958, vol.II, pp.32–3.

45 Lenin, *Collected works*, vol.10, p.216.

46 The quotation is from his hard-hitting pamphlet of 1920, *Left-Wing Communism – an Infantile Disorder*, in which he was even more ready than usual to call a spade a spade. See Lenin, *Collected Works*, vol.31, p.41.

47 See Elwood, pp.271–2.

48 This figure, based on a careful analysis of the patchy surviving data, first appeared in A.S. Bubnov, 'Statisticheskie svedeniia o VKP(b)', *Bol'shaia sovetskaia entsiklopediia*, 1st edn, (Ogiz, Moscow), 1930, vol.XI, col.531.   More recently, some Soviet historians have suggested a substantially higher figure. Cf. V.V. Anikeev, 'Svedeniia o bol'shevistskikh organizatsiiakh s marta po dekabr' 1917 goda', *Voprosy istorii KPSS*, 1958, no.2.

49 A.A. Timofeevskii *et al.*, eds, *V.I. Lenin i stroitel'stvo partii v pervye gody sovetskoi vlasti*, (Gospolitizdat, Moscow), 1965, p.64.

50 For discussion of the conflicting evidence, see T.H. Rigby, *Communist Party Membership in the USSR 1917–1967*, (Princeton University Press, Princeton), 1968, pp.59–62.

51 Ibid., pp.63–7.

52 The breakdowns on which the present analysis rests appear in *Shestoi s"ezd RSDRP (bol'shevikov). Avgust 1917 goda. Protokoly*, (Gospolitizdat, Moscow), 1958, pp.294–300.

53 Robert Service gives an excellent summary of the party's mode of operation in this period in his *The Bolshevik Party in the Revolution 1917–1923.* Chapter 2.

54 See *Perepiska Sekretariata TsK RSDRP(b) s mestnymi partiinymi organizatsiiami (Mart - oktiabr' 1917 g.) Sbornik dokumentov*, (Izdatel'stvo Politicheskoi Literatury, Moscow), 1957.

55 See *Shestoi s"ezd RSDRP(b)*, pp.37–8.

56 Service, pp.59–60.

57 *Shestoi s"ezd RSDRP(b)*, pp.297–8.

58 The CC membership was not made public at the time, but is listed in *Vsesoiuznaia Kommunisticheskaia Partiia (bol'shevikov) v rezoliutsiiakh s"ezdov, konferentsii i plenumov TsK KPSS*, (Gospolitizdat, Moscow), 1936, p.270. The CC elected at the April Conference numbered only nine voting, and four alternate, members.

59 An excellent brief account with useful guide to the literature is Leonard Schapiro, *1917. The Russian Revolutions and the Origins of Present-Day Communism*, (Maurice Temple Smith, Hounslow), 1984. Also particularly recommended are A. Rabinowitch, *The Bolsheviks Come to Power: The Revolution of 1917 in Petrograd*, (Norton, New York), 1976; W.H. Chamberlin, *The Russian Revolutions*, 2 vols, (Macmillan, New York), 1935, reprinted 1965, and E.H. Carr, *The Bolshevik Revolution*, 3 vols, (Macmillan, London), 1950–3.

60 The best analysis is John L.H. Keep, *The Russian Revolution. A Study in Mass Mobilization*, (Norton, New York and G.J. McLeod, Toronto), 1976, Parts I–III.

61 See Astrid von Borcke, *Die Ursprünge des Bolschewismus. Die jakobinische Tradition in Russland und die Theorie der revolutionären Diktatur*, (Johannes Berchmans Verlag, Munich), 1977.

62 Lenin, *PSS*, vol.34, pp.242–3.

63 Ibid., vol.31, p.183.

64 Ibid., p.341.

3 Traditional, Market and Organisational Societies and the USSR*

This article represents an attempt to describe Soviet society, and particularly the Soviet political system, in terms of a typology of society based on modes of coordinating social activity. It is felt that this approach may be of value in pointing out some of the similarities and some of the differences between communist and non-communist industrialised societies.[1]

Society arises from the possibility of achieving by combined effort ends which cannot, or cannot as well, be achieved by individual effort. Any combination of effort, however, whether it involves a division of functions or merely the collective performance of the same function, produces a problem of coordination. Human society exhibits three main modes of coordinating combined effort.

The most obvious of these is *command*. Command is a relationship in which one party is active and the other is passive in the determination of what is done. The complement of command is obedience. One actor formulates or transmits goals, assigns tasks, and prescribes methods; the other carries out his assigned tasks in the manner prescribed.

*World Politics, vol.XVI, no.4 (July 1964), pp.539–57.

The second mode of coordinating social activity is *contract*. In contract, both parties are active, though not necessarily to the same degree, in determining what is done. Contract involves a commitment by each party to perform certain actions which have the effect of furthering the goals of both parties: these goals may be shared or separate. A mutual assistance pact between states, a business partnership, and a wage agreement between employers and workers are various examples of the coordination of activity on the basis of contract. A special and most important type of contract is the contract of sale.

The final mode of coordination is *custom*. In a purely customary relationship, both parties are passive in determining what is done. Objectives, roles, and methods are all 'given'. Like habit for the individual, custom economises effort by providing standard solutions to recurrent problems. Like habits, customs tend to evolve from more or less deliberate solutions reached in the past: that is, they can often be regarded as routinised commands or contracts.

In amplification of this classification, three main points need to be made.

First, these three modes approach the problem of coordination from different angles, and it is possible for more than one of them to be brought into play in a particular segment of social activity. For example, on a feudal manor, the duties owed by the serf to his lord were prescribed by custom, but in carrying out these duties the serf was subject to the commands of the lord's steward.

Second, although there are many activities whose conduct *requires* one or another of these modes of coordination, there is a wide range of activities which can be conducted, though not necessarily equally effectively, on the basis of two or all of them.

The third point of amplification relates to the comparison of societies. It is probable that all three modes of coordination can be found to some degree in all societies. Nevertheless it does seem that one mode or another tends to predominate in most societies; and, further, that as societies become technologically more developed and more complex, coordination by contract and command tends to replace coordination by custom.

The tendency of one particular mode of coordination to predominate makes it possible to classify societies in terms of this criterion, and it will be useful to introduce such a classification into the discussion at this point. Custom-dominated societies will be called *traditional societies*; contract-dominated societies will be called *market societies*; and command-dominated societies will be called *organisational societies*. The terms chosen are rather arbitrary, and would require some discussion in a fuller exposition. They are intended to suggest the predominance of particular modes of coordination without implying that any society can be fully identified with a particular mode of coordination.

Traditional society in anything like its pure form did not long outlast the advance from food gathering to food-production. The society of medieval Europe, while retaining a marked traditional quality, contained well developed contractual features, especially in the regulation of relationships within the élites, and the role of command was also significant, notably in the military and ecclesiastical spheres.

The narrowing scope of custom and the expanding role of contract and command in the later Middle Ages were connected with the growth of two activities: trade, and the exercise of the central political authority of the state.

It is obvious that, once either the ramifications of the market or the command activities of the state spread beyond certain narrowly circumscribed limits, they will act as powerful solvents of the customary mode of coordination, because the latter depends on a constant environment, which can be relied upon to throw up only standard problems for which it has ready-made solutions. For the same reason, since both contract and command presuppose the possibility of *ad hoc* solutions, every customary relationship presents them with a potential obstacle. In Europe, everywhere from England to Muscovy, the state and the market went hand-in-hand and reinforced each other in undermining the traditional society of the Middle Ages. As both command and contract were expanded in scope beyond their old limits, they came into conflict not only with customs specific to their concrete field of operation, but with the whole legal, political, and ideological context within which these customs were set. The main theme of European history from the sixteenth to the twentieth century is the impact of the contractual and command spheres in refashioning this legal, political, and ideological context in their own image. The competition between these different modes of coordination was also reflected in conflicts of interest between the different segments of society-based on them, and particularly their élites – the feudal nobility, the bourgeoisie, and the bureaucracy. Prominent bourgeois and bureaucrats not only struggled against the traditional privileges of the nobility, but sought admission to the nobility themselves, and thereby helped to transform it from within; or they went further and sought to destroy and supplant the nobility as a class.

One further aspect of this process should be noted. As the spheres of contract and command increased, they soon met with obstacles set up by each other as well as by the older customary relationships. While the decline of custom was universal, countries came to manifest considerable variety in the relative weight of the three modes of coordination, and the way these were distributed through different areas of life. Here one might risk the generalisation that, whereas in Eastern Europe the main heir to customary forms was command, in North-western Europe (and North America) it was contract.

In pre-reform Russia, repeated expansion of the role of the state command structure took the country a long way on the *direct route* to an organisational society. Important steps in this direction were the replacement of the traditional nobility, not by a bourgeoisie, but by a 'service nobility' created by and dependent on the state; Peter the Great's 'revolution from above'; and the defeat of the Decembrist revolt, which left the nobility as a class little more than a decorative but a functional facade for the bureaucracy.

Nonetheless, Russia did not develop into a fully-fledged organisational society until the twentieth century. This was partly due to deficiencies of ambition and resources, especially technical resources, and partly to the prolonged freezing of organisational forms at a fairly primitive level. Although command played the decisive role in many areas of life, including some sectors of the economy, the most important sector, agriculture, was still governed predominantly by custom. This helped to maintain the supremacy of the state command structure by inhibiting the development of market relationships, but it did so at the price of crippling the organisational *resources* of the state itself. The abolition of serfdom in 1861 and Stolypin's reforms fifty years later, which promised the dissolution of the peasant commune, opened the way for a vast extension of *either* organisational *or* market relationships. The reforms of 1861 certainly gave a great fillip to the growth of contractual forms and of the bourgeoisie, and the market began to impinge on political life even before the granting of representative institutions. It expressed itself, for instance, in the struggles within the central bureaucracy at the end of the nineteenth century, when the Ministry of the Interior often spoke for landed interests and the Ministry of Finance for industrial interests. The creation of representative institutions after the 1905 Revolution, with all their limitations, promised a further extension of contractual relationships; and these might well have assumed crucial importance within a generation or so if it had not been for Russia's involvement in the First World War. The collapse of the state command structure as a result of the war opened up two possibilities: *either* a reassertion of the dominant organisational pattern of Russian society, its possibilities now enormously enhanced by the destruction of prematurely frozen organisational forms and of the traditional survivals in the economy, *or* a breakthrough by contractual forms and the bourgeoisie that would put Russia on the path to becoming a market society. In the event, it was the first of these possibilities which was realised.

The most distinctive feature of modern Western countries is the tremendous scope of contractual relations – so much so that we are justified in describing these as market societies. The original focus of these contractual relationships was trade and access to revenue from land, and economic life has always provided the main dynamic for the spread of such relationships.

But the essence of a market is competition and choice, and the economic market is bound to be distorted by, and to struggle against, everything that obstructs choice and competition by prescribing obligatory roles, goals, or methods, either by custom or by command of state or other authorities. The economic market requires, and increasingly wins for itself, a market in ideas and a market in leaders. It is alien to the ascription of status, which cripples the market's role as determinant of the division of labour, and favourable to a doctrine of 'inalienable rights' which guarantees to all some degree of autonomous participation in the market.

The ideal market would be one in which each individual is an autonomous and equal agent. But it is one of the ironies of history that the wider market relationships have spread in the modern Western world, the farther they have tended to depart from this ideal. The causes of this are the advantages of combination and scale in a market situation. Factory production, trade unions and employees' associations, and political parties are various responses to this situation in different fields of activity. In advanced market societies, the autonomously competing and contracting actors therefore increasingly tend to be groups, rather than individuals. The more complete the elimination of traditional elements in such societies, and the narrower the scope of the command structure of the state, the closer their politics will approach the model of our group theorists. Group theory may thus represent an appropriate method of analysing the politics of such societies, but we must note the special conditions which make this so, conditions present only in rudimentary form, if at all, in other types of society.

Looked at from the point of view of its internal, rather than its external, relationships, each of these groups shows features of a 'market' or an 'organisation' or a mixture of the two – that is to say, the relationships between its members may be based on contract or command or both. In production units organisational relationships predominate, whereas in organised interest groups market relationships play a much bigger part, and usually include internal competition between subgroups over the choice of aims, methods and leaders. It is worth noting that greater cohesiveness and therefore often greater effectiveness of the group tend to arise from emphasis on the organisational rather than the market aspects in its internal relationships. If a trade union is to be an effective bargainer with employers, it must work for compulsory union membership and place its members under strong discipline in the case of a strike. And the greater the stress of competition to which the group is exposed, or the stronger the threat to its integrity or survival, the more its command structure tends to be reinforced and the closer its internal market is constrained. We see this even in market societies taken as a whole. In wartime there is a wholesale replacement of coordination through contract by coordination through command, and predominantly market societies are transformed into proto-organisational societies. We see, then, that the spread of market relationships provides an umbrella, as it were, beneath which organisational relationships grow, just as the command structure of the state at an earlier historical phase provided an umbrella for the growth of market relationships.

And a further apparent paradox: the growth of these organisational relationships does not always restrict the scope of contractual decisions, but may even expand them. For example, a strong trade union organisation, while narrowing the area of individual contract between employers and workers, may greatly widen the range of negotiable issues and cover a greater proportion of workers by negotiated contracts.

Nevertheless, the more the organisational forms grow within the womb, as Marx would say, of the market society, the greater are the chances of the fully-fledged organisational society being born. Britain could not have been turned into an organisational society during the Crimean War. It could during the Second World War. There is thus, an *indirect* route, as well as a direct one, to the organisational society.

Without necessarily implying a monogenetic theory of social change, one must note the peculiar importance here of technological advances (whether these are seen as motive impulse or simply as transmission belts of change). The possibilities opened up by improved technique were obviously of central importance in the transition from traditional to market societies. I have suggested that market relationships themselves have played a large part in the fostering of organisational forms: but at all stages, available technique has set limits to the growth of these forms. The advance of technology constantly opens up new possibilities for large and more effective organisation and gives those organisations which employ such technology an advantage in the competition of the market. But whereas in the transition to a market society it was technological changes in the field of *production* that were of greatest importance, in the transition to an organisational society the key role was played by advances in the techniques of *communication* and *transport*.

By the twentieth century it had become technically possible to run a large nation as a single organisation. The pioneers in attempting this were Italy and Russia, although in both cases achievement fell well short of ambition, owing to the relative technical backwardness and largely agrarian economy of the two countries. Later it was taken up by Germany, to a lesser extent Japan, and during the Second World War by a group of English-speaking countries. In the latter, particularly in Britain, high technical levels combined with the experience accumulated by government agencies since the 1920s to produce a comprehensiveness of organisational coordination exceeding in important respects that yet achieved anywhere else. The resurgence of strong market elements in these societies since the war should warn us against taking for granted that the universalisation of coordination by command is an inevitable process in contemporary human society. In the early post-war years Russia was for a time the only basically organisational society in existence, but the communist regimes established along her eastern and western borders soon gave a strong organisational stamp to the society of these areas. The various societies identified above as 'organisational' varied greatly not only in the purity of their organisational character but in the location and strength of residual market and traditional elements. Their transformation into organisational societies also followed a number of different patterns: a sudden vast extension of the range of activities coordinated by the state command structure; a combination of violence and of manipulation of the political forms of the market society; the establishment of a miniature organisational society in one corner of the country and its extension by military conquest to the rest of the country, and so on. But in all cases what you had was a particular organisation (the government, the party) taking overall other organisations within society, placing them under its command and eliminating market relations both between them and within them.

The organisation which carried this out in Russia was of course the Bolshevik wing of the Russian Social Democratic Workers' Party. We are all familiar with the picture of the Bolsheviks as a clandestine, highly disciplined, and centralised organisation aiming at the domination and manipulation of other organisations and ultimately of the state, and at employing this domination and manipulation to refashion society totally. While there is much truth in this picture and we should allot it considerable weight in explaining the genesis of Russia's organisational society, it is, as it stands, an oversimplification, and to lose sight of this is to run the risk of neglecting important contingent factors and of exaggerating the inevitability of later developments. For one thing, the Bolshevik leaders certainly had no 'blueprint', as it were, for a system of overall command, and both the structure and the scope of the system were developed empirically. The most vivid illustration is what happened to the party command structure after the seizure of power. Between November 1917 and March 1919 the party as an organisation practically atrophied. Senior Bolsheviks were nearly all assigned to key posts in the hierarchy of executive committees of the soviets, and it was through this hierarchy that the leadership governed the country. The local party committee was reduced to the status of propaganda department of the soviet executive committee. This reached a point where there were even serious suggestions that the party, having obviously performed its historic role, might now be abolished. The main reason for this was that Yakov Sverdlov, who was both secretary of the CC of the party and chairman of the Central Executive Committee of the Congress of Soviets, saw no great virtue in duplicating his lines of command and found it more convenient to channel nearly all matters through the better-staffed soviet apparatus. When Sverdlov died suddenly in March 1919, the Bolshevik leaders took a long hard look at their mechanism of rule, decided that the atrophy of the party organisation had gone too far, set up the basis for a new party command structure, and placed the party and soviet hierarchies under different members of the leadership. During the next two years the party hierarchy replaced that of the soviets as the leadership's principal chain of command, through which it coordinated the administration of the whole country. Incidentally, we now have a pretty good picture of *how* this happened, but *why* it happened as it did is still far from clear.[2] The point I wish to make here, however, is that this sequence of events suggests reasons for doubt that the role the party has come to perform in the Soviet society flows with some inevitable logic from

Lenin's principles of party organisation and relations with extra-party organisations as we have them in *What Is To Be Done?*.

The other qualification that should be made to the common stereotype of the Bolshevik organisation is that Lenin's Bolsheviks always fell short of the ideal, military-type organisation of professional revolutionaries. To employ my own terminology, they were not just a command structure, but contained many market elements, even if these were often only latent or potential. It is easy to forget that the Bolsheviks were an integral part of the Russian Marxist movement, which was one of the main transmission channels for certain ideas and procedures generated in the market societies of the West, such as the election of leaders, decision by discussion and persuasion, the free competition of ideas, and the rights of individuals and minority nationalities, all of which Marxists connected with a vaguely conceived ideal of democracy. Although the Bolshevik organisation provided less congenial soil for this ideal than some other sections of Russian socialism, and although the Bolsheviks perhaps more than any other group were prepared to violate the ideal in the interests of the organisation, it was always implied that these violations were an unfortunate and temporary necessity, justified even in terms of the ideal, because victory for the organisation would alone ensure the full and genuine realisation of the ideal later. And indeed, when the end of the Civil War seemed to make possible an easing of organisational pressure, the leadership not only tolerated but even fostered some practical expression of the democratic ideal – in other words, some dilution of organisation by market forms. The high point of this was the trade union discussion on the eve of the 10th Congress and the contest for electing delegates to the Congress on the basis of rival platforms. At this time the party, having suppressed all competing centres of ideas and leadership, looked as if it might itself come to serve as a limited market for ideas and leadership for the new Soviet society. In the event this did not happen, and the intra-party market was itself suppressed, but the seeds of the market have nevertheless been kept alive by the so-called 'democratic' principles embedded in the party's ideology and formal rules of organisation, and they have shown themselves capable of putting forth shoots when conditions are favourable. All this amounts to a significant difference between Soviet Russia and Nazi Germany: the 'leadership principle' is a purer recipe for the organisational society than is 'democratic centralism'.

The organisational character of the Bolshevik movement and the comprehensiveness of its goals are not, then, the only factors one would need to invoke in explaining the building of an organisational society in Russia. Another factor of great importance was the precariousness of the regime during its early years. We have seen that stress of competition tends to favour command rather than contractual internal relationship, and that even a strongly market-oriented society may take on a predominantly organisational character in the throes of a serious struggle for survival.

No one would contest that the Civil War was largely responsible for the tremendous spread of coordination by command during the early years of the Soviet regime. After the Civil War the leadership found it both possible and expedient to replace command by contract and the market throughout a wide area of economic life. As we have just seen, this happened in some degree in political life as well, and if the tendency did not last long and did not go far in this sphere, this was primarily due to the realisation that the threat to the integrity and survival of the organisation remained greater than had been thought, a fact that was brought home to the leadership by the Kronstadt revolt, the spate of peasant disturbances, and the strength of the 'workers' opposition'. Realising that the regime was still pretty precarious, the leadership felt justified in moving against its critics within the party, since public conflict among party members was obviously giving encouragement and ideological weapons to disaffected sections of the population, and an opposition group within the party was now the most likely rallying point for opposition to the regime in the country at large.

The reinforcement of the party command structure after the Tenth Congress, and in particular the ban on 'fractionalism' on pain of expulsion from the party, were decisive steps in the building of an organisational society in Russia. Up to this time organisational measures had not been widely used to settle policy disputes within the leadership. After 1921 it became increasingly possible to do so, should any leader perceive these possibilities and have a will to use them. The appointment of Stalin as General Secretary in 1922 and his subsequent manipulation of the party organisation to gain domination of the leadership and to eliminate all who questioned his commands raise in an acute form the problem of whether the occasion made the man or the man the occasion. To the present writer, the personality of Stalin seems another of those contingent factors which helped to determine the character of the Soviet political and social system, and without which these would have taken a substantially different form.

Let me now briefly describe the Soviet system as it developed under Stalin. First, Stalin's struggle to ensure his individual dominance of the party command structure went hand-in-hand with a struggle to intensify party supervision of other organisations and to extend it to ever new fields of activity. The logic of this was in large part the need to occupy the actual or potential organisational bases of his rivals. This is an example of how sharp *internal* as well as *external* conflict can intensify the organisational character of a system, once organisational features reach a certain level of development. But the expansion and intensification of the organisation also arose in part as a response to obstacles encountered to the implementation of Stalin's goals in the society at large. The so-called collectivisation of agriculture was essentially a device to place peasant labour under a system of command when Stalin became convinced that direction through the market was proving inadequate to the needs of industralisation.

By the mid-1930s there was no sphere of social activity, from retail sales to internal security, and from farming to the arts, which was not directed by a chain of command culminating in Stalin. Soviet society had been welded into one large organisation: to adapt Alfred Meyer's apt phrase, it was 'Joseph Stalin, Incorporated'.[3] But Stalin was evidently still not satisfied that he was assured of the unquestioning obedience of those around him or that the discipline of the population was yet adequate to meet the demands he might wish to make on it. Although he probably intended the terror of 1936–38 to serve a number of purposes, the main one was just this: to reduce every individual, right up to the members of his immediate entourage, to simply an organisation man of 'Joseph Stalin, Incorporated', to eradicate any tendencies to serve *two* masters: not only Stalin, but also, say, one's local or national interests or ideals, the standards of one's profession, the interests of one's occupational group, artistic or humanitarian values, or what have you. After the trauma of the *Yezhovshchina* had effected this adjustment, a reduced level of terror was sufficient to keep it in force. And the logical complement of this was the Stalin cult, since everyone was, indeed, living for Stalin and at his pleasure.

This general picture requires some qualifications, for there remained important areas of socially relevant activity which were subject to a wide degree of individual choice and only slight organisational control: many aspects of consumption, for instance, and leisure-time activities, not to mention mating and childrearing. The production and distribution of agricultural products were only partly organised; a considerable part was still in the hands of the individual peasant and was market-coordinated. There was still a market in labour, although it was suppressed for about ten years after 1940. In addition, people often did succeed in diverting effort and resources from assigned purposes for the sake of personal gain or in the service of one or another of those group interests or ideals mentioned in the preceding paragraph. Indeed, in the economic field the regime clearly recognised that such diversions of resources were not always dysfunctional, that they were sometimes evoked by, and helped to compensate for, defective organisation. In this way, some elements of a market were allowed to develop in the interstices of the command structure.

It is now necessary to consider some special features of this system: the role of the party, mobilisation, and the nature of intra-organisation struggle; and then to look briefly at some of the changes in the system since the death of Stalin.

The Communist Party is described in the Soviet Constitution as the 'guiding nucleus' in all Soviet institutions. Sometimes Western writers, impressed by the abundant evidence that the formally democratic structure of the soviets is just a facade, seize on this statement about the 'guiding nucleus' as an admission that the party 'really' rules the USSR. There is a confusion here, arising from failure to take sufficient account of the character of intra-party relationships. In the early years of the regime, when there was still a significant market of ideas and leaders within the party, there was a certain sense in which one could speak of the party, as such, as ruling. But in the mature organisational society after the 1930s, when the party itself was totally manipulable by the supreme leadership, no amount of party supervision over other organisations entitles us to speak of party rule. A recent article by C.W. Casinelli[4] introduces a useful corrective in regard to this question. But Casinelli goes much further. He not only argues that the CPSU does not rule the Soviet Union, but that, in common with the parties found in other totalitarian systems, it is not even one of the important instruments of rule; in other words, not only are the soviets a facade, but the party is a facade, too.

This view would scarcely stand up in a close empirical study of the Soviet system. So far as the CPSU is concerned, it appears to be based on a misreading of certain evidence from secondary sources. For example, Casinelli draws attention to the well-known fact that factory directors often do not take the meetings of their primary party organisations very seriously and treat the factory party secretary as a subordinate. What is left out of account here is that the party instance to which the factory director is effectively answerable is the bureau of the district or city committee; and he takes directives and criticism from these people very seriously indeed, since they can have him sacked and also substantially determine his promotion prospects.

Now it is true that Stalin, as he established his dictatorship, was careful to diversify his lines of command; he was not content to direct other organisations *through* the party command structure but made the leaders of the most important of these organisations directly accountable to him personally, and he also established outside controls *over* the party, particularly police controls. All the same, the party remained not only an important instrument of rule, but the most important of such instruments throughout the Stalin period.

The party was responsible for a number of distinct operations. At places of work it was supposed to provide political and ideological leadership and supervision, to act, as it were, as the eyes, ears and mouthpiece of the regime. For this purpose it attempted to maintain a nucleus of party members in all workplace groups.

In the instruments of coercion – the armed forces and the police – a party chain of control duplicated the formal line of command, and this served as the leadership's main safeguard against these organisations becoming autonomous centres of power which might be used against it.

But the most important function performed by the party was (and remains) to provide overall coordination at various levels to all other territorially-based organisations. A less generalised job of coordination is carried out by the politico-administrative mechanism of the state – the hierarchy of the central and republican governments and the executive committees of regional, city, and district soviets. But coordination through this channel is incomplete. If you take an administrative region (*krai* or *oblast*), for example, this will contain a great variety of economic, education, welfare, and control organisations administered by the state; but some of these will be directly responsible to agencies of the central or republican governments, while in others government direction will be exercised through the regional executive committee. In addition you will have a whole range of organisations not directed through government channels at all: trade unions, the consumer cooperatives, the law courts, the Young Communist League, writers' and artists' unions, and so on. The regional party committee is the one body which can provide generalised leadership and coordination for all these organisations. The same thing applies at the republic, city, and district levels.

There are many misconceptions about the character of the control exercised by the territorial party hierarchy. Sometimes its ideological aspects are overstressed. The party is sometimes conceived of as a kind of priesthood with police powers, which is there to prevent other agencies from slipping into apolitical attitudes to their job – to remind them, for instance, that they are not just making steel; they are building the technical base of communism. In actual fact, the *agitprop* side of party activities, though important, is a subordinate concern of local party committees, and the party officials responsible for it always play second fiddle in the local secretariats.

Another mistaken view of the party's role is to regard it as just another supervision agency, differing from, say, the old Ministry of State Control, the Inspectorate of the Ministry of Finance, the State Establishments Commission and so on, only by being larger, more authoritative and more generalised in its impact. It is regarded as an organisation responsible solely for checking to see that the more specialised agencies carry out their jobs properly, and for chivying them into doing so. Again this draws attention to part of the truth. What is described as 'verification of the fulfilment of party decisions' is indeed one of the major tasks of party committees vis-à-vis non-party agencies in both fact and theory. But in both fact and theory it yields in importance to two other tasks – namely, giving guiding directions on matters of importance, and selecting and assigning leading cadres.

The local party committee exists not just to preach at, or jolly along, the administration from outside. It is an integral part of the administration – its central core. The relationship of the party command structure to the various specialised agencies, both governmental and otherwise, is partly analogous to the relationship of line to staff in a business corporation. The party committee is responsible for deciding issues which arise in any field of activity, which involve coordination at the level concerned, and which cannot be settled exclusively within the specialised agency directly responsible. Economic agencies throw up by far the greatest number of such issues. And just as cabinets everywhere in wartime find that a tremendous range of local or specialised issues are channelled up to them for decision, so in the Soviet Union at times of stress, or on questions of crucial important the bureaus and secretariats of party committees, may become responsible for running things in very considerable detail. During the blockade of Leningrad, departments of the district party committees were in charge of even the transfer of individual workers from one factory to another and the allocation of spare parts among different factories.[5] In one district near the mouth of the Volga, where fishing is the main industry, the district party secretary used to cross all matters relating to the fishing industry off the agenda of sittings of the soviet executive committee and put them on the agenda of the bureau of the district party committee.[6] Until recent reorganisations, it was notorious that, during the spring sowing and at harvest time, the office of the district party secretary became the nerve centre from which all the farms in the district were really run.

Failure to grasp this relationship, to realise that the party command structure is an integral part of the administration, focused particularly on the running of the economy, is at the root of much of the confusion about the nature of Soviet politics, of crude dichotomies between 'apparatchiks' and 'technocrats', and so on. A regional party secretary is not only likely to have received the same technical education as the factory director or the industrial minister, but may well be the factory director of yesterday and the industrial minister of tomorrow.

Two other special aspects of the Soviet system as it developed under Stalin will have to be treated rather schematically. 'Mobilisation of the masses' is a phrase much used by Soviet political writers. What they understand by it is perhaps not too remote from what we mean by 'public relations'. Its significance is best brought out by drawing a contrast. In modern Western countries the competitive processes of the market tend to build up in the public, and particularly in those groups whose interests are most directly involved, in awareness of public issues and their likely implications while these issues are still being settled. There are, however, large public and private corporations whose decision-making processes are little influenced by the market and whose major decisions nevertheless are likely to affect large numbers of people. Such corporations tend to find a particular need for what we call 'public relations'. In the Soviet Union nearly all decisions are made in this way – that is, the members of the public are not led to an understanding of them by the processes of the market, and need to have the decision 'sold' to them after it is taken. Hence we have 'mobilisation', which aims at informing people as to what has been decided and what new benefits, sacrifices, or responsibilities it will involve for the country as a whole and for whatever special groups they belong to in particular, and at building a positive attitude of acceptance of the decision. 'Mobilisation' is not left to the mass communications media; it is the main aim of thousands of *ad hoc* workplace and other meetings, and the pseudo-democratic processes of elections, meetings of soviets, party conferences and congresses, and so on have been largely shaped to serve its purposes.

Finally, a word about political conflict under Stalin. The form this took was largely a function of the methods by which Stalin found it convenient to exercise and preserve his domination. As we have seen, Stalin reduced the market elements in the system to such a marginal role that it was impossible for potential economic or other interest groups to cohere and take action to advance their interests. He also saw to it that particular organisational divisions based on sectors of the economy, national or territorial units, professional groups, or what have you could not be manipulated to serve sectional interests or aspirations. And finally, Stalin was particularly active in restricting any tendency for the various chains of command – the party, the police, the economic administration, the army, and so on – to develop into autonomous centres of power. He did this by an elaborate system of mutual controls and by giving the various members of his entourage – the potential manipulators of these potential power centres – divided and overlapping responsibilities for them. Three possible ways that political conflict *might* have been structured were thus excluded by Stalin.

Some students of the Soviet system may question whether Stalin did in fact prevent the third of these possibilities from being realised. Since there is evidence that Stalin's 'lieutenants' managed to build up something like personal followings in sections of the organisations under their command, some writers have concluded that particular leaders were identified with the interests of the particular sub-élites associated with these sections: the military, the police, the managers, the *apparatchiki,* and so on. They then go on to explain the ups and downs of particular leaders and their most prominent supporters in terms of rivalries among these sub-élites.

The trouble with this view[7] is that, when you succeed in identifying networks of supporters, they appear typically to cut right across formal divisions between chains of command and fields of activity. For example, the officials identified as having been executed or imprisoned in connection with the so-called 'Leningrad Case' enable us to build up a picture of the 'patronage' exerted by the late Central Committee secretary, Andrei Zhdanov. This evidence suggests that Zhdanov's patronage predominated in the state and party organisations of Leningrad Region and City, and that it was prominent without predominating in the Central Committee apparatus, the government of the RSFSR, the State Planning Committee, certain fields of ideology and the party apparatus in a broad zone in northwest Russia. Study of the various purges and counterpurges in Georgia between 1951 and 1953 gives a similar picture of the ramifications of patronage networks there.   And finally, the diverse organisations from which Khrushchev drew old subordinates to fill responsible posts under his command after 1953 indicate the extent to which his patronage had spread by the end of the Stalin era.

This was not accidental. It was a direct result of Stalin's own particular method of 'divide and rule'. From his point of view it was not only necessary to deprive particular command structures of the unity and continuity of organisation and leadership which might enable them to be brought into play as weapons against him; it was also necessary to prevent the command level immediately below him (that is, his 'lieutenants') from coalescing to limit his power or remove him. By allowing superiors right down the line a good deal of say in the appointment of their subordinates, to the point that this strongly affected career expectations and career rivalries, and at the same by having his own immediate subordinates *share* responsibility for particular command structures, by giving one the direction of control agencies working within the command structure run by the other, by giving them interlocking responsibilities for territorial, functional, and organisational supervision, and finally by redistributing responsibilities with considerable frequency, Stalin was able to achieve both these objectives at the same time. He thus managed to distribute power in such a way as to keep it in manipulable chunks, without these chunks taking a form that could easily be wielded against him.

Space will permit only a brief sketch of some of the main modifications in this system since the death of Stalin.

First, the post-Stalin leadership found that it could dispense with two major supports of the organisation without endangering its survival: the actual as distinct from the potential terror, and the leadership cult. This was made possible by the greater intrinsic viability of the organisation due to a reduction in internal hostility, and this in turn was due to a number of factors, which included the killing off or dying out of many of the most embittered elements in the population, the improvement in economic conditions, and the long-term effects of education and indoctrination.

Second, the new leaders found that effective execution of policies by the ever more complex organisation under their control called for a considerable decentralisation of systems of command and for allowing more administrative discretion and initiative at lower levels. Moving in this direction, however, they quickly encountered new dilemmas. In combination with the changes referred to in the previous paragraph, decentralisation afforded wider scope for individuals and groups to further particular interests or ideals independent of, or even contrary to, the intentions of the supreme leadership. Hence the many disciplinary measures to counter such deviations as minority nationalism, economic parochialism, 'partylessness' in the arts, and so on. And this drew attention to a more fundamental problem. Could the evils and inefficiencies of overcentralisation be overcome by administrative devolution without necessitating a greatly expanded control apparatus which virtually amounted to recentralisation, or could this objective be achieved only by allowing an increased role to contractual, competitive 'market' elements? This problem has been firmly posed in both the economic and the intellectual spheres, but the leadership has not yet squarely faced up to it.

And finally, there were of course changes in the locus of supreme power and consequent alterations in the forms of political struggle. The death of Stalin appears to have provoked a deal, a contract, between those occupying the next level of command; the terms of this deal involved the distribution among them of control over the various command structures, each leader apparently enjoying a good deal of autonomy in those structures under his command, and the settling of major issues by negotiated agreement. These arrangements gave a distinct impetus to market elements in the political system, and these gradually increased in the years that followed. One most important manifestation of this was that some of the command structures took on something of the nature of interest groups, which temporarily imbued Soviet politics with some of the characteristics imputed to it by the school of Kremlinology criticised above. Another manifestation was the emergence of proto-democratic procedures both in the Central Committee and at the base of the party hierarchy.

These trends, however, were partially reversed once one of the leaders succeeded in subverting the deal of March 1953 and establishing his personal dominance. Khrushchev has reduced (though not entirely eliminated) the flavour of pluralism which the system was beginning to acquire. He has also shown that one of Stalin's devices for controlling the exercise of power by his subordinates – the manipulation of rival and interlocking patronage systems – can work successfully even without the dimension of terror.

The Soviet Union is the most long-lived and one of the most highly developed of twentieth century 'organisational' societies. Soviet experience amply demonstrates the viability of his new type of society and its relative efficiency for the achievement of many social goals. It provides no unequivocal evidence, however, of superior efficiency as compared with advanced market societies, at least at current levels of technological development. Moreover, any hypothesis of the inevitable maximisation of the spread and intensity of command relationships in organisational societies (an assumption often implicit in discussions of 'totalitarianism') could only be argued at this stage on the theoretical level; it certainly cannot be demonstrated empirically from the Soviet example. Here the spectacular extension of such relationships came to a halt in the late 1930s, and, despite some fluctuations since then, they have tended, if anything, to retreat somewhat.

Similarly, Soviet experience provides little evidential support for the view that there are particular mechanisms of control or particular relationships between different mechanisms of control which *must* be employed by their rulers in order to remain in power. The spread, intensity, and character of mechanisms of control have varied considerably in the history of the Soviet regime. Such variations seem to have been largely due to changes in the opportunities and dangers facing the regime and, as in any highly centralised system, to differences in the predilections and abilities of its leaders. These are factors whose future operation it would be impossible to predict.

Notes and References

1 The conceptual framework employed here was suggested in the course of a critical study of Max Weber's typology of society based on forms of domination (*Herrschaft*), which will be reported elsewhere. An earlier version of this paper was read at a seminar on the sociology of power held at The Australian National University. Many matters touched on in the following pages involve thorny issues of historical interpretation, which must await examination in a more extended exposition of the writer's views, but it was felt that a general outline of the latter might be of some value at the present stage.

2 See Leonard Schapiro, *The Communist Party of the Soviet Union*, (New York), 1960, 242ff.

3 See Alfred G. Meyer, 'USSR, Incorporated', *Slavic Review*, vol.XX (October 1961), pp.369–76.

4 C.W. Casinelli, 'The Totalitarian Party', *Journal of Politics*, vol.XXIV (February 1962), pp.111–41.

5 *Partiinoe stroitel'stvo*, nos 9–10 (1946), p.19.

6 *Partiinaia zhizn'*, no.4 (1948), p.40.

7 The writer has considered this question at greater length elsewhere. See T.H. Rigby, 'Crypto-Politics', *Survey*, no.50 (January 1964), pp.188–91.

4 Stalinism and the Mono-organisational Society*

The policies and methods pursued by Stalin played a vital part in establishing the Soviet social and political system as we know it today. And yet these policies and methods were also means to, or attributes of, a form of personal rule that disappeared with its founder. Is there a paradox here? What *was* the role of Stalinism in the genesis of modern Soviet society?

The Soviet Sociopolitical System

The Soviet Union may be termed a mono-organisational society, since nearly all social activities are run by hierarchies of appointed officials under the direction of a single overall command.[1] Organisations are also, it is true, the most characteristic social structures in modern Western society, but here traditional and especially market structures not only retain a significant role in various societal subsystems, but are crucial to overall coordination of the society, which is achieved largely through processes of competition and mutual accommodation within the framework of established rules and conventions. In the Soviet Union, by contrast,

*Robert C. Tucker (ed.), *Stalinism: Essays in Historical Interpretation*, (Norton, New York), 1977, pp.53–76.

overall coordination of the multifarious discrete organisations operating in the various societal subsystems is itself achieved *organisationally*, that is, through superordinated structures of command, much as in wartime the Supreme Command directs and orchestrates the numerous formations, branches, and services operating in a particular theatre of war.

The problems of coordination are obviously stupendous in an organisational complex that seeks to embrace nearly all the socially relevant activities of scores of millions of people, and in its efforts to cope with these problems the system has evolved a number of distinctive devices and processes. Structurally most of these are focused on the Communist Party, which has been largely redeployed from its earlier purposes to serve the needs of societal coordination. Most obvious here is the hierarchy of full-time party officials staffing the so-called party committees at the various territorial–administrative levels, which are primarily engaged in steering, monitoring, and reconciling the operations of the numerous specialised organisations in their area. The activities and responsibilities attaching to ordinary party membership have also been reoriented to serve the purposes of societal coordination. The party sees to it that some scores of thousands of responsible and other sensitive posts are restricted to its members, that substantial membership levels are maintained in all influential occupations, and that every work group has its leavening of communists. Intra-party indoctrination and information programmes, discipline and accountability procedures are employed to orient members, both 'cadres' and rank-and-file and, through them their non-party colleagues, towards overall party goals and current priority tasks as defined by the leadership, rather than the special values and interests of the group concerned.

The running of practically all sectors of social activity by organisations which are themselves integrated organisationally into a single vast structure has given rise to one of the most influential ways of looking at Soviet society. This is sometimes referred to as the 'bureaucratic model',[2] although it requires a good deal more than a perception of the fundamentally bureaucratic character (or organisational, administrative, or managerial character – at a certain level of generalisation the terms may be used interchangeably) before one has a 'model'; for there are many varieties of 'bureaucracy', and we cannot yet claim to have a satisfying specification of the essential structures and processes of Soviet society as a bureaucratic entity and of the systemic inter-relationships of these structures and processes.

The nature of this problem may be better appreciated if we recall the 'classical' accounts of bureaucratic or managerial systems. These envisage a hierarchical pyramid with a more or less elaborate division of labour, the activities of each participant being governed by rules and instructions handed down by his superior. Goals, formulated at the apex of the pyramid, are broken down at successive levels to ever simpler sets of tasks, and organisational success depends on each participant precisely performing his tasks as prescribed, without his needing to understand the system as a whole or even support its goals (in fact, if participants substitute for the instructions of their superiors their own view of what will best serve the organisation's goals, the system will tend to be disrupted). Conversely, the information required for the formulation of goals and the assignment of tasks is progressively assembled as it is funnelled upwards, and the full picture is visible only at the apex. In a large system, top management will usually have at its disposal, in addition to the pyramid of reporting and command (the 'line' officers), groups of specialists ('staff' officers) to vet performance with respect to personnel and technical standards, to provide related services, and to assist with the organisation's external relations.

All of this will look familiar enough to connoisseurs of Soviet society. Whatever activity you engage in in the USSR, will you not find yourself at some point in a hierarchical chain of command where the main expectation will be that you fulfil the *zadaniia* assigned to you from above, under the watchful eye of various control agencies? Do not all lines converge on the Politburo, where alone, allegedly, the full picture is available for orienting decisions on all fields of activity? Could not all Soviet institutions be seen as the various line and staff divisions of a single hierarchical pyramidal structure?

This is all very well as far as it goes, but deeper probing reveals other aspects of the Soviet system that do not fit at all well into this 'classical' bureaucratic model. I will briefly refer to three of them.

First, there are the parallel party and governmental hierarchies, with their overlapping jurisdiction and blurred division of labour. Party bodies are supposed to 'guide and check' the work of governmental and paragovernmental agencies and their field units without 'supplanting' their officials. Party officials should not become involved in the routine administrative work of bodies subject to their supervision, but must be prepared to closely direct operations in situations of crisis or where matters defined as urgent or important are at stake. In seeking to satisfy these ambiguous requirements, the party official will get some help from rules, instructions, and objective criteria but must rely largely on his political judgement.

Second, the totality of demands that Soviet officials receive from their direct superiors and other bodies authorised to instruct them is frequently such that some demands cannot be met without sacrificing others, either because of inadequate resources or because in the given conditions the different demands conflict operationally. This phenomenon, first noted in the study of Soviet industrial management,[3] can be detected in various forms and degrees in most fields of activity. Seemingly both a product and a source of inefficiency and confusion, it can also have important advantages. Operatives down the line, obliged constantly to make decisions about which demands to meet and what to sacrifice in meeting them, become more responsive to the current priorities of the most important relevant authorities. This introduces greater flexibility into the organisation, decentralises effective decision-making, and in Weberian terms generally fosters substantive rationality at the expense of formal rationality.[4]

A third major departure of the Soviet system from the 'classic' bureaucratic model is the salience of mobilisational methods. In Soviet parlance 'mobilisation' may simply mean a campaign, usually involving a mixture of exhortation and coercion, for achieving some collective objective in the normal sphere of responsibilities of those concerned; for example, fulfilling their production plan. But it may also involve, for example, in getting in the harvest, the redeployment of persons from their normal tasks, the suspension of normal rules, and the substitution of an *ad hoc* role allocation and authority structure in place of those normally applying.

To emphasise such 'anomalies' is not to deny the bureaucratic character of Soviet society but to point up the question of *what kind* of bureaucracy it is. And we are now in a position to provide a partial answer to this question by reference to the distinction which some contemporary organisation theorists have drawn between 'mechanistic' and 'organic' systems of management and administration. The mechanistic system, appropriate to stable conditions and routine programmes, corresponds by and large with the 'classic' model of bureaucracy outlined above. By contrast, 'the *organic* system is appropriate to changing conditions, which give rise constantly to fresh problems and unforeseen requirements for action which cannot be broken down or distributed automatically arising [*sic*] from the functional roles defined within a hierarchic structure'.[5] In these circumstances participants are constantly faced with problems that oblige them to redefine their tasks and make *ad hoc* decisions in collaboration with others directly involved (whatever their place in the formal organisation), and such decisions must be informed by an appreciation of the overall goals of the organisation and its immediate priority objectives. These two forms must be seen as 'ideal-types', the poles of a continuum, and actual organisations will usually evolve some mixture of mechanistic and organic elements in their actual mode of operation.

I would suggest that the 'anomalous' features of the USSR as a bureaucratic system are largely explicable as vehicles for a partially organic mode of operation, which represents a response to the frequently unstable and volatile conditions generated by social and technical innovation, organisation growth and change, and the disruptions attendant on complexity. Thus, while the state apparatus can be largely left to itself so long as mechanistic processes suffice, the party can come to the fore where circumstances necessitate operating more organically. Mobilisational methods and the action-patterns evoked by mutually conflicting demands are textbook organic devices. The shared 'culture' and orientation towards the organisation's goals, values, and programmes which are necessary for it to function effectively as an organic system are facilitated by the permeation of all groups with party members, whose special indoctrination, information and accountability sensitise them to the general thrust and changing priorities of the system.[6]

Soviet society, then, can be seen as a single vast and immensely complex *organisation*, displaying a distinctive blend of mechanistic and organic characteristics. This picture, however, will remain misleadingly incomplete unless we take account of certain further features which derive precisely from the fact that this is a *society-wide* organisation, which not only runs the production and distribution of nearly all goods and services, but seeks to monopolise the socialisation and moral guidance of its members and has full responsibility for such basic functions of 'the state' as military defence and internal order. What we must note here is not merely the global range of functions but the effects of combining them in a single organisation. There is no space here to explore all the ramifications of this but certain aspects require our attention.

First, I shall deal with the salience and distinctive characteristics of ideology and repression in the Soviet mono-organisational system. As anyone soon becomes aware on joining a large organisation – be it an industrial firm, military formation, or government department – it will always have its own peculiar 'ideology' or 'culture', and this, for the reasons we have noted, can become crucial to successful performance where the system is operating 'organically'. At the same time any state must possess its legitimating beliefs and symbols, enjoying a wide degree of acceptance in the population. Furthermore, people growing up in any society must not only acquire the technical skills necessary for their future work roles but also the values, attitudes, and behaviour-patterns enabling the society to cohere and operate effectively as a system. What is peculiar to the mono-organisational society is that all three of these phenomena – the organisational culture, the political legitimation and the socialisation of individuals – come together in a single purportedly comprehensive ideology. For this is what 'Marxism–Leninism' has evolved into in the USSR. Further, while we now understand that the 'goal-system' governing the behaviour of members in any large organisation cannot be reduced to a single all-embracing goal (for example, making soap, winning the war, saving souls), such a 'basic' goal will always be there as the *raison d'être* of the organisation and the ultimate (even if rarely invoked) touchstone of action. In the ideology of the Soviet mono-organisational system the 'construction of communism' performs this role.

The combination and consequent interpenetration of functions in this system has other important consequences for the ideology. This may be illustrated from the example of the arts. Since the 'production' and 'distribution' of artistic values is directed by the same organisational system that is responsible for, *inter alia*, material production, the civic training of youth, and national defence, the system's managers will naturally be concerned that the impact of their artists on, say, work motivation, acceptance of existing authority-patterns, or attitudes to military service should be entirely positive.

It follows from what has been said that the ideology of the mono-organisational system will be not only global in scope but also monopolistic in its claims. Cultural pluralism and tolerance for heterodox ideas may be not merely acceptable but actually functional in a 'market' society, with its largely autonomous subsystems and coordination through processes of competition and mutual accommodation. In a mono-organisational society, by contrast, while they might be functional to the subsystems, they will be *dys*functional to the system as a whole. The very comprehensiveness and internal coherence of the ideology mean that a challenge to any part of it threatens the whole. It is an intangible seamless web which, if torn, will reveal the emperor naked. Hence it is no mere perversity when Soviet leaders apprehend heresy amongst historians or poets as ultimately threatening their overthrow. And, along with the legitimacy of the rulers, the whole pattern of shared attitudes, symbols, and concepts in terms of which societal coordination is achieved (largely through the mediation of the party) both within and between its constituent subsystems, is similarly vulnerable to the voicing of discordant facts or ideas.

All human societies set limits to deviant expression and behaviour and to opposition to established authorities and institutions, beyond which they will be prepared to employ coercive controls. In the Soviet mono-organisational system one tends to run up against such limits far more quickly than in modern Western societies, and coercive controls are correspondingly more salient. There are three main reasons for this. First, the monopolistic position of the official ideology in all its ramifications needs to be policed and enforced: not just its social and philosophical doctrines, but its democratic symbols and forms so manifestly at variance with the bureaucratic structure of power and its claims about the character of Soviet life so often inconsistent with the personal experience of citizens. Second, the Soviet political system lacks legitimate channels of opposition to existing leaders and their policies – like other large-scale formal organisations, and also like *most* historically known political systems, but unlike those of the modern West, where such arrangements can be seen as functional to the processes of competition and mutual accommodation through which societal coordination is achieved. And finally, since the effective functioning of the mono-organisational system depends on the faithful transmission of messages (bearing commands, reports, etc.) through its immensely complex communication channels, special controls and sanctions are required to ensure that such messages are not intentionally or unintentionally distorted.

It is clear, then, that the salience of coercive social controls has an objective basis in the functional needs of the system and does not merely flow from the repressive attitudes of its leaders. These functional needs also explain the relative prominence of the political security and auditing–inquisitorial components in the pattern of coercive controls rather than the protection of persons and private property component which predominates in the West.

The effort to embrace practically all social activities within a single organisational system also has important consequences for the character of politics in the USSR. This has much in common with the politics one finds in any large organisation or bureaucracy: that is, it is for the most part 'crypto-politics', not overt and channelled through specialised 'political' institutions, but covert, masquerading as the faithful performance of assigned organisational roles.   It involves competition between constituent organisations and their formal subdivisions, biased reporting of information relevant to the formation or vetting of policy, informal networks or cliques, the use of personnel powers to reward friends and punish enemies, and bias in the execution of policy so as to facilitate or prejudice its success or to favour certain affected interests rather than others.

The crypto-politics of this organisational system, however, also displays some distinctive features deriving from its societal scope. On the one hand the full coercive and informational resources of the society are involved, both as instruments and prizes, in Soviet bureaucratic politics. On the other hand, all social cleavages and special interests, be they local, professional, ethnic, generational, or what have you must feed into, and be played out in, the bureaucratic political arena if they are to be reflected in policy outcomes.

Essentially Soviet crypto-politics may be regarded as an aspect – but only one aspect – of the 'informal organisation' of the system. In all large organisations informal arrangements evolve to supplement and often modify or even supplant their formally prescribed structures and rules, serving to adapt the operation of the system to the interests, convenience, and limitations of the participants. They inject contractual and customary elements into what usually purports to be a 'pure' command hierarchy. The informal organisation may assume such importance in the operation of a system that 'working to rule' would lead to its speedy breakdown, and this is notably the case in many parts of the Soviet system. The informal arrangements in and between Soviet organisations arise, in part, from their quasi-organic mode of operation, and to this extent enjoy a qualified legitimacy. These, however, shade through numerous grades of strictly improper, but usually tolerated, plan-fulfilling devices into the labyrinthine underworld of *blat*.

Despite the vast scope of the mono-organisational system there are important areas of human action in the USSR which the system seeks only to regulate without, however, directly managing them. On the one hand, a considerable autonomy of choice is vested in an acknowledged personal–family–domestic sphere, to which the system concedes a major influence over such societally important matters as quantitative and qualitative changes in the population, childrearing, personal consumption and leisure-time activities. On the other hand, the substantial (though varying) element of self-selection in job allocation and the private plot sector in farm production represent significant market enclaves in the centrally managed economy. Further, the retention of pre-existing ethnic entities with their languages and much of their élite and folk cultures

– however pruned and channelled to serve the interests of the system
– entails considerable traditional influence on the behaviour, beliefs,
and loyalties of the population. A special and uniquely anomalous
case here is the tolerance – however limited, grudging, and
combined with repression – of religion: for this involves permitting
organised activity aimed at perpetuating behaviour and beliefs
deemed to conflict fundamentally with the basic goal of the system.

Stalinism

This, then, is how I would characterise Soviet society. It is a society
in which most activities, despite significant traditional and market
'survivals', are directly managed by innumerable organisations or
bureaucracies, all of which are linked up in a single organisational
system. In its operation this system displays a distinctive blend of
mechanistic and organic aspects, and the party, which combines a
bureaucracy superordinated over all other bodies with a membership
permeating all segments of the system, plays a crucial role in its
coordination. The range and combination of functions performed by
this mono-organisational system have engendered an ideology
comprehensive in scope and monopolistic in its claims, a highly
salient system of coercive social controls dominated by its political
security and vetting–inquisitorial aspects, and a lively crypto-politics
within and between its bureaucratic structures, on whose outcome
the conflicting ambitions and interests of individuals and groups
primarily depend.

While this account of the USSR as a mono-organisational society
has been presented in the present tense, it would be applicable, as I
hope any reader who has followed the discussion so far would
concur, at any time from the 1930s on. As I shall argue later,
however, only with crippling qualifications could it be applied to the
Soviet Union of the 1920s. The fully-fledged mono-organisational
society, in fact, crystallised simultaneously with the establishment of
Stalin's dictatorship. The question logically suggests itself,
therefore, whether what I have been presenting is actually an
analysis of *Stalinism:* but only to be answered, surely, with a
resounding negative. For who would be satisfied with a
characterisation of Stalinism that left out the police terror and the
personal power and cult of the dictator? It follows, then, that the
history of the Soviet mono-organisational society can be divided into
two stages: a first, 'Stalinist', phase, during which the
characterisation I have given above is applicable but inadequate, and
a second, 'post-Stalinist', phase, during which it is both applicable

and adequate. 'Stalinism' in other words, was the mono-organisational system in combination with something else, and we must now look more closely at what this 'something else' was.

Let us begin by bringing to mind some of its main ingredients. First and most obvious was one-man rule, contrasting with the oligarchical pattern of power before and afterwards. This does not mean, of course, that Stalin personally decided everything, which would have been physically impossible, but that he personally decided anything he wanted to, unconstrained by the power of any individual, group, institution, or law.[7] Even the most powerful of his officials knew better than to query his commands.[8] This untrammelled power extended to the liberty, and indeed existence, of any individual or group in the population. He could have members even of his immediate entourage incarcerated or killed without his needing to inform, let alone consult, the others. For such purposes he had at his disposal a political police enjoying arbitrary powers of arrest and punishment and maintaining a spy network permeating the whole of society. This enabled him not only to destroy opposition but to forestall it, by removing 'over-mighty subjects', by striking at suspect segments of the population, by inhibiting discussion, and by the 'atomising' effects on human relationships of the prevalent mutual distrust.

Stalin's fiat not only ran in all fields of practical policy, he was also the final arbiter in matters of faith, truth, and public taste and morals. His spoken and written utterances were accorded the reverence of received truth, and ritually repeated in season and out. They formed the core of a body of official doctrine which drew also on the writings of Marx, Engels, and Lenin, and which, like the dictator himself, was not subject to critical discussion but only affirmation. Truth was what conformed to this doctrine rather than what conformed to observed facts. This was of course deadly to true art and scholarship, and artists and scholars of independent mind were arrested or otherwise silenced, leaving the field to sycophants and time-servers.

It goes without saying that overt association to further particular interests or policies was out of the question in these circumstances, and crypto-political life, though persisting very actively, came to centre mainly round the rivalries of personal followings and cliques. The public arena, emptied of spontaneous political life, was, however, noisy with contrived activity as the citizens were kept busy acclaiming the leader and his regime and policies in meetings, processions, and other manifestations, and engaging in 'voluntary' services at the behest of the soviets, Komsomol, trade unions, and a host of other official organisations. Moreover, 'building communism' meant under Stalin the sacrifice of mass living standards to grandiose industrialisation projects, imposing an exhausting and enervating burden on the ordinary citizen in merely coping with the conditions of day-to-day life. Thus, between his 'heroic labours' and all these extra demands, the latter was left with little time, heart, or energy to engage in self-motivated activities.

Many features of Stalin's regime may be subsumed under the principle *divide et impera*. Resentments engendered by the dictator's policies were redirected against target groups in the population: against 'bourgeois specialists', '*kulaks*', 'enemies of the people', 'homeless cosmopolitans', and so on. Younger, technically better-trained officials were set against the generation of their superiors, who had won their positions through political loyalty (and thus knew not only too little, but also too much). The dictator's lieutenants and the bureaucracies they commanded were given overlapping jurisdictions, and thus brought into conflict.

The term 'cult' is appropriate to the presentation of Stalin in the media, at meetings, in school and kindergartens, and in the arts. But the pseudo-religious character suggested by this term permeated the whole ideology, which partook of the quality of holy scripture, subject to constant public affirmation in ritualistic and sometimes even incantational terms.

Now, all this is familiar enough – indeed all too familiar. But this is precisely the point. For, whereas those features of Soviet mono-organisational society common to both its Stalinist and its post-Stalinist phases constitute a system qualitatively new in human experience, that 'something extra' that we must add to the first phase to get an acceptable account of Stalinism consists of ingredients that have recurred with singular unoriginality throughout the history of complex societies. It is indeed the sort of thing you are *likely* to get when one man attains absolute power, and 'tyranny' will serve as well as anything else as our name for it.

'What kind of Sovereign is this that cannot take away any life that she pleases!' exclaimed the Chamberlain of Emir Nasrullah of Bokhara, when informed of the constitutional position of Queen Victoria.[9] Periander of Corinth, the Emperor Tiberius, the Emperor Ch'in Shih-Huang, or Cesare Borgia might have reacted with the same incredulous scorn. Tyrants everywhere are apt to be deified, to impose their standards of truth and beauty on all, to crush all signs of independence, and to carry out prophylactic purges.[10] For a brief, systematic characterisation, we still cannot do better than Aristotle's summary of what he called the 'traditional method' of maintaining tyranny:

> Here belong all the old hints for the preservation (save the mark!) of tyranny, such as 'Cut off the tops and get rid of men of independent views', and 'Don't allow getting together in clubs for social and cultural activities or anything of that kind; for these are the breeding grounds of independence and self-confidence, two things which a tyrant must guard against', and 'Do not allow schools or other institutions where men pursue learning together, and generally ensure that people do not get to know each other well, for that establishes mutual confidence'. Another piece of traditional advice to a tyrant tells him to keep the dwellers in the city always within his view and require them to spend much time at his palace gates; their activities then will not be kept secret and by constantly performing servile obligations they will be used to having no minds of their own.
>
> Similarly a tyrant should endeavour to keep himself aware of everything that is said or done among his subjects; he should have spies like the Tittle-tattle women, as they were called at Syracuse, or the Eavesdroppers whom Hiero used to send to any place where there was a meeting or gathering of people. It is true that men speak less freely for fear of such men, but if they do open their mouths, they are more likely to be overheard.
>
> Another traditional way is to stir up strife amongst all possible opponents of the tyranny, by slander setting friends against friends, class against class, and one monied set against another. It is also in the interests of a tyrant to keep his subjects poor, so that they may not be able to afford the cost of protecting themselves by arms and be so occupied with their daily tasks that they have no time for rebellion. As examples of works instituted in order to keep subjects perpetually at work we may mention the pyramids of Egypt....Friends are a source of protection to a king but not to a tyrant; it is part of his policy to mistrust them as being potentially more dangerous to him than the rest....
>
> The typical tyrant dislikes serious and liberal-minded people. He regards himself as the only authority; if anyone sets himself up in rivalry and claims the right to speak his mind he is felt to be detracting from the supremacy and absolute mastery of the tyrant. Thus his dislike of intellectual pretensions is based on fear; such people are potential destroyers of his rule.[11]

Does not this, allowing for incidental features deriving from the conditions of the Greek city-state, read like a paraphrase of large parts of our characterisation of the rule of Stalin? Aristotle does not set out to list all the 'traditional' devices of tyranny, but argues that they can be summed up under three headings: namely that the tyrant's subjects should '(a) have no minds of their own, (b) have no trust in each other, and (c) have no means of carrying out anything'.[12] He goes on, however, to point out that while it is along these lines that the tyrant usually seeks to maintain his rule, he has an alternative method, namely to cultivate the image of a 'king'– that is a *good* absolute ruler who seeks the public benefit rather than his own. To this end he will avoid squandering the people's money on personal ostentation and gifts to favourites; he will represent his demands for services as necessary to the economic well-being of the people; he will take advantage of war to establish a reputation for military leadership and to pose as the saviour of the nation; he will link himself personally with the bestowal of honours but not, if he can help it, with the infliction of repression, and so on.[13]

Aristotle's two patterns of tyranny should, perhaps, properly be regarded as 'ideal-types', since actual tyrannies have frequently combined elements of both. Even the most obnoxious of tyrants, including Adolf Hitler, have sometimes displayed attributes of 'kingly' rule alongside the traditional devices of tyranny. And this, it should be plain, was true of Stalin as well.[14]

Now, the argument here is not one of *plus ça change...* – quite the contrary. Tyrannies vary, and not only because tyrants vary, but also because of the particular circumstances of their assuming and exercising power, and the character of the societies they rule. It is this last factor that interests us here. In the past, tyrannies have been limited for technical reasons either in geographical scale or the depth and generality of their penetration. It was possible for a tyrant acting within the confines of an ancient Greek or Renaissance Italian city-state to exercise a profound and continuing influence over the lives of all his subjects, though even here the traditional and market relationships which governed routine daily activities tended to cushion his impact. In the great despotic empires the ruler's hand was directly, continually, and profoundly felt only by limited (mainly élite) segments of the population and in specific fields of activity. The more humble the subject, the more remote from the capital and major administrative centres, the more indirectly, superficially, and intermittently would he feel that hand (though if it chanced to fall, say, to summon him to military or labour service or to inflict exemplary punishment, his life might never be the same). Hence Russian folk wisdom enjoined: 'Do not keep your household near the prince's household, or your settlement near the prince's settlement'

(*Ne derzhi dvora bliz kniazha dvora, ne derzhi sela bliz kniazha sela*), for 'Near the Tsar, near to death' (*Bliz tsaria —bliz smerti*), even if 'Near the Tsar, near to honour' (*Bliz tsaria —bliz chesti*). In such empires the tyrant, in effect, ceded vast segments of the life of society to the virtually autonomous operation of traditional and market forces.

Stalin's tyranny, by contrast, disposed of the technical resources, most crucially in the fields of communication and transport, that enabled it to achieve on an imperial scale the deep and generalised penetration of society previously possible only on a mini-state scale. More than this, however, the drastic curtailment of the role of autonomous traditional and market forces in the regulation of social activity, and the substitution of hierarchical organisations, culminating in the person of the tyrant, for managing most areas of life, opened up a series of channels for transmitting the tyrant's will *directly* to *every* subject: one to order his work; one to demand his manifold manifestations of submission and acclaim; one to guide his thinking; one to spy on him and punish his actual, suspected, or potential misdemeanors; and so on. And now we are ready for definitions. Stalinism was not just the mono-organisational society, nor was it just tyranny. It was tyranny exercised under the conditions of a mono-organisational society, or, as I would prefer it, the mono-organisational society as run by a tyrant.

Here, however, a further question immediately arises: if Stalinism was a combination of these two components, was this combination purely fortuitous, or was some necessary relationship involved? Since the Soviet mono-organisational society has now functioned for nearly a quarter-century without the ingredient of personal tyranny, the latter is evidently not an essential feature or condition of such a society. Yet, as mentioned earlier, the establishment of Stalin's tyranny and of the mono-organisational society did coincide closely in time. Was the one therefore necessary to the *establishment* of the other? And if so, what was the historical connection between the two phenomena? It is to these questions that we must now turn.

The Making of Stalinism

It is easy to detect factors in pre-Stalinist Russia making for both personal tyranny and a mono-organisational society. These factors are reasonably familiar, and it will suffice to recall them briefly. Russia entered the twentieth century as an autocratic monarchy in both theory and practice, and the attendant attitudes were deeply embedded in both the 'élite' and 'mass' political culture: 'Truth is

God's but freedom [to decide] is the tsar's' (*Pravda bozh'ia, a volia tsarskaia*); 'No one judges the tsar's judgement' (*Tsarskoe osuzhdenie bessudno*). It is true that conventions of restraint and elements of a *Rechtsstaat* had been painfully evolving for some generations, and the political reforms following the 1905 Revolution, despite the reaction that soon set in, represented significant steps towards a constitutional monarchy which ultimately *might* have led to some genuine form of elected parliamentary government. However, liberal and anti-authoritarian politics had little chance to take root before being swept away, along with the middle classes, where such support as they enjoyed mainly lay.

The traditions of the Russian revolutionary intelligentsia, out of which the Bolshevik movement emerged, were predominantly and often scornfully anti-liberal and had no patience for procedural democracy or compromise with opponents. Although these traditions did not focus on individual leaders or saviours – despite all that has been written about Russian 'messianism' – they invested the revolutionary organisation (as such) with an unqualified claim to rule which flowed from its 'correct' doctrine; and in the inevitable struggles to establish what *was* correct doctrine, dominant personalities were bound to emerge and establish followings, so that in practice the thrust of these traditions was towards dictatorship, a fact that was clearly recognised by such of Lenin's fellow-Marxists as Leon Trotsky and Rosa Luxemburg when he set about grafting these organisational traditions (in the form of 'democratic centralism') on a section of the infant Russian Social Democratic Workers' Party.

Lenin, admittedly, although always prepared to fight tooth and nail for the policies he believed right, was not despotic by personality, and could tolerate being contradicted, criticised, and overruled on non-essential issues. This partly explains why the potential for personal dictatorship embodied in his organisational methods was not realised in Lenin's lifetime. In practice what emerged was an oligarchy of party leaders, resting on a state machine from which they had extirpated all opposition, and a party machine run by officials formally elective but in practice chosen from the centre. The panic reaction of this oligarchy, in the form of its ban on 'factions', to the surfacing of intra-party opposition groups in 1920–21, ensured that henceforth no effective alternative to their collective dictatorship could develop – so long as they hung together.

Aristotle's perception of the inherent instability of oligarchy, of the tendency of such collective dictatorships to soon break down, failing special efforts and particularly favourable conditions, has been abundantly borne out over the intervening two millenia – and in the Soviet case neither the efforts nor the favourable conditions were forthcoming. Without assuming that a personal dictatorship was 'inevitable', we must recognise it as now a likely outcome.

Turning to those elements in pre-Stalinist Russia making for the crystallisation of a mono-organisational society, one may again detect relevant antecedents well back in the tsarist past. First there was the great preponderance of the state over society, marking tsarist Russia, as some would have it, as an oriental despotism.[15] Because social forces were too constrained to allow much scope for spontaneous evolution, change, when it occurred, mainly took the form of 'social engineering' from above, most dramatically in the reforms of Peter the Great and Alexander II. Related to this was the notion of society as consisting of 'estates', each of which was defined in terms of its distinctive obligations to the state, which were enforced by a centralised bureaucracy. The realisation of this notion in actual practice was always somewhat untidy and became progressively more so, but its influence remained important. A further point was the major involvement of the state in a variety of social activities, from the promotion of industrial development to science and higher education.

We must beware of exaggerating these features of pre-revolutionary Russia. For one thing, capitalist market relations made considerable headway in the generation or so before the Revolution. The dominance of tradition in the villages, where four-fifths of the population still lived, modified the picture even more drastically. Yet these qualifications should themselves be qualified. Russian industrial capitalism remained heavily dependent on the state. As for the peasantry, the commune – the main vehicle of tradition – operated as a kind of 'primitive totalitarianism' which left little scope for autonomous individual choice and on top of this was also caught up in administering important programs of the state, for instance the poll tax and army recruitment before the 1861 reforms, and subsequently implementing the terms of the emancipation.

Nonetheless, caution is called for in drawing comparisons with the 'West'. In the salience of features which seem partly to prefigure those of the mono-organisational society, tsarist Russia stood out in sharp contrast, say to England, but less so to both pre- and post-revolutionary France, and even less to Prussia–Germany. There is no justification for assuming that, even without the Bolsheviks' coming to power, Russia would necessarily have been the country to pioneer the mono-organisational society.

Once the Bolsheviks were in the saddle, however, the probability of such an outcome was enhanced enormously. For the two main components of their movement, namely their Marxism and their Russian revolutionary traditions, conspired mightily to this effect. From their Marxism they received the concept of a society totally remade from the basic economic structure up, their confidence in the feasibility and indeed inevitability of this, and their resort to the state as the main instrument of this transformation. From the Russian revolutionary tradition, as we have noted, they received and perfected the centralised 'military' pattern of organisation and their belief in the absolute claims of the revolutionary will, which should brook no opposition or resort to avoidable compromise. Pestel as early as the 1920s looked to a 'temporary' dictatorship of revolutionary leaders to bring about *his* good society. The two components came together in the concept of the 'dictatorship of the proletariat', an *obiter dictum* of Marx's unearthed by Lenin and borne aloft like the Holy Grail. This dictatorship, defined as 'power unlimited by any laws', was to be exercised, as Lenin acknowledged, 'essentially' by the 'revolutionary vanguard'.

The measures collectively known as War Communism went a long way towards transforming Soviet Russia into a centrally managed society during the very first years of the regime, although how far this was due to the drive to remake society and how far to improvisations provoked by the demands of the Civil War it is not easy to say. Much of industry was nationalised and run by centralised government agencies, and the rest of the economy was placed under close supervision and direction. The market in goods and services for both production and consumption was almost entirely replaced by centralised allocation. Official agencies moved in busily to take charge of non-economic activities such as the arts, media, science, education, and health care. Opportunities for expressing views at variance with Bolshevism were progressively curtailed, while massive campaigns to transform people's beliefs and attitudes were mounted. Moreover, the party was already asserting a major coordinating role in keeping the specialised bureaucracies entrusted with various aspects of national life running in harness.

Despite this mammoth surge towards the centralised bureaucratic management of society, Soviet Russia even in the full tide of War Communism fell considerably short of the mature mono-organisational society as we have described it above, and the substantial abatement of centralised economic and, in some degree, other controls during the NEP further widened this gap. Nonetheless the USSR in the mid-1920s was much closer to the mono-organisational pattern than any other society that had yet existed, and especially any society in peacetime.

Thus the ground was now well prepared for both the constituent elements of Stalinism. It would be a mistake to infer, however, that Russia was already teetering on the brink, that one sharp push was all that was needed to plunge it into the Stalinist abyss. There remained a number of restraining factors, and these must be examined before we can grasp the dynamic relationship between the two components of Stalinism.

First, there was still much that was not centrally managed. In the economy agriculture formed one vast exception, and after 1921 most small-scale industry and distribution was also in private hands, while market relationships again came into their own as the major coordinating mechanism in the economy. In non-economic activities, although access to resources was for the most part determined by official agencies, there was a considerable degree of autonomy at operative levels. This leads to a second point: there was still substantial scope for independence of thought during the 1920s. Of course, 'counter-revolutionary' views could not be publicly expressed, but in most fields this left a wide range within which conflicting opinions and attitudes could compete. This was most conspicuously so in the case of science but was also marked in the arts, the aspirations of Proletkul't notwithstanding. On matters with more direct political implications, such as legal or economic policy, the forums within which open debate could occur tended to be more restricted, but sharply differing views were nevertheless vigorously pressed throughout the 1920s. In general, differences of opinion enjoyed a degree of legitimacy, and there was no assumption that there must be a 'correct' line authoritatively dispensed on all issues.

Finally, significant obstacles to one-man rule were built into the Russian communist movement itself. I said earlier that Lenin bequeathed an oligarchical power–structure institutionalised in the Politburo, which seemed likely to degenerate into a personal dictatorship unless the oligarchs could, rather improbably, hang together. This picture now needs to be qualified. To start with, the oligarchy was not wholly restricted to the seven or eight members of the Politburo. On the one hand, the party Central Committee, numbering three to four dozen at this period, was not yet a mere rubber stamp for 'its' Political Bureau. On the other hand, both the Council of People's Commissars and the party executive machinery (run by the Orgburo and the Secretariat) remained important, if subordinate, decision-making centres. Further, the authority of the major oligarchs lent a degree of autonomy to the official bodies directed by them (the industrial administration (VSNKh), the political police (GPU), the Army and Navy Commissariat while Trotsky was in charge, the trade unions, the Leningrad party organisation while dominated by Zinoviev, the Moscow party organisation while dominated by Kamenev, and so on), and so injected a considerable element of bureaucratic pluralism into the operation of the system.

There was also a more general and pervasive inhibition on dictatorship, deriving from democratic elements in the party's traditions and structures. Largely under the influence of German Social Democracy, Marxism as a political movement came to Russia heavily imbued with democratic values. The tradition of democracy, moreover, was one that rejected populism of either a Rousseauesque or charismatic variety, and stressed such procedural aspects as free and open discussion of policy, collective decision-making by majority vote, election of executive bodies and officials, etc. It is this, of course, that explains the widespread disquiet within the infant Russian Social Democratic Workers' Party at Lenin's quasi-military, centralist concepts of organisation, and it explains why he had to present these as 'democratic' centralism. At the same time the Bolshevik affirmation of procedural democracy was not pure sham, despite their readiness to make a virtue of the necessity of operating *un*democratically in the conditions of the conspiratorial underground. While accepting the authority of directives and 'cadres' sent from the centre, local party organisations did elect committees, did discuss policy issues, did take votes. In the language of genetics, the organisational patterns and concomitant attitudes that established themselves in the pre-revolutionary period may be characterised as centralism dominant and democracy recessive.

These patterns were further reinforced during the Civil War, as the necessity of curbing democracy in the interests of strict discipline and the centralised deployment of personnel was accepted. It was only as peace and victory were in sight that the centralist and democratic strands of the party tradition came sharply into conflict. The resolution of this conflict in favour of the former, through the leadership's success in rallying the Tenth Congress to support its suppression of intra-party opposition and factions, can be regarded as a reconfirmation and entrenchment of the established centralism dominant–democracy recessive patterns. The leadership was now armed with the disciplinary and personnel powers to break up centres of opposition, to install compliant secretaries and committees, and to keep criticism and discussion on a low key.

Nevertheless the democratic forms were observed so far as consistent with these purposes, as was the right of party members to debate 'unresolved' issues, a right that was exercised with marked vigour at the annual conferences and congresses.

The Soviet political system as bequeathed by Lenin may be described as an oligarchy focused in the Politburo but overflowing to a second level of several dozen other officials, an oligarchy marked by a considerable degree of bureaucratic pluralism, and operating in a climate of limited freedom of thought and under democratic forms possessing some residual substance. Through a variety of bureaucratic structures this oligarchy sought to manage a great deal that went on in Soviet society, but substantial areas of activity still lay outside its direct administration.

The only trouble with this picture is that it is too static. For the oligarchy had hardly consolidated its power before it began to break up. And as it broke up the constituent elements of the regime assembled and reassembled themselves in a kaleidoscopic succession of patterns. Without attempting to trace these patterns here, we should note some underlying consistencies. First and most obvious, the divisions within the oligarchy intensified the elements of bureaucratic pluralism in the system. Their effects on freedom of speech and intra-party democracy were more complex and contradictory. As the contending leaders sought to outdo each other in getting supporters elected as committee members and congress delegates and in securing favourable resolutions from local conferences, they in effect revived the very factionalism they had united to suppress a few years earlier. And since their struggles were fought out in terms of issues, there was a sharp stimulus to policy debate, which overflowed from the party conclaves into the press and scholarly institutions. Controversy largely centred around such central economic problems as how to handle the peasant and strategies of industrialisation, but erupted at various times on a surprising range of other issues. Moreover, since the divided leadership was rarely able to provide agreed guidelines in specialised fields like the arts and sciences, law, education, and so on, each of these tended to become a battleground of ideas and rival groups and personalities in its own right. From a liberal–democratic viewpoint all this may seem normal enough, but in terms of Bolshevik traditions the constant fever of policy debate, the public displays of party disunity, and the recurrence of 'factionalist' tactics within the party were decidedly pathological. Which is why those in the dominant faction of the movement could usually count on widespread support within the party when they resorted to the same measures to crush their opponents as had been employed against the anti-oligarchy oppositions of 1920–21: to use the personnel and disciplinary powers vested in the party's central executive organs to remove their rivals' supporters from party positions; to get resolutions against them passed by local committees and conferences; to deny their adherents election to party congresses and the Central Committee; to use the party's authority over the other agencies of the regime to remove these from their rivals' control; to use the party's authority over the media, scholarly institutions, etc., to deprive their rivals of a public voice; and, finally, if the latter, denied all legitimate platforms, resorted to clandestine meetings, circulation of protest declarations, etc., using the political police to expose them and render them liable to direct disciplinary measures. These methods were used successively against Trotsky and his supporters, Zinoviev and Kamenev and their supporters, and finally Bukharin, Rykov, and Tomsky and their supporters. Thus while the divisions within the oligarchy activated the machinery of intra-party democracy and stimulated public debate, they simultaneously provoked counter-measures that were fatal to both.

The Soviet Union in the 1920s, then, revealed a strong potential to develop into a mono-organisational society and a similarly strong potential to develop into a personal dictatorship, but substantial obstacles would have to be overcome to realise these potentials. Their realisation would thus not occur automatically, but required deliberate acts of human will – acts, moreover, that called for great determination and political skill, and a strong initial power base. This point deserves special emphasis. While circumstances were favourable to the emergence of Stalinism, they by no means fully explain its emergence. A full explanation must also give weight to the deliberate acts of Stalin. We must therefore consider these acts, but in doing so there is one question of particular interest to our analysis: could Stalin have become dictator without taking Russia that extra mile to the fully fledged mono-organisational society or achieved the latter without making himself dictator – for it should be reiterated that it was their combination, not the dictatorship alone, that constituted Stalin*ism*. The reader will perhaps guess at my answer to this question from what has gone before: it would have been very difficult to attain the one without the other and any step towards the one tended to involve a step towards the other.

For the oligarchical structure of power both made for and rested on a relatively dispersed and pluralistic pattern of decision-making and a level of subsystem autonomy that was incompatible with a mono-organisational system. Clearly the oligarchs could never have achieved sufficient mutual trust and unity of purpose to deliberately sacrifice their individual power bases in the interests of creating such a system – even it they could agree on its desirability. The way to both a mono-organisational society and a personal dictatorship, therefore, lay through capturing the oligarchs' power bases, liquidating the limited subsystem autonomy, and concentrating decision-making in a single centre. Now this, in fact, was what Stalin's tactics amounted to, and although it is an oft-told tale[16] we shall need briefly to recall these tactics in order more fully to appreciate this point.

It is generally agreed that the crucial resource enabling Stalin to establish his dictatorship was control over the party's organisational machinery, through his being (from 1921) the only Politburo member with a seat (and therefore the key seat) in the Orgburo and (from 1922) general secretary of the party. It is also clear that control of this machinery was essential to undermining the authority of his fellow oligarchs and depriving them of *their* various organisational power bases, both inside and outside the party itself. The transformation of the oligarchy into a dictatorship required that this machinery be in the hands of a man possessing the skill to operate it, the drive to use it to extend his power, and the capacity to retain control of it to a point when the change in the power structure was irreversible. This last aspect is often overlooked. For why was Stalin allowed to *go on* using his control of the machine so as to reward his friends and punish his enemies, to build up compliant majorities in committees and conferences, and to place more and more of his supporters in key positions at the centre and in the provinces? After all, Stalin's fellow oligarchs did not need Lenin's 'Testament' to tell them that he was 'abusing his powers' in these ways.

The answer to this has already been foreshadowed. The successive dominant factions in the Politburo needed precisely such things to be done in order to defeat their opponents in the leadership and get their policies implemented, and Stalin was both willing and manifestly capable of doing it for them. Of course they could see he was benefiting from it, but so, it seemed to them, were they. Playing this role required of him special qualities additional to those of a machine boss: skill in coalition-building, flexibility (or cynicism) in falling in with the policies of the temporary majority, and an acute sense of political timing in changing allies and policies. There is also a further aspect: if Stalin's fellow oligarchs licensed him to manipulate the officials and rank-and-file of the party, the latter still had to comply with such manipulation. That they mostly did so is usually explained by a combination of the party's centralist organisational patterns and careerism.   These factors were undoubtedly of great importance.   As we have seen, the centralist side of 'democratic centralism' was emphatically reasserted with the suppression of the opposition groupings of 1920–21 and the prohibition of factionalism. This latter enabled Stalin's organisers to get their nominees elected simply by labelling as 'factionalism' any attempt by party members to consult in putting up alternative candidates. Careerism, evident enough even during the Civil War, notoriously blossomed thereafter, whether due, as variously suggested, to the 'petit bourgeois' atmosphere of NEP, to weariness, disillusionment, and the craving for comfort and security, to the greater likelihood of idealists perishing in the war or suffering expulsion through opposition activity, or to the influx of worker and peasant cadres who tended to identify the emancipation of their class with their personal elevation.   There was, however, a third factor explaining the compliance of the party's lower echelons to manipulation by the Stalin machine: the widespread disquiet over public displays of disunity and the sense that it was pathological and un-Bolshevik for party meetings and media to be constantly taken up with conflicts of policy and personality. Stalin knew how to harness such misgivings to his cause as well, playing the practical, reliable activist who simply wanted to get on with the job of implementing agreed programs as laid down by Lenin rather than haring off after theoretical subtleties: an image of the party worker, the *partrabotnik*, with which the ordinary Communist making his way in the party could easily identify.

Thus while Stalin's use of the organisational weapon was crucial to his achievement of supreme power, he also needed to employ political skills of a high order, so as to secure and maintain sufficient élite and mass backing and to 'legitimate' his organisational measures.

Stalin was most adept at exploiting his organisational strengths and neutralising his organisational weaknesses. Perhaps the best example is his promotion of the 'full' Central Committee vis-à-vis the Politburo, a gambit that had the virtue of appearing in line with both intra-party democracy and proposals of Lenin's shortly before his death, but which also had the special advantage that Stalin, through his control of party congress elections, enjoyed a majority in the Central Committee well before he was able to begin stacking the Politburo with his adherents. Though constitutionally master of the Politburo, the Central Committee had lapsed into a subordinate and dependent position before the death of Lenin, but Stalin worked to revive its authority, employing it – particularly in joint meetings with the Central Control Commission, which was even more heavily dominated by his supporters – as a captive court of appeal from Politburo decisions, as a forum to harass his opponents, and eventually as an instrument to restructure the Politburo membership.

A rather similar manoeuvre was employed with the Council of People's Commissars, or Soviet 'Government'. Under Lenin's chairmanship this body enjoyed enormous authority, and even though its subordination to the Politburo had become clear well before Lenin's death and its prestige declined sharply with Rykov as chairman in place of the founder of Bolshevism, its potential role as an alternative focus of power remained considerable. The direct influence Stalin could exercise within the Government through his powers in the party Secretariat was, moreover, quite limited. On the other hand there was the Central Executive Committee (CEC) of the Congress of Soviets, and especially its Presidium, to which bodies the Government was formally responsible. These bodies, also very significant in the early years of the regime, had long been lapsing into a primarily decorative role, but now they began to be revived. Again a crucial consideration was that these 'soviet' bodies, through party control over the election of their members, were far more susceptible to direct influence by Stalin than was the Council of People's Commissars. The Presidium of the CEC now began to assume much of the business formerly handled by the Government, to hold joint meetings with it, and to assert its superior constitutional status, thus substantially cutting into the power base of Rykov, a man of independent mind whom Stalin must have regarded as an obstacle to his power even before they came into open conflict at the end of the twenties. The building up of the CEC and its Presidium as a counter-weight to the Government was given an added impetus by the election to the Politburo in 1926 of CEC Chairman Kalinin, a man more pliant to Stalin's will than Rykov. The tactical motivation of these developments is reflected in the fact that once Stalin was in a position to stack the Politburo and Government the Central Committee and CEC (including its Presidium) were both allowed to atrophy as working bodies.

If Stalin's organisational power was instrumental in capturing the citadels of Politburo 'outs' on behalf of Politburo 'ins', it was also extended by every such capture. Thus when Trotsky lost the Army and Navy Commissariat in January 1925, it was taken over by Stalin's ally Frunze and, on the latter's death, his close supporter Voroshilov. Shortly afterwards, when Kamenev and Zinoviev went into opposition, their power bases in the Moscow and Leningrad party organisations respectively were restaffed with loyal Stalinists. Dzerzhinsky's death in 1926 was a windfall for Stalin, for his authority would have been a serious obstacle to Stalin's penetration of the political police (now the OGPU), which henceforth, under humbler and more compliant leadership, went rapidly ahead. Finally, in 1930, with the defeat of the so-called Right Opposition and the removal of Rykov from chairmanship of the Council of People's Commissars, Tomsky from the chairmanship of the Central Council of Trade Unions, and Bukharin from chairmanship of the Comintern, they were replaced by Stalin's protégés Molotov, Shvernik, and Manuilsky respectively. Such appointments could be recognised by most Communists as proper and legitimate, since the new incumbents were invariably men with distinguished records of service to the party, and who, if not the general secretary, was best placed to make recommendations to such positions? Of course, as the new leaders were installed, more or less extensive staff changes soon followed, consolidating the hold of Stalin's supporters on the organisation concerned. The effect of these developments was to liquidate the semi-autonomy of one major bureaucratic structure after another, and *pari passu* and semi-autonomy of the areas of activity they administered, binding them into an ever broader and ever tighter organisational network in which the last word on all important matters was reserved for Stalin himself.

Thus by 1930 the transition to the mono-organisational society and to Stalin's personal rule were both well advanced. And meanwhile the biggest remaining gaps in the mono-organisational pattern were being removed with the replacement of NEP by a 'command economy' based on centralised directive planning and administration of industry and distribution, and collectivisation of agriculture. We may be tempted to see in Stalin's espousal of these changes a manifestation of his psychological compulsion to maximise control and bend all to his will, but even without invoking such psychological factors it is easy to understand his resort to *organisational* measures to solve the problems of rapid industrialisation and peasant recalcitrance, since these were the measures at which he was adept, which were most obviously at hand, and which had served him so well in the past.

All the essential ingredients of the mono-organisational system were now present, and they rapidly shook down into the patterns described at the beginning of this paper. Stalin's personal rule, however, had not yet taken on the unmistakably 'tyrannical' features we associate with mature Stalinism. True, his critics could be deprived of a public voice and centres of independent thought constrained and harassed (as RAPP was licensed to do, for instance, in literature); but there was not yet an official orthodoxy on all matters to which everyone must adhere. True, a leadership cult was well established, but Stalin was not yet ascribed superhuman qualities and the masses were not yet being constantly assembled to give exultant displays of their devotion. Most vital of all, though Stalin's power to punish his critics had been amply demonstrated, and fear was already an important ingredient in his rule, he still lacked that truest hallmark of the fully established tyrant – the unlimited power of life and death over all his subjects. And because he lacked that power those in authority under him could still assert a voice of their own and might still, conceivably, combine against him. Hence vestiges of the oligarchical pattern of power survived, especially in the Politburo and other inner executive bodies, but also, to some extent still, in the Central Committee. The men at these levels, moreover, though loyal supporters of Stalin in the past, and therefore presumably satisfied that 'their' man was in the saddle, and satisfied too with the social and political transformations he had effected in getting there, had certainly not bargained on becoming the helpless subjects of an arbitrary despot. They may also have had some sense that while Stalin's dictatorship was a necessary condition of the triumph of 'socialism' (or the mono-organisational society in our terms), its perpetuation and entrenchment were not essential, and might be harmful, to the further development of 'socialism': whether it was indeed some such perception or merely fear that provoked the tentative moves in 1934 to replace Stalin by Kirov will perhaps never be known. The outcome, however, we know all too well, and it gave Stalin, by 1937, the power to have anyone he wanted killed. Once that was there the remaining attributes of tyranny bloomed abundantly.

Epilogue

Our subject is Stalinism, and not what followed it. Yet what followed is important for our theme since it showed that the two constituent elements of Stalinism were separable, that you could, in other words, have the mono-organisational society without the personal dictatorship. The contemporary failure to perceive them as separable was perfectly understandable, since they had come into being together and were organically linked in a single 'Stalinist' system. Furthermore, other contemporary dictatorships, namely Mussolini's and especially Hitler's, had displayed sufficient tendencies towards the comprehensive centralised management of society to suggest a new socio-political type: the 'totalitarian dictatorship'. Indeed the organic combination of personal absolutism with total social control was a key assumption of the most influential models of totalitarianism until some years after Stalin's death.[17] If the subsequent efforts to salvage the concept of totalitarianism in characterising the Soviet system have proved singularly unenlightening, this is primarily because existing models, once the attributes deriving from personal dictatorship are subtracted, can tell us so little about the remaining attributes of the system.[18] As a more general term signifying patterns of thought and action that tend to total social control, 'totalitarianism' still deserves a place in the lexicon of the social sciences; in this sense Soviet mono-organisational society is strongly marked by totalitarianism, but then so, too, in various degrees have been many other societies quite differently organised,[19] and a quite different concept is required, such as that of the mono-organisational system, if we want to focus attention on the salient defining characteristics of societies like the USSR.

If, as I have argued, personal dictatorship went hand-in-hand with the establishment of the Soviet mono-organisational system, why was it not needed to maintain it?[20] Here I can do no more than sketch out an explanation. Establishing the system was not simply a matter of extending to all segments of social activity a centralised network of administrative subordination; it involved changing, in myriad ways and various degrees, the attitude and behaviour patterns of a whole population. Until these patterns became second nature – and this certainly could not happen overnight – any relaxation of the dictatorship and division of power at the top involved a strong danger of the system falling apart. By the time Stalin died, however, older people had had almost a quarter-century to adapt to the system, and there was a whole new generation socialised, from the kindergarten up, to its roles and expectations. In the period that followed, when none of the old dictator's entourage managed to take sole power, it soon became apparent that the system had put down deep enough roots to be viable without such supports as a leader cult and massive arbitrary repression.

An oligarchical sharing of supreme power painfully established itself and gradually acquired a fairly settled institutional shape. Those features of 'Stalinism' that had flowed from and supported the personal rule of the tyrant were now increasingly found to be inconsistent with oligarchical rule as well as costly to societal performance, while the defence of those features that constituted the mono-organisational system became the common ground on which the oligarchical consensus rested. That the system could now tolerate and even profit from a measure of bureaucratic pluralism and freedom of thought and expression also became clear, but so also did the strict limits beyond which the system was endangered by such things: limits indicated as much by experiences in Poland, Hungary, and Czechoslovakia as in the Soviet Union itself.

It might be argued that this analysis ignores the personal dominance enjoyed by Khrushchev between 1957 and 1964 and by Brezhnev from about 1970. In neither case, however, was this dominance comparable in degree or character with Stalin's, and it is dubious whether the power of Khrushchev and Brezhnev within their respective regimes was greater than that of many chief executives in liberal–democratic systems. If we further take account of the 'interregna' of 1953–57 and 1964–69, the Soviet regime since Stalin must be seen as having a *relatively weak* chief executive role. This probably reflects more than anything else protective measures taken within the oligarchy itself, whose members recognise that a strong chief executive might quickly make himself dictator in a system lacking serious societal checks on the supreme echelon of. power. It remains problematical, however, whether the oligarchical structure of power could survive a profound or prolonged crisis situation requiring expeditious and decisive leadership.

Should some future chief executive attempt 'to escape from the control of the collective', as Khrushchev was alleged to be doing on the eve of his removal, he will need speedily to assume the powers and methods of a tyrant if he is to escape a similar fate. Such an outcome may now seem improbable but cannot be ruled out. Should it occur, we would again have 'a mono-organisational society ruled by a tyrant' – our definition of Stalinism. But would it be *Stalinism*, with a society so much richer, better educated, and more complex than that of 1953, with a new political élite, and above all a *different* tyrant? For if, as Tolstoy tells us, 'all happy families resemble each other, every unhappy family is unhappy in its own way', every tyrant will impose his own particular variant of misery on his subjects. For the same reason, it probably casts more confusion than light to extend the 'Stalinist' label even to those other Communist regimes with strongmen at the top; it is confusing in the same way, for instance, as labelling the various fascist dictatorships of the 1930s 'Hitlerite'. Still, as Stalin was the man whose tyranny was built in tandem with the first mono-organisational society, there is some justice in invoking his name whenever such a society throws up a new tyrant.

Notes and References

1 A fuller characterisation of the Soviet social and political system in the terms presented here will be found in Andrew C. Janos, ed., T.H. Rigby, 'Politics in the Mono-Organizational Society', in *Authoritarian Politics in Communist Europe: Uniformity and Diversity in One-Party States*, (Berkeley, Calif.), 1976.

2 The ordinary Soviet citizen did not, of course, require a scholarly 'model' to convince himself of the salience of bureaucracy in the USSR, and, indeed both Trotsky in *The Revolution Betrayed* and his subsequent writing and James Burnham in *The Managerial Revolution* long ago focused their respective characterisations of Soviet society on the dominance of the bureaucrats or managers. However, it has taken a later generation of scholars familiar with the work of Max Weber and modern organisation theory and prompted by post-Stalin developments to challenge the prevailing concept of 'totalitarianism', to look seriously at the structural characteristics of the USSR viewed as a bureaucratic system. A pioneering role was played here by Alfred G. Meyer in his article 'U.S.S.R. Incorporated', *Slavic Review*, vol.XX (1961), pp.369–76, and his book *The Soviet Political System: An Interpretation*, (New York), 1965.

3 See Joseph Berliner, *Factory and Manager in the U.S.S.R.*, (Cambridge, Mass.), 1957.

4 The positive aspects of this phenomenon are ably discussed by Andrew Gunder Frank in his article 'Goal Ambiguity and Conflicting Standards: An Approach to the Study of Organization', *Human Organization*, vol.17 (1958–59), pp.8–13.

5 Tom Burns and G.M. Stalker, *The Management of Innovation*, (London), 1966, p.121. In this book, originally published in 1961, Burns and Stalker provided the pioneering, and still the most elaborate and satisfying, characterisation and explanation of this distinction. The basic concepts have since gained wide acceptance, but some have seen the term 'organic' as misleading, and in a recent edition of their book Burns and Stalker have substituted 'organismic'.

6 The view proposed in this paragraph is argued at much greater length in my article 'Politics in the Mono-Organizational Society'.

7 Khrushchev makes and illustrates this point repeatedly in his memoirs. See *Khrushchev Remembers: The Last Testament*, tr. and ed. Strobe Talbot, (Boston), 1974, pp.11, 20, 45, 158, 177, 238, 241, 357.

8 See, e.g., ibid., p.93.

9 Fitzroy Maclean, *A Person from England and Other Travellers*, (London), 1958, p.87.

10 Han Fei Tzu, whose prescriptions were well regarded by the first Ch'in emperor, recommended that 'the ruler of men must prune his trees from time to time and not let them grow too thick for, if they do, they will block his gate....If the trees are pruned from time to time, cliques and parties will be broken up. Dig them up from the roots, and then the trees cannot spread....Search out the hearts of men, seize their power from them. The ruler himself should possess the power, wielding it like lightning or like thunder'. Han Fei Tzu, *Basic Writings*, tr. Burton Watson, (New York), 1964, pp.41–42.

11 Aristotle, *The Politics*, tr. T.A. Sinclair, (Penguin Books, Harmondsworth), 1961, pp.225–27.

12 Ibid., p.227.

13 Ibid., pp.228–31.

14 For a comparative analysis of tryannical regimes, including that of Stalinist Russia, resting heavily on Aristotle's approach, see Maurice Latey, *Tyranny: A Study in the Abuse of Power*, (London), 1969.

15 See especially Karl A. Wittfogel, *Oriental Despotism: A Comparative Study of Total Power*, (New Haven), 1957.

16 See, for example, Leonard Schapiro, *The Communist Party of the Soviet Union*, (New York), 1960, especially Chaps 15, 16, 21; Robert C. Tucker, *Stalin as Revolutionary, 1879–1929: A Study in History and Personality*, (New York), 1973, Chaps 8–11; and Robert V. Daniels, *The Conscience of the Revolution*, (Cambridge, Mass.), 1965, Chapters 7–13.

17 See especially Hannah Arendt, *The Origins of Totalitarianism*, (New York), 1951; and Carl J. Friedrich and Zbigniew K. Brzezinski, *Totalitarian Dictatorship and Autocracy*, (Cambridge, Mass.), 1956.

18 This view, which cannot be argued here at length, would not, of course, command universal assent. For an excellent discussion of the value of the totalitarian concept, see Carl J. Friedrich, Michael

Curtis, and Benjamin R. Barber, *Totalitarianism in Perspective: Three Views*, (New York), 1969. Cf T.H. Rigby, 'Totalitarianism and Change in Communist Systems', *Comparative Politics*, vol.4, no.3 (April 1972), pp.433–53 (this volume, Chapter 6).

19 Cf. Leonard Schapiro, *Totalitarianism*, (London), 1972; Barber, in *Totalitarianism in Perspective*.

20 Unfortunately there is no space here for comparative analysis of the role of personal dictatorship in the USSR and other countries with a fully or partly developed mono-organisational system. Certainly a dominant leader pattern with repressive and obscurantist features resembling those found under Stalinism has been usual in countries 'going' mono-organisational, but much study is required to sort out how far common determinants are at work. More generally, on the concept of the mono-organisational society as a framework for comparison of Communist systems, see Rigby, 'Politics in the Mono-Organisational Society'.

5 The Embourgeoisement of the Soviet Union and the Proletarianisation of Communist China*

It is now clear that, despite a high level of coincidence between the interests and outlook of the USSR and the Chinese People's Republic, differences nevertheless exist. Most discussion of this question has focused on six main groups of issues:

1. Status within the bloc and authority in the international Communist movement.

2. Competition for influence in the uncommitted countries.

3. How far the Chinese path to Communism may properly stray from the Soviet model.

4. Different views over the possibility and desirability of improving relations with the imperialists and avoiding war.

5. The amount and timing of Soviet economic aid.

6. Border areas – Sinkiang, Mongolian People's Republic, etc.

There are, moreover, strong indications that each of these groups of issues has contributed to tension between the two allies at some stage or other of their ten-year-old alliance.

---

*Kurt London, ed., *Unity and Contradiction: Major Aspects of Sino-Soviet Relations*, (Praeger Publishers, New York), 1962. Copyright © by Frederick A. Praeger, Inc. Reprinted with Permission.

There is another series of factors which, I believe, are already exercising an influence upon Sino-Soviet relations, and whose influence will probably grow during the next two decades. These are factors deriving from differences in the character of the two societies – factors that I have alluded to in pseudo-Marxian terms in my title. Industrialisation in all societies involves recruitment of a new wage-earning class from other classes existing in pre-industrial society, primarily from the peasantry and petty bourgeoisie of artisans and shopkeepers. For most individuals, the change of class is accompanied by some or all of the following consequences: a real or apparent worsening of material living conditions, at least in certain basic aspects; subjection to an unwonted and often harsh labour discipline; loss of the standing and satisfactions that go with independence and traditional skills; uprooting from a local community in which the individual's behaviour was clearly prescribed for all common circumstances of life.

These objective and subjective deprivations tend to alienate the new wage-worker from society at large, and this is what is meant here by proletarianisation. The classical description of the proletarian given by Marx and Engels in the *Communist Manifesto* pictures him as possessing 'nothing to lose but his chains'; his wages are sufficient only 'to prolong and reproduce mere existence'; 'modern industrial labour...has stripped him of every trace of national character. Law, morality, religion are to him so many bourgeois prejudices, behind which lurk in ambush just as many bourgeois interests'.

Of course, no proletariat has ever fully conformed to the *Manifesto* pattern. Before the factors making for the proletarianisation of the new worker have taken full effect, new processes are under way tending to integrate him into society at a new level. Even in England, which provided the chief model for the *Manifesto* proletarian, influences as varied as the Wesleyan chapels, the mutual-aid societies, and the mechanics' institutes were early at work to render the working man less of an outcast and to link him up with the emerging urban community in which he found himself. At a later stage, working-class organisations ostensibly directed against the existing order–trade-unions and socialist political parties – to the extent that they were legally tolerated, themselves became potent forces integrating the industrial workers in the nation and the state. Alongside psychic factors tending to moderate the proletarianisation of the wage earner, material factors soon made themselves felt. As the first rigors of early industrialisation passed and the capital created thereby began to be reflected in a rising per capita national income, benefits started trickling down to the workers in the form of improved working conditions, housing, community services, more leisure, and, most important of all, consumption levels rising above mere subsistence and permitting the accumulation of a modest store of personal and family property. One must not minimise the importance of the psychic factors, but their impact would probably have remained very limited without the driving force of improving material conditions; the two acting together constituted a process of deproletarianisation which assumed growing importance in the maturing industrial society.

These two overlapping processes of proletarianisation and deproletarianisation of the new wage-earning class are aspects of the adaptation of traditional societies to industrialisation. The timing and intensity of the various factors contributing to these processes varied greatly from country to country, and also between different sections of the working class within particular countries. Their political expression also took various forms. However, the usual pattern showed a greater or lesser degree of intensification and radicalisation, with more or less violent movements of protest, followed by a period of increasing regularisation, institutionalisation, and moderation (in which, however, established radical traditions continued to receive lip service, and sometimes influenced action when war or recession brought psychic disturbance or a worsening of material conditions).

The Proletarianisation of Russia

The beginnings of modern factory production in Russia can be traced back well into the eighteenth-century, with serfdom and the Czarist autocracy producing some interesting distortions of Western European models – notably the assignment of families or whole villages of state peasants as hereditary labour in particular enterprises. However, the influence of these early feudal elements in the Russian factory should not be exaggerated, and in particular, left no great legacy of paternalism in employer–worker relations, such as that which in Japan, for instance, exercised such a profound influence upon the social and political effects of industrialisation. It was in the 1860s that industrialisation got under way, with the stimulus of the liberation of the serfs and the building of railways. By the 1890s, it was proceeding apace (pig-iron production trebled between 1886 and 1896), and on the eve of the First World War, Russia had a substantial class of wage earners in industry, transport, mining, and construction, amounting to over 10 per cent of the employed population.

This was a proletariat *par excellence*. All the ingredients were there: the exchange of traditional village life – with its omnipresent spiritual and secular authorities and the built-in social insurance of household and commune – for the squalor, insecurity, and confusion of the industrial centre – with low wages, long hours, and often appalling working conditions. Hence, the radical moods of this class, which erupted in the great strikes of the 1890s and played a prominent part in the revolutions of 1905 and March, 1917.

The Russian proletariat was also *one* of the instruments of the communists in the 'proletarian revolution' of November 1917, and in the Civil War that followed. Consequently, alongside the populist slogan of 'land to the tillers', Bolshevik tactics found a place for the syndicalist slogan of 'workers' control'. The contrast between urban-based Russian communism and village-based Chinese communism can be exaggerated; it is probably true that the Bolshevik victory in the Civil War was ultimately due to the fact that, for the majority of peasants, the Reds seemed the lesser evil, since a White victory threatened loss of their new-won acres. Nevertheless, working-class participation was undoubtedly a much greater factor in the Russian Revolution than in the Chinese. This lends special significance and irony to the fact that while the final victory of the Bolsheviks entailed for the peasants satisfaction of their basic grievances, it brought for the workers merely confirmation of their proletarian status. The collapse of the syndicalist dreams of workers' control and equality played a part in the Kronstadt revolt and in the 'workers' opposition' within the party. This disappointment, together with the disillusioning experience of the New Economic Policy, help to explain the persistence of proletarian attitudes of mind among the Soviet working class and their alienation from the 'workers' state'.

On the eve of the First Five-Year Plan, this still essentially proletarian working class constituted some 10 per cent of those employed; 80 per cent were peasants – most of them now independent proprietors. The next ten years saw the proletarianisation of this peasant mass. On the one hand, there was a resumption of large-scale industrialisation, which had been interrupted by 14 years of war, civil war, and rehabilitation, and by 1937, nearly a third of the peasants had been shifted into wage-earning jobs. These Russian peasants entering industry in the 1930s were subjected to essentially the same proletarianising pressures, material and psychic, as had been their predecessors of 40 years earlier.

On the other hand, a frontal attack was made on the petty-bourgeois character of peasant life itself. A minority of peasants were converted directly into wage-workers (state farms and machine-tractor stations provided less than 10 per cent of rural employment in 1940), while the majority were dragooned into 'collective farms', which were in form voluntary cooperatives. The distinctions between the two, though invested with great legal and theoretical significance by communist writers, are of secondary importance for our present purposes. The collective farmers, too, were deprived of their family enterprises and set to work in the 'public' sector, where they were directed by managements chosen by the local party and government authorities, allotted targets under the state plan, and paid according to 'the amount and quality of work done' out of profits primarily determined by state-fixed prices.

Thus, between 1928 and 1933, the petty-bourgeois masses of Russia were converted into employees of enterprises directly or indirectly controlled by the state. At the same time, there was a drastic decline in their material living standards. According to one estimate, workers' real wages, even in 1938, averaged 57.5 per cent of their 1928 levels. In the countryside, the decline in consumption levels reached famine proportions in some areas during the early years of collectivisation and it was probably only in the 1950s that the standards of the 1920s were regained. The social transformation effected during these years has often been described as a 'revolution from above'. The ironically-minded might call it a 'proletarian revolution from above' – but one made to *create*, not to emancipate, a proletariat. Politically the conversion of the bulk of the Soviet population into proletarians had the same consequences as similar transformations elsewhere – the alienation of the proletarianised masses from society and the regime.

The proletarianisation of Soviet society was never complete. It was limited by the following three factors:

1. Creation of privileged strata. Marxist writers, in seeking to explain the failure of the population in capitalist countries to behave in a revolutionary fashion, have often pointed to the 'bribing' (a) of the managerial–technical–clerical strata, which are given material and status privileges and encouraged to orient themselves toward the employers rather than the workers, and (b) of sections of the working class itself (the phrase 'aristocracy of the proletariat' was once popular), who are given higher wages and encouraged to lead the workers in a conciliatory and reformist direction. In the Soviet

Union, the 'bribery' of these two groups was undertaken as a part of party policy and opposition to it labelled 'petty-bourgeois egalitarianism'. During the First Five-Year Plan, income differentials were radically widened so as to create relatively high rewards for the managerial–technical intelligentsia, and also (by virtue of wide margins for skill and often steeply progressive piece rates) for a section of the industrial workers themselves. The creation of this privileged intelligentsia and of the Stakhanovite aristocracy of the proletariat tended to behead any potential movement of protest.

2. Granting of fringe benefits. In the early decades of industrialisation in England, when real wages were at their lowest, other determinants of working-class living standards (conditions of work, social protection, etc.) were also at their most unfavourable. In Germany and some other countries where industrialisation came later, the debasement of working-class conditions was soon significantly mitigated by social legislation. In the Soviet Union, such social legislation assumed a scale unprecedented in any country at a similar stage of industrialisation. Hours of work were limited to 48 in 1940, cut to 46 in 1956, and are currently being reduced to 40, with a further reduction to 36 promised in the next few years. Regular holidays, pensions, and protection from arbitrary punishment and dismissal were provided, and the workers and their families were included in ambitious state education and health programmes.

3. Survival of elements of private enterprise in the countryside. The attempt in the early stages of collectivisation to concentrate all production in the public sector and eliminate the peasant household altogether as an economic unit was soon discontinued, and by 1935, the right of each household to its auxiliary plot and a small amount of livestock was confirmed. The produce of these plots was not restricted to consumption by the household, but might be traded in the collective-farm markets. Due partly to government price policies, which often rendered the return from work on the public sector negligible, and partly to the power of traditional attitudes toward property, the peasants tended to be oriented primarily toward their private plots, and the peasant household remained, as it had been for centuries, the basic unit of rural economic and social life, while work on the collective sector was widely regarded as a sort of corvée. Thus, strong petty-bourgeois elements remained to moderate the proletarianisation of the peasantry.

These three factors limiting the proletarianisation of the Soviet population also clearly moderated its political effects. The compromise permitting the peasants to retain their private plots took some of the fire out of their hostility, which had reached such desperate proportions at the beginning of the collectivisation era. Fringe benefits narrowed the resentment of the urban working class. The 'bribery' of the managerial–technical intelligentsia and the Stakhanovite aristocracy of the proletariat meant that the most able and energetic tended to do relatively well under the regime and were thus inclined to identify their interests with *its* rather than with those of the masses.

Nevertheless, by the 1930s, substantial sections of the proletarianised population of the USSR appear to have become politically and socially alienated from the regime, and, as has happened in other industrialising countries, this found expression in more or less violent movements of protest. These took such varied forms as spontaneous strikes during the early 1930s, the destruction of property and assassination of communists by the peasants at the time of collectivisation, and the Vlasov movement and other anti-Soviet manifestations during the Second World War. That protest movements did not assume such proportions as to overwhelm the regime was of course due to the strength of Soviet physical, organisational and ideological controls.

The aggravation of internal security problems characteristically accompanying industrialisation has usually been met by intensified police and often internal military controls. Nowhere has this been truer than in the Soviet Union. But, as was mentioned, it is also characteristic for the proletariat to generate its own organisational and psychic links with society, which tend ultimately to moderate this alienation and the security problems arising therefrom. In the Soviet Union, such links were a deliberate creation of the regime. The Soviet regime sought to involve the masses organisationally and ideologically to a degree unprecedented in the world, though subsequently surpassed in China. In this way, they strove to direct resentments and political and intellectual energies into safe channels. A central part in this involvement was played by a mythological world view, to whose demands Marxist theory, history, science, journalism, and the arts were all subordinated, and whose dominant expression was the cult of the God-King Stalin.

The Embourgeoisement of Russia

The embourgeoisement of the working class in developed capitalist countries has sometimes been understood in terms of property rights: Workers become house-owners, have savings-bank deposits and perhaps other investments, and consequently develop the bourgeois outlook of men of property. It is, however, now clear that the emphasis should rather be placed upon consumption in a wider sense. As the real wages of the working class increase, are they used to create a distinctive working-class material style of life? Rarely to any significant extent, and never for long. On the contrary, the workers' increasing income is applied to emulate bourgeois standards of dress, house-furnishing, and decoration, and the workers soon show themselves as anxious as their middle-class fellow citizens to keep up with the Joneses in the acquisition of cars, television sets, and refrigerators.

The political consequences of embourgeoisement are a matter of common experience. The working-class movement ceases to be millenarian, ceases to be revolutionary, becomes reformist, and ultimately becomes geared to the attainment of small specific material benefits within the existing socioeconomic system. This reflects the transformation of the outlook of the individual worker. No longer required to concentrate all his efforts on attaining mere subsistence, with no prospect of improving his position so long as society is organised as it is and his place in it remains unchanged, he now finds his basic needs guaranteed, and his aspirations are turned toward the 'extras', toward material luxuries, and the existing system seems to promise him a growing share of these. In capitalist countries, this does not mean that the workers necessarily become advocates of capitalism. But they can no longer be seriously interested in radical measures to change the system. Like the middle classes before them, they are now basically oriented toward stability.

In the Soviet Union, embourgeoisement is implicit in the very policy of material incentives, said to be the main distinctive feature of socialism, the lower stage of communism – 'from each according to his ability, to each according to his work'. It might be recalled that Lenin pointed out in *The State and Revolution* that payment in proportion to work done implies the persistence of 'bourgeois right' in the domain of distribution. My argument here, however, rests not upon Marxist theory but upon the consequences of the policy of incentives in practice. The additional income of those who have benefited from this policy has been applied, not to the creation of a

distinctive socialist material culture, but, no less than in the case of
the working class in capitalist countries, to the emulation of
bourgeois standards of consumption. Modest and discreet at first
(up to the mid 1930s, even Politburo members wore cloth caps), it
became increasingly open and blatant, following the replacement of
the Old Bolsheviks by Soviet-bred 'organisation men' during the
Great Purge. As a reward for helping to build a socialist society,
Soviet citizens are encouraged to build a bourgeois personal life.

Until recently, embourgeoisement was limited to the 'bribed'
categories of managerial–technical intelligentsia and Stakhanovite
aristocracy of the proletariat. The great social change that is now
taking place in the Soviet Union is the extension of this process to
wider and wider sections of the population. As in other countries,
marginal social benefits and ideological factors were not in Russia
sufficient to eliminate the essentially proletarian character of the
masses so long as their material standards remained at about
subsistence level. It is the achievement of relatively high and rising
real income that is now carrying the Soviet masses through the
process of deproletarianisation on to embourgeoisement.

This is true even though we cannot say with too much confidence
just how high this real income is and how fast it is rising. There
would be general agreement that average real income, after a
catastrophic fall during the First Five-Year Plan, a gradual rise
during the 1930s, and a further drastic setback during the Second
World War, did not regain the levels of the late 1920s until around
1950. Since then, the official claim is that between 1950 and 1958, the
real income of workers and white-collar employees rose by 55 per
cent and of peasants by 85 per cent. This claim is probably
exaggerated, but not wholly misleading. Money wages at present
appear to average about 80 rubles a month. Though comparisons of
this kind are notoriously treacherous, we would probably not be too
far wrong in suggesting that these 80 rubles will purchase food,
drink, clothing, and household goods and furniture equivalent to
about one-third of those currently purchasable by one month's
average wages in Great Britain, and no more than a quarter of what
may be bought with a month's average wages in the United States.
But one must also take into account the far lower cost of housing in
the USSR, the scale of publicly provided services (comparable with
those provided in Great Britain and considerably greater than in the
United States), and the fact that in the overwhelming majority of
Soviet families, both husband and wife have full-time jobs. In short,
though real wages in the Soviet Union are still well below Western

European, let alone North American, standards, these have now ceased to be quite absurd as a basis for comparison.

Reverting to the official figures, the physical volume of Soviet retail trade is said to have more than doubled between 1950 and 1958. Sales of meat, butter, and eggs – crucial items where living standards are advancing from subsistence levels – increased two and a half or three times. The expansion of clothing and footwear sales was on the same level. Turning to consumer durables, a more telling case for the purposes of our thesis, we get the following picture: in the same years, 1950–58, sales of radios rose from under a million to 3.67 million, of sewing machines from 500,000 to nearly 3 million, of bicycles from 650,000 to nearly 3 million, of television sets from 12,000 to nearly a million, refrigerators from 1,000 to 330,000, washing machines from 280 to 500,000, of vacuum cleaners from 6,000 to 250,000. The number of passenger cars produced rose from 60,000 to 120,000, and of motorcycles from 120,000 to 400,000. There is, so far as I know, no reason to think these figures seriously misleading. What they show is this. Although many items that have been standard home equipment in the more prosperous capitalist countries for a quarter century or more are only now becoming available to the general public in the USSR, and other items that are *becoming* or have just become standard equipment in the former are still limited to a small minority in the latter, the Soviet Union has nevertheless now entered the era of the mass consumption of durable consumer goods. In this respect, it is probably at a stage comparable with Western Europe between the wars. The progress, however, is quite rapid, and there is probably nothing fantastic in the aim to increase real income per head by 40 per cent during the current Seven-Year Plan. Whatever the exact rate may be, each year extends the availability of many important items several rungs down the social scale. And by now, almost the whole population is involved to a greater or lesser extent in this process.

This applies even in the countryside. The official estimates that the value of the labour day trebled between 1953 and 1957, while the average money income of the *kolkhoznik* more than doubled between 1952 and 1957, are probably not too far from the facts. Here a complex social process is going on. Despite the removal of the tax on the products of the private plots and the lifting of other restrictions on the peasants' 'private enterprise', there is a general cautious move toward limiting the role of the latter (cutting down and consolidating plots, raising the compulsory minimum of work on the 'public' sector, sale of *kolkhozniks'* cows to the collective, and so on). The most important factor has been the change in price policy, which has made work on the 'public' sector a paying proposition, and it should not be long before the peasants are relying on this as their main source of income. These trends indicate a decline of the petty-bourgeois element in peasant life. However, it is clear that the peasants will never be fully proletarianised, as they are now being caught up in the nationwide process of embourgeoisement in the area of consumption.

I believe that all this is effecting a profound change in the outlook and mentality of the Russians. One American writer has described this as the coming of the 'consumer ethic'. Since 'bourgeois right' reigns in the area of consumption, and Soviet consumer standards are a direct reflection of those of bourgeois Europe and America, we can also regard this as the era of the embourgeoisement of Russia.

This process has only recently begun and will really get under way during the next decade. Present plans provide for the rehousing of the bulk of the population from single rooms in 'communal' flats to small family flats during this period. Even if construction plans fall well below present targets, it is clear that, for a large part of the Soviet people, the next few years will see the great undertaking of furnishing and equipping their new-won living space. The spreading of high levels of mass consumption has a peculiar excitement and adventurous quality to it which, I think, is beginning to infect the atmosphere in the Soviet Union. The new concern shown by the top leadership with the retail trade mechanism is symptomatic of this, and has found such varied expressions as experiments in the introduction of self-service, the establishment of instalment-buying arrangements, and the 1960 decisions on internal trade, which, among other things, provide for a great expansion in retailing facilities.

Anyone who has spent much time talking to Soviet people recently must have been impressed by the way individuals in all social classes and in all areas are taken up with saving for and acquiring luxuries: clothes in fashionable styles and good materials, furniture, household appliances, cars. Resentment tends to be directed no longer against the system as a whole, or against some scapegoat such as the internal or external enemy or the backward past, but against shortages or poor quality in the ranges of durable consumer goods into which the individual has now moved.

This is obviously fraught with great political implications, perhaps not dissimilar in certain important respects to those produced by the embourgeoisement of the working class in capitalist countries. In the view of the present writer, the underlying alienation of the bulk of the Soviet population from the Soviet system is passing. It is being replaced, not by a militant dedication to the official ideology, but merely by an acceptance of existing society as normal, as providing for their interests, and not fundamentally a conspiracy against them. The existing order seems to promise satisfaction of their current aspirations for durable consumer goods, and the opening up of ever-new possibilities beyond these. Thus, like the masses in the more prosperous capitalist countries and, like their own privileged sections in the past, the Soviet masses have now acquired a vested interest in stability. In the past, a *section* of society was 'bribed' by material incentives to support the regime's exploitation of the masses. Now everyone is 'bribed' to accept the existing order. The antagonism between privileged and unprivileged is therefore undermined, and the way opened up for a new consensus in Russian society, based on the maintenance of ever rising consumption standards for all classes.

This involves a fundamental change in the security problem. Formerly, the proletarianised condition of the masses produced such powerful pressures toward protest that the system could only be maintained by means of the most elaborate and violent physical and ideological counterpressures. These counterpressures can now be eased. Hence, developments varying from a curtailment of the powers and activities of the police to a certain modification of the mythological character of the official world view.

The Proletarianisation of China

No one would question the historical fact of the proletarianisation of China, as the term is here defined. What should be noted is that it seems to be going further, and promises to last longer, than in Russia.

Communist China began its industrialisation efforts with a far smaller industrial base in proportion to population, and with lower mass-consumption levels, than did the Soviet Union. The road to the achievement of high average levels of real income is proportionately longer and more difficult to traverse. It is not surprising that the Chinese Communist leaders have sought so diligently for short cuts. What they have found are various ways of maximising production effort and minimising current consumption, and of reinforcing physical and ideological controls to counter the resentments so caused.

In considering the impact of the changes wrought on Chinese society since 1949, one should not forget the relative strength of petty-bourgeois elements in the old China. Without romancing about the sturdy independent peasant or minimising the role of landlordism, one cannot but be impressed by the firm place traditionally occupied by the peasant family holding as an economic unit, as compared, for instance, with the Russian peasant household, whose role was for so long distorted by the authority of the commune (*obshchina*) and the centuries of serfdom. Chinese towns, too, were still strongholds of the trading and artisan classes, which in early twentieth century Russia were already largely overshadowed by the new factory proletariat. Commercial values seem to have enjoyed an acceptance in China which they were always denied in Russia. Chinese society, therefore, would appear to have been far worse prepared than Russian society to undergo the experience of total proletarianisation.

Up to 1958, the Chinese Communists nevertheless contrived to proletarianise their country in a more gradual, less cataclysmic manner than had their Soviet comrades. Collectivisation of the peasantry was approached through graded steps of mutual aid and cooperation and, when completed in 1955–56, contained concessions to family holdings such as were not granted in Russia until after the first crisis of collectivisation was past. Expropriation of industrialists and traders in the towns was also eased by intermediate stages of mixed ownership and participation in management. Rationality and moderation, however, were completely overwhelmed by the tidal wave of communisation that swept over the country in the second half of 1958.

The communes have brought changes in the domains of both production and consumption which carry proletarianisation in China beyond Soviet levels. Despite the partial reversal in December, 1958, of the policy of totally eliminating the peasant family enterprise by confiscating private plots, livestock, and implements, the private economy of the peasantry appears destined to play a far more subordinate role in the Chinese rural scene than it has so far in Russia. In the time that remains after they have cultivated the communal fields, the peasants are required to devote their energies to communal industrial undertakings or public works rather than their private plots.

If the communes have restricted and threatened the existence of petty-bourgeois elements in agricultural production, they have done the same thing for 'bourgeois right' in the area of distribution and consumption. It is true that the principle of material incentives, of 'to each according to his work', has never been discarded (though sometimes treated cavalierly or with impatience), and sections of the population are 'bribed' by fairly wide wage differentials and discriminatory rationing procedures.   However, the impact of material incentives is severely limited under commune conditions. Although there has been a retreat from the immediate pooling of personal and family property and even dwellings, the atmosphere in the communes is clearly hostile to the private accumulation of luxuries, and the cadres and other relatively privileged strata are expected to set an example in austerity. Communal mess halls and care of old people and children – practices whose primary aim is no doubt the release of women for 'production' – and the system of free supply (now rather in abeyance), have the effect of minimising the role of the family as a consumption unit.

These are the main distinguishing features of the Chinese experience of proletarianisation. Comparison of actual material living standards with those prevailing in Russia at a similar stage of development can have little relevance. What is, perhaps, worth noting is that China is incapable of supporting a programme of social services and other fringe benefits that mitigate the effects of proletarianisation comparable with those provided in the Soviet Union even during the 1930s. The Chinese worker, urban or rural, seems to have little defence against arbitrary disciplinary measures by his superiors, and extremely long hours of work appear typical.

Such an extreme form of proletarianisation as has been imposed upon the population of China gives rise to pressures which could assume explosive force if not subdued by commensurate counterpressures generated by the regime. The CCP leadership has made ample use of internal police and military controls and of mass-communication media, but has made to this stock-in-trade of all totalitarian states some additions of its own. In this connection, the militarisation of rural commune life may be mentioned, in its aspects both of organisation of the 'people's militia' and of regimentation of work activities. Even more important, however, is the control exercised over every individual through his work-study group. The universal obligation to engage in regular directed 'study' and 'discussion' requires the rank-and-file worker to remould his attitudes and actively commit himself to a degree that in the Soviet Union is expected only of party members.

Implications

It has been argued that in certain fundamental respects, the societies of China and the Soviet Union are diverging radically in their character at the present time. These divergent social trends will tend to produce certain political consequences, both within the two countries themselves and in their relations with each other and with other states. Nevertheless, it is obvious that they constitute only one factor among the many influencing political behaviour. All I shall do here is to suggest the direction of pressures arising from this particular factor, without attempting to estimate how effective these pressures might be expected to be.

One would expect it to produce, I think, a growing mutual irritation and difficulty of communication, arising from the sharp contrast in the tone and atmosphere – one might almost say the rationale – of life in two societies. Let us look at one or two points that highlight this contrast.

Since 1958, the Chinese communists have been engaged in attempting to supplant the family cooking stove, as far as possible, by communal mess halls. Meanwhile, in the Soviet Union, a great housing programme is in progress, aiming (among other things) at providing family kitchens for millions who formerly shared their cooking facilities with others in 'communal' flats. The striving for cosy and 'cultured' family living conditions is a natural and long-accepted corollary of Soviet policy on material incentives, but it seems quite alien to current Chinese ideas on how to move toward communism.

The last few years have seen a growing respect for hard facts in the Soviet intellectual sphere, and an increasing concern to relate plans consistently to objective reality. In China, on the other hand, the tendency has been in favour of subjective against objective factors, excessive concern with the latter even becoming one of the criteria of 'rightist opportunism'. The Chinese taste for 'letting politics take command' accords ill with the current Soviet stress on practical economic studies as the dominant element in party education. Connected with this is the Chinese attitude on incentives. Relying on incentives has been vigorously attacked in China as another of the errors of the 'rightist opportunists', whereas in Russia their central importance has never been called in question, and at no time more than the present has greater reliance been placed on material incentives as a built-in stimulus to production, overshadowing the role of all external organisational and ideological pressures.

In such ways, the two societies are becoming remote and, I should say, out of sympathy with each other. Soviet administrators and executives, not to mention more ordinary citizens, may increasingly find it easier to establish a rapport with, for instance, Americans than with Chinese communists.

It might be objected here that all this, whether right or wrong, has no bearing on international relations, which are decided by a few individuals at the top. But these few do not move in a vacuum. While largely moulding the societies around them, they are to some extent moulded in their turn by the societies. Attention has been drawn to the contrast in the atmosphere and tone of life between present-day China and Russia. But the leaders of both are very much in tune with the current tone and atmosphere of their countries. No one who has studied Khrushchev carefully over the past seven years could seriously doubt his involvement in the enterprise of raising mass-consumption levels. Nor is it likely that the commune, 'leap forward', and 'walking on two legs' mentality is merely manipulated by the Chinese leadership without it infecting them too.

No little importance here attaches to the upper- and middle-level officials, who form the human environment within which these top leaders move. In China, these are predominantly old, pre-1949 cadres, whose administrative apprenticeship was served under harsh material circumstances and military conditions. For them, the austerity of extreme proletarianisation, the regimentation, improvisation, and reliance on organisation and propaganda rather than objective conditions must appear natural features of the struggle for Communism. Their opposite numbers in Russia, in their overwhelming majority, are anything but revolutionaries, but are drawn from the pioneers of embourgeoisement in the USSR – members of the new technical–managerial intelligentsia who were placed on the power escalator by Stalin's purging of the Civil War generation of cadres. For these men, career-making in the party, administrative, or managerial hierarchy has meant constantly raising the levels of family consumption and acquiring a comfortable, well-furnished multi-room flat, a nice *dacha*, expensive holidays. Nothing could be more natural for *them* than to equate the spread of ever higher consumption levels with progress and the march toward communism. What is of particular interest to note is that not only is China not administered by such people *now*, but, if it turns out that the more ambitious forms of communisation are established, she never will have such a group as administrators. The road to communism in Russia has been via embourgeoisement. If China attempts to avoid this path, the end result in the two cases may be very different.

The implications of all this for relations with the 'imperialists' seem fairly plain. The notion of achieving victory over capitalism in peaceful economic competition, with the population of capitalist countries 'choosing' communism when they realise what high living standards it opens up, is obviously very congenial to the present state of mind among Russians. At the same time, the idea of a destructive war, robbing them of the comforts they have so long been deprived of and are now beginning to enjoy, is deeply repugnant, and I believe this repugnance reaches very high into the Soviet hierarchy. In China, tension is needed to support the mythological world view which the regime requires to control its proletarianised population. The threat of 'imperialist' attack is an integral part of this (compare the 'capitalist encirclement' in Stalin's Russia), essential to justify austerities, hard work, and regimentation as well as that Iron Curtain without which the mythology could not survive. International tension is no longer necessary to the Soviet leadership in the same way to ensure internal control. But the contrast goes further than this. Atomic war would render meaningless the strivings and achievements of Soviet society over the last 30 years; this is not true of the proletarianised society of China, which has nothing to lose but its chains.

6 'Totalitarianism' and Change in Communist Systems*

There are certain Christian theologians who would have us desist, at least for a time, from using the word 'God', not because they reject the reality of the divine, but because the word has acquired such conflicting and misleading connotations and become embedded in such dubious social attitudes that its use tends to obscure rather than to communicate the reality behind it. For much the same reason, I have long advocated a taboo on 'totalitarianism' in our discussion of communist political systems – to which at least some of the contributors to these volumes would breathe 'Amen'. But alas! whatever may be said about 'God', 'totalitarianism' is very much

---

*Comparative Politics, vol.4, no.3 (April 1972), pp.433–53; a review article discussing the following books: Hans Buchheim, Totalitarian Rule: Its Nature and Characteristics, (Wesleyan University Press, Middletown), 1968; R. Barry Farrell, ed., Political Leadership in Eastern Europe and the Soviet Union, (Aldine Publishing Co., Chicago), 1970; Carl J. Friedrich, Michael Curtis, and Benjamin R. Barber, Totalitarianism in Perspective: Three Views, (Praeger, New York), 1969; Chalmers Johnson, ed., Change in Communist Systems, (Stanford University Press, Stanford), 1970; H. Gordon Skilling and Franklyn Griffiths, eds, Interest Groups in Soviet Politics, (Princeton University Press, Princeton), 1971; and Philip D. Stewart, Political Power in the Soviet Union: A Study of Decision-Making in Stalingrad, (Bobbs-Merrill, Indianapolis), 1968.

alive. Not only has there been a renewed spate of books and articles employing, explaining, or defending the term[1] but even in volumes aimed at improved conceptual orientations, such as those edited by Chalmers Johnson and by Gordon Skilling and Franklyn Griffiths, it keeps cropping up with its usual astounding versatility of connotation.

A spirited defence of 'totalitarianism' is offered by Carl J. Friedrich, who argue that 'reviews of the divergent use or abuse of the term do not prove anything about the reality, especially if no more suitable term is suggested'.[2] Its distinguishing features are now defined as '(1) a totalist ideology; (2) a single party committed to this ideology and usually led by one man, the dictator; (3) a fully developed secret policy; and three kinds of monopoly or, more precisely, monopolistic control: namely that of (a) mass communications; (b) operational weapons; (c) all organisations, including economic ones, thus involving a centrally planned economy'.[3]   The main change from the Friedrich–Brzezinski 'syndrome' of 1956 is the de-emphasis of terror.[4] Friedrich argues that, despite changes in theory and practice, existing communist regimes, in particular the Union of Soviet Socialist Republics, still manifest these six defining features of totalitarian dictatorship. Michael Curtis, in his contribution to the same volume, contends that they do not.   On some points there is direct confrontation of argument, as when Curtis denies that the Nazi and Fascist regimes had anything worth calling an ideology,[5] and Friedrich retorts that you must not confuse ideology, an 'action-related system of ideas', with a static doctrine.[6] For the most part, however, the arguments move on different planes or, where they address themselves to the same point, emphasise different facets to arrive at opposite conclusions.   Thus, what appears to Curtis as evidence of 'intellectual dissent', a consequence of the relaxation of the official intellectual monopoly,[7] Friedrich sees as examples of 'resistance', a normal feature of totalitarianism resulting precisely from this monopoly.[8]

It is always hard to decide who wins this kind of dispute, and for the sovietologist the difficulty in this case is compounded; for, whereas both authors illustrate their arguments largely from Soviet experience, one scarcely recognises the actuality of the USSR in the pages of either of them. To take one example, when Friedrich speaks of physical terror giving way to psychic terror in the Soviet Union, and places such instrumentalities as the comradely courts in this context,[9] he comes nowhere near a realistic characterisation of the changed nature and impact of repression since Stalin. It was then, not now, that 'psychic terror' was a real – indeed a mass – phenomenon, that is, people's lives were constantly clouded by anxiety engendered by the danger of arbitrary arrest. At the present time, though the limits of permitted utterance and activity are set far more narrowly than in the West, one knows well enough what they are, and can normally avoid anxiety unless one chooses to violate these limits – as indeed some of the nation's finest spirits do. Friedrich is likewise wide of the mark on several other aspects of post-Stalin change he selects for discussion. Nor, unfortunately, does Curtis come much closer; indeed, he is inclined not only to misinterpret the facts, but to misreport them.[10]

These papers are chiefly valuable for some of their less central themes. Curtis offers a powerful statement of the differences between the Nazi, Fascist, and Soviet regimes,[11] leaving one wondering, indeed, why he still considers 'totalitarianism' to have been a useful classificatory concept in the past.[12] Friedrich views 'the development of a substantial consensus' as the main change in the theory and practice of Soviet totalitarianism,[13] and sees terror and consensus operating as 'Siamese twins'. 'There may be much freedom of expression, and even license, in such a regime, provided sacred taboos of ideology and official policy are avoided, and provided such dissent is strictly individual and does not aspire to organised support.'[14] This seems to come closer perhaps than Friedrich would wish to Herbert Marcuse's concept of 'repressive tolerance';[15] and it is similarly vulnerable to charges of circular argument and unverifiability. A further thought of Friedrich's is that totalitarian regimes, like other forms of autocracy, are evidently subject to oscillation between tight and loose control. He says that not only should post-Stalin changes in communist countries be seen in this light,[16] but so also should the Hitler and Stalin regimes which 'far from providing the typical model of a totalitarian dictatorship, were rather extreme aberrations'.[17] He scarcely comes to grips with the well-known arguments against the likelihood of renewed 'Stalinism' in the USSR, restated here by Curtis,[18] nor does he appear to observe that if Nazi Germany was atypical and Fascist Italy not really totalitarian, the study of totalitarianism logically resolves itself into 'comparative communism'.

The Friedrich–Curtis discussion is complemented and, for my money, upstaged by Benjamin Barber's carefully argued, profound, and witty paper on the conceptual origins of 'totalitarianism'. Barber begins with an analysis of the scholarly uses of the term, identifying three major distinctions: between whether the definition offered is phenomenological (listing objective attributes) or essentialist in character; whether or not totalitarianism is seen as a peculiarly modern phenomenon; and whether it is seen as logically antithetical to democracy or compatible with it. He draws also several secondary distinctions which tend to covary with the first major distinction: between emotive and non-emotive usages, between simple and complex definitions, between those that are rigorously political and those that focus on economic and social determinants, and between those regarding totalitarianism as qualitatively unique and those identifying it as a particular combination of quantitatively variable attributes found in lesser degrees also in other systems. What emerges is a picture of mutually cancelling usages discrepant on so many planes that one is tempted to conclude that 'totalitarianism is to modern science what reason was to Luther: a conceptual harlot of uncertain parentage, belonging to no one but at the service of all'.[19]

Nevertheless Barber does descry a common focus in most definitions of totalitarianism in their concern with the *scope* of government – 'the relationship between the public domain (the state) and the private realm (defined in terms of social groups [society] or atomised individuals)'.[20] He does not, however, find in this sufficient justification for salvaging the term, and discusses two kinds of difficulties in doing so. First, while the level of political analysis to which writers on totalitarianism are primarily oriented is that of scope (the boundaries of the political system) they usually make 'unstated, unfounded and often unperceived' assumptions about connections between variables on this level and on the levels of rulership (inputs) and ends (outputs).[21]

The other kind of difficulty derives from the assumption implicit in all varieties of totalitarian theory that 'totalism' (the disappearance of boundaries between the public and private domains) may be equated with 'statism', whereas these boundaries may equally 'be absent either by custom (as in tribal societies) or by choice (as in...communitarian examples), or they may simply melt away as a function of a natural evolution of political or social processes'.[22] One effect of totalitarian theory has been to distract attention from this last path to totalism, along which some observers consider contemporary American society to be well advanced, and which may in some respects prove more pernicious than the statist path. Finally, while it would be open to us to agree, in full awareness of what we were doing, to employ 'totalitarianism' to denote statist totalism, this would probably not prove a useful analytical tool; for the very notion of statism implies 'a dualistic cleavage between abstract public and private spheres' which modern political research has shown to be unrealistic, even in the updated pluralist version where 'groups' substitute for atomised individuals as the units of the private sphere.[23]

Barber's article calls for little comment except that no one should again utter the word 'totalitarianism' without first giving serious thought to his analysis. Nevertheless the problem remains, as the author would doubtless agree, that a number of modern political systems have aspired to statist totalism and achieved in high degree something that looks very like it. It would be useful to have a single term to denote such systems.

In terms of Barber's classification of approaches to totalitarianism, Hans Buchheim stands squarely in the 'essentialist' camp. 'Totalitarian rule', he writes, 'is the demand for unlimited control over the world and hence social life, translated into political action.'[24] Friedrich, himself resolutely 'phenomenological' in approach, dismisses this definition for unrealistically neglecting organisational aspects and for failing to distinguish a specifically modern form of rule from past systems with totalist claims.[25] Barber has a quicker way with Buchheim's approach, simply excluding it from his analysis as too 'exotic and garish'.[26] Perhaps both were unduly moved by aesthetic revulsion from Buchheim's admittedly grotesque image, 'the creeping rape of man'.[27]

Buchheim's short book may be mistaken for an extended statement of an 'ideal-type', oriented primarily toward the cases of Nazi Germany and Stalinist Russia, accompanied by a discursive comment on its historical and intellectual context. As such it would be vulnerable to many of Barber's strictures and to other empirical and logical criticisms. What Buchheim offers is not really social science at all, however, but rather a meditation on an experience: 'The concept of totalitarian rule', he writes, 'cannot be determined by purely logical means. It was explicated and clarified only by our own bitter experience with this form of government.'[28] And again: 'Man's craving to be master of his fate allows him to accept – at times even enthusiastically to support – matters which, as he himself senses, overwhelm his core. Here is one of the strange inner contradictions of life under totalitarian rule, which cannot be understood from the outside and through the categories of normal political reasoning.'[29] The book is valuable as a body of reflections precisely from this 'inside' perspective, and it would be a pity if the Anglo-Saxon reader were deterred by its unfamiliar modes of thought and language from savouring its insights – which, to be sure, apply far more directly, as do the often similar insights of

Hannah Arendt – to Nazi Germany than to any other 'totalitarian' society.[30]

On the face of it, a view of Soviet or Communist politics that allots importance to group interaction is as incompatible with the (any!) concept of totalitarianism as with the official Soviet self-image.[31] In a recent paper, H. Gordon Skilling has offered a taxonomy of communist systems along a totalitarianism–pluralism axis in terms of the role of groups in political life,[32] and such an approach would probably command wide assent.[33] And yet the relevance of a 'group' approach to some aspects, at least, of Soviet politics has long been accepted by some major specialists.[34] Nor should we forget that assumed links between leadership factions and 'political forces' in the wider society were a standard analytical device of old-style Kremlinology.[35] Certainly he who would stalk the 'group' will find his path beset by many a semantic maze and conceptual pitfall. Much has been done since the appearance of Skilling's pioneering article in 1966[36] to chart the path and its dangers,[37] and the new volume edited by Skilling and Griffiths notably advances this work. Yet consensus on defining 'groups' and conceptualising their involvement in the political process remains an elusive goal.

Skilling opens the volume with two general papers, in the first of which he reviews the drift in the post-Stalin period from a totalitarian image of communist politics to one 'that took account of the conflicting groups that exert an influence on the making of policy by the party'. He terms this revised image a 'pluralism of élites', which is less a genuine pluralism than 'a kind of imperfect monism in which, of the many elements involved, one – the party – was more powerful than all others but was not omnipotent'.[38]

In his second paper, subtitled 'Some Hypotheses', Skilling begins by stressing that a group approach to Soviet politics cannot arbitrarily employ concepts derived from Western experience, nor does it necessarily involve an interpretation of Soviet politics solely in terms of interest groups and group conflict. The groups with which he is concerned are defined not by shared characteristics, but by common attitudes and common claims; he would prefer to designate them 'demand groups'. Such groups in Soviet society may articulate not only their own distinctive interests and attitudes but also 'the innumerable raw demands arising from society as a whole'.[39] They are more likely to be loose associations of individuals than organised groups. Such 'demand groups' are located primarily within, and sometimes straddling, the various 'groups in strategic location', namely such categories of officials as party *apparatchiki*, managers, the military and security police, and such professional categories as economists and writers. Leadership factions 'perform significant functions of articulating and amalgamating the interests of social and political groups'.[40] Such 'social groups' as workers and peasants, 'groups based on age or sex', and 'regional, national, or religious groupings', are denied direct participation in Soviet group politics by their lack of political resources. Soviet interest groups seek to exert influence on policy-making primarily through the specialised departments of the central party and government machines, but some use is also made of formal representative bodies like the Central Committee and the Supreme Soviet, and especially of the party and specialised press.

Despite Skilling's careful definition of interest groups as 'demand groups', the focus of discussion tends to shift to his 'groups in strategic location', and it is around these, in fact, that the specialised chapters are organised. While the authors of these chapters all offer a characterisation of their particular category of officials or professionals, usually discuss the main cleavages within it, and have something to say about their orientation toward, or involvement in, political issues, each conceptualises the 'group' aspect of Soviet politics in his own way, so that there is no systematic verification of Skilling's hypotheses. In some cases the participating collectivities identified show the features of his 'demand groups'; more often they are defined in terms he rejects by shared characteristics (organisational affiliation, career experience, and so on); and sometimes the whole occupational category figures as a group actor.

There is valuable material here, of which space permits us to give only the barest indications. Frederick C. Barghoorn traces the evolution of security police structures and of their political role. Roman Kolkowicz, while identifying divisions in the political role of the military, based on organisational, age, career, personal association, and other factors, concludes that they offer a fairly unified response when their basic professional interests seem threatened. John P. Hardt and Theodore Frankel argue that the industrial managers are primarily concerned with operational autonomy, professionalism, and personal enrichment and status, and discuss their fortunes in pursuing these aims under and since Stalin. They see an emergent dichotomy between 'engineer' and 'businessmen' managers. Richard W. Judy analyses the cleavages among economists based on institutional affiliation, age, and degree of mathematical proficiency and traces historically the involvement of groups of economists in policy issues, ending with a most useful classification of positions adopted on the 'Liberman' debate and post-Stalin discussions of theory. While the Writer's Union itself has always been a tool of the party, Ernest J. Simmons sees the struggle between liberal and conservative elements within it as endemic since its inception; in the post-Stalin era liberal writers have come to 'give purpose and direction' to the whole reform movement in the USSR. Soviet jurists may never challenge party policies, but as Donald D. Barry and Harold J. Berman demonstrate, the very exercise of their functions involves the assertion of legal values against the arbitrary use of power, and their participation in the framing of legislation gives them a consultant role qualitatively different from that of other specialist groups. Jerry F. Hough's contribution on the party *apparatchiki* is outstanding both in the richness of its data and rigor and sophistication of its analysis. Structural affiliation and related career and educational differences are the most important sources of cleavage among the *apparatchiki*; and groups so based, in pushing particular interests, are more likely to align themselves with related state officials than with other party functionaries. Specialised groups of party officials figure to a degree as the recognised spokesmen of those interests in the community at large acknowledged by the regime as legitimate, much as do the officials of voluntary associations in the West.

Franklyn Griffiths makes an important theoretical contribution to the study of the 'group' dimension of Soviet politics with his paper, 'A Tendency Analysis of Soviet Policy-Making'. To summarise, and unavoidably to oversimplify, he argues that we should go back beyond David Truman and beyond 'reified' groups to Bentley's original notion of 'tendencies of articulation' with respect to particular issues. This is a promising approach, which seems an appropriate framework for conceptualising several of the cases studied elsewhere in terms of group conflict.[41] Yet it remains incomplete, for reasons I shall attempt to indicate below. Skilling himself takes up in a final chapter Griffiths' and other criticisms of the group approach, and summarises the findings of the specialised chapters, identifying wide differences in the legitimacy, autonomy, ends, methods, and cohesiveness of group action.

One can agree with Hough that the presence or absence of autonomous voluntary associations for the furtherance of sectional concerns does not in itself always and necessarily generate radical differences between Western and Soviet-type polities in the feeding of such concerns into the policy process.[42] Yet it is symptomatic of a more basic difference, a fuller recognition of which would resolve some, at least, of the semantic disputes about 'groups' in Soviet politics. Since direct and open struggle on behalf of both personal and shared concerns is accorded only marginal legitimacy in the

USSR, the furtherance of such concerns occurs for the most part 'parasitically' upon the performance of other, legitimate activities – principally assigned tasks. Thus, speakers at meetings of soviets or party committees, the primary function of which is mobilisational, may insert sectional 'demands' into their presentation of issues. Specialists, employed to provide expertise, will inject their own value preferences into their treatment of issues, as government consultants or in scholarly articles. In such cases one could, perhaps, fairly speak of the 'articulation' of 'interests'. However, 'articulation' would seem a curious term to apply to the general process of furthering group concerns as envisaged here, since its efficacy often depends on such concerns remaining tacit, if not concealed. For the most part it occurs not in public but in the day-to-day work of officials, and figures as much in the implementation of policies as in their formation. While 'allies' are often influenced by an awareness of each others' activities, direct collusion is probably rare. Thus, the term, 'group' might also best be avoided. It is primarily along such lines, I would assert (but cannot here demonstrate), that occupational, regional, ethnic, moral, and other shared concerns are advanced, and come into conflict in the Soviet political process.[43] If this is correct it is only the iceberg-tip of the politics of furthering shared concerns that finds enough public resonance to permit detailed case studies, and it would therefore be rash to generalise conclusions drawn from such studies for this whole dimension of Soviet politics.

Philip D. Stewart, the author of one of the most interesting of these case studies,[44] also discusses the 'group' dimension of Soviet politics in his *Political Power in the Soviet Union: A Study of Decision-Making in Stalingrad*. This book, based primarily on the scrutiny of *Stalingradskaia pravda* for the years 1954–61, provides generous and interesting documentation of familiar aspects of Soviet politics as manifested in one particular region. Unfortunately, despite its subtitle, the book provides little qualitatively new information to help fill those tantalising gaps in our knowledge of political processes in the USSR, and specifically of the decision-making process. Indeed, where hazier areas are treated, such as the procedures of the *obkom* bureau and secretariat or party elections, Stewart is repeatedly forced back on inferences based on the general literature, both Soviet and Western.[45] This reflects not on the competence of the author – quite the contrary – but on the absurd Byzantine or Mafia-like secrecy with which the Soviet regime persists in surrounding its internal processes.

Stewart's richest information relates to the personnel of regional party bodies. It is here, too, that he seeks a point of entry into the 'group' question, by analysing the extent to which the occupants of different posts participate in the discussion of various topics at regional committee meetings. While stressing that this does not provide a measure of *actual* influence (since the role of committee meetings, like party conferences, is a mobilisational rather than a decision-making one), he suggests that there should be some correspondence between such participation and the *potential* influence of 'institutional groups'. How far potential influence is actualised depends on the willingness of the party secretaries – who monopolise access to the decision-making process – to consult the leaders of other bodies; and this willingness, as he quite reasonably argues, seems to have increased since the 1930s.

Stewart's book thus illustrates the main problem of evaluating Soviet political changes, or at least its empirical dimension: these changes reside not so much in the structures, with which we are reasonably familiar, as in their operation, about which we are relatively ignorant. This empirical focus comes out very clearly in most of the contributions to the volume edited by Chalmers Johnson. But these also reveal no less clearly the conceptual or theoretical dimension of the problem: the current lack among political scientists of a common language for analysing intersystemic differences and intrasystemic change. For this book, and the 1968 Workshop on the Comparative Study of Communism on which it was based,[46] are in large part an essay in bridge-building between 'sovietology' and contemporary political science, in conformity with the main thrust of communist political studies over the past six or seven years.[47]

There is ample evidence here of the relevance and value for a better understanding of communist systems of concepts developed in various areas of comparative politics and political sociology. Yet one is also struck by the persistence of preoccupations, perspectives, and even terminology traditional in the sovietological literature; this is especially noticeable at the more 'macro' level of analysis. 'Totalitarianism' provides the most interesting example. Of the 11 papers, the term figures to a greater or lesser extent as an organising concept in those of Richard Lowenthal, Alexander Dallin and George W. Breslauer, Paul Cocks, Gordon Skilling and Chalmers Johnson (with whom it is expelled through the front door but returns through the back); in addition Zvi Gitelman speaks of 'post-totalitarian communist systems'. At the same time most of these authors, as well as R.V. Burks and the economist John Michael Montias, give greater centrality to the comparatists' concept of a 'mobilisational system'. While several writers point to the limitations of the totalitarian concept, the emphatic anti-'totalitarians' are in a minority. Dankwart A. Rustow sees the concept as an updated version of the autocratic fantasy of Louis XIV, 'overpessimistic' in its estimate of the degree of control achievable under actual conditions over human behaviour, and 'overoptimistic' in ignoring that far fuller control may be on the cards in the future;[48] whereas Montias suggests a parallel between the totalitarian model in studying communist political systems and the preoccupation with integral planning in analysing communist economic systems.[49]

The book's most prominent theme is a version of what might be termed the 'gravediggers of communism' image: totalitarianism (or Stalinism, or communism, or the mobilisation system) of its nature produces forces which ultimately lead to its transcendence (like Marx's capitalism generating its proletarian destroyers). A harbinger of this image was Wendel Willkie's comment to Stalin in 1942 that if he continued to educate the Soviet people he would end up educating himself out of a job.[50] Later we had the 'Macht im Hintergrund' theory, which assigned the managers the role of the party's 'gravediggers'.[51] In the 1950s a 'gravediggers of communism' assumption was apparent in much of the discussion of 'de-Stalinisation', and now it is often implicit when changes in communist countries are analysed in terms of 'liberalisation', 'modernisation', or 'convergence'.

The version offered here is sophisticated and carefully non-determinist. As Johnson sees it, the communists, initially inspired by their Utopian vision, impose on the population a 'mobilisation system' which engenders a high level of alienation; this system achieves modernisation in some directions at the cost of frustrating it in others. The consequences of its very successes, however, especially in fostering functional differentiation and societal complexity, engender a 'deep-seated crisis of the mature mobilisation regime, a crisis characterised by the need for fundamental reform and the possibility of internal explosion'.[52] The controls of the mobilisation stage have now become dysfunctional, but the remedies, which would tend toward a market system, would threaten with redundancy the very leaders and structures that would have to apply them, and so remain problematical. Lowenthal sees the differences between communist regimes and other modernising mobilization regimes as springing from the Utopian goals of the former. The contradiction between 'development' and 'Utopia' endemic in communist systems grows steadily in intensity since the developmental achievements suffer increasing damage from successive 'revolutions from above'. With the consequently probable triumph of 'development' over 'Utopia', communist movement regimes will be transformed into conservative bureaucracies. Currently the Soviet regime, no longer a force for imposed social change, but insistent on acting as authoritative arbiter of the pressures and demands of society, is 'neither totalitarian nor democratic, but *authoritarian*'.[53]

Employing a similar developmental model, Alexander Dallin and George W. Breslauer see terror as changing from a dominant feature of communist systems to a brake on development, while the achievements of the mobilisation stage[54] foster certain functional equivalents of terroristic coercion in the normative and material spheres. The role of devil's advocate falls mainly to Jeremy Azrael, who considers the concept of mobilisation a dubious improvement on 'totalitarianism', since a similar confusion prevails as to its objective referents. He points out that the post-Stalin period has seen *increased* efforts at mobilising the masses in the Soviet Union as well as in China and Yugoslavia, and argues that post-Stalin reforms are more plausibly explained in terms of the ideas and personalities of individual leaders rather than of underlying socioeconomic pressures.

Meanwhile, other contributors make little or no use of the mobilisation model. Alfred G. Meyer offers stimulating discussion of the main types of convergence theory. Paul Cocks analyses the history of the two main approaches to rationalising party control: that is, by scientific organisation and by public participation. He argues that while the aim of these efforts is 'to preserve the substance of totalitarian power'[55] they produce unintended consequences which could result in 'systemic transformation'.[56] Gitelman discusses the 'authority crisis' in 'post-totalitarian communist systems' and the alternative strategies open to the leadership, namely 'national performance' and 'authentic participation', the latter attempted only in Yugoslavia and Dubcek, Czechoslovakia. Burks also considers the need for new bases of legitimation in his paper on technology and political change, and envisages a choice between 'market socialism' and 'radical decentralisation'. Montias proposes a classification of communist economic systems based on three main variables (the degree of mobilisation, the reliance placed on hierarchically transmitted commands, and the relative importance of markets in producer goods), one virtue of which is to accommodate certain non-bureaucratic aspects of communist economies. Skilling, classifying communist polities in terms of such aspects of the political role of groups as their legitimacy, autonomy, degree of organisation, and objectives, concludes that, 'if we take a greater degree of pluralism as the criterion of progress, we cannot assume that change in the Communist world is necessarily moving in a liberal or progressive direction'.[57]

In a final paper Rustow properly praises the contributors for avoiding the fallacies of unilinearism and economicism, and even more for restoring *purpose* as a factor for political change – the theorising away of which he sees as a major defect in most Western schools of political science. Yet there remains something odd about this book. In a collection of essays describing and accounting for changes that are frequently discussed in terms derived from the name of the former Soviet dictator, one might have expected somewhere a systematic consideration of the central leadership dimension of change. It is true that several contributors refer in passing to the shift from personal to collective rule or to the importance of the personalities and ideas of leaders.[58] Yet no one analyses the *structure of leadership* as a defining characteristic and itself a source of systematic change rather than merely an epiphenomenon. We turn hopefully, therefore, to the volume edited by R. Barry Farrell, only, however, to be disappointed again for, although the book addresses itself to several important problems, this is not one of them.

Political Leadership in Eastern Europe and the Soviet Union opens with three theoretical chapters. Alfred G. Meyer traces Marx's ambiguous legacy on the question of class-leadership relations, pointing out that Leninism has failed to resolve this ambiguity. Andreas Hegedus of the Hungarian Institute of International Relations offers a Marxist analysis of bureaucracy in relation to alternative politico-administrative–managerial structures in developed socialist societies. Carl Friedrich discusses the evolving leadership styles of communist 'totalitarian' regimes in the light of a distinction between initiating, maintaining, and protecting leadership (which often overlap in practice), concluding that these regimes 'should not be seen any longer as dictatorships, but as a novel form of autocratic rule'.[59]

Part Two is concerned with the characteristics of Soviet and East European leaders and 'élites'. Farrell discusses the educational equipment of Politburo members in the European socialist countries, and compares the education and specialist experience of party and government foreign service personnel. Carl Beck presents an elaborate analysis of changes in the composition of the politburos, secretariats, and central committees of five East European states in terms of their representation of 'career types' ('party bureaucrat', 'ideologue', 'Social Democratic Party', 'military', 'technician', among others). Frederick Barghoorn gives biographical information on the post-Khrushchev Politburo and Secretariat in the USSR, and discusses participation in Central Committee meetings. Michael Gehlen offers a valuable analysis of the party officials elected to the Soviet Central Committee between 1952 and 1966 in terms of their background and career patterns. Frederic Fleron focuses on an aspect also examined by Gehlen, namely the increasing number of Soviet political leaders and senior *apparatchiki* with extensive early experience in industry, agriculture, or some other specialist field. Fleron's approach is to dichotomise the political 'élite' into those with more than average early specialist experience ('coopted' officials) and those with less than average ('recruited' officials), and to measure the extent to which the latter have grown at the expense of the former in the post-Stalin period.[60]

Space is lacking to discuss the particular conclusions (generally interesting and sober) that these authors draw from their data, but a general comment may perhaps be permitted. We have been analysing the background and careers of Soviet and other communist-regime officials for some two decades,[61] and both the quantity and technical sophistication of such studies have greatly increased in recent years;[62] however, the growth in our understanding of the political impact of such factors has scarcely kept pace. The facile assumption that the categories we invent to order the incidence of such variables represent politically significant 'groups' is now encountered far less frequently.[63] However, the circumstances and mechanisms through which they may acquire such significance have not yet been systematically elucidated. A useful first step might be to scrutinise in detail the political history of the last couple of decades for indications of relevant cases. Until such cases have been identified and studied, the conclusions we draw from 'élite' data must remain largely on the *a priori* level.

A number of disparate chapters form Part Three of the book, which is entitled 'Leadership and Society'. Using a decision-making framework, Dennis Pirages identifies the inappropriateness of the traditional communist 'custodial' model for the 'second stage' of industrialisation, particularly with respect to information and motivation, illustrating his argument from the findings of Polish attitudinal surveys. M. George Zaninovich reports on a survey he conducted in Yugoslavia, which shows substantial differences between communists and non-communists with respect to socio-economic distribution, a number of politically relevant attitudes and values, and 'situational' attributes such as nationality, religion, and education. Jindrich Zeleny and the late Ota Klein, of the Czechoslovak Academy of Sciences, discuss the socio-political implications of the 'scientific–technological revolution' for socialist countries, without, I fear, dispelling one's skepticism as to the capacity of Marxism to illuminate this problem. Gordon Skilling applies his group approach to an interesting analysis of Czechoslovak politics up to February 1969. Jeremy Azrael summarises his work on the political role of the managers,[64] arguing that no 'managerial revolution' is to be expected, although the managers could play a part with other groups in fostering a more pluralistic polity in which the primacy of the party apparatus would be more limited. Finally, Jan F. Triska reports on a discussion held on the final day of the conference from which the book emerged (including such participants as Merle Fainsod and Harold Guetskow in addition to the paper contributors) in which many different views were expressed as to the significance of the material presented and most promising lines of further research.

Without presuming to develop here a detailed general model of Soviet and communist politics, it may be useful in conclusion to sketch out a rough framework, within which some of the main problems discussed earlier may be located.

The most salient feature of communist systems is the attempt to run the whole society as a single *organisation*, in which almost no socially significant activities are left to autonomously interacting individuals and groups, but instead are managed by centralised, hierarchical agencies, themselves subject to close coordination, principally by the apparatus of the party. As in any large organisation, 'market' elements (decision by mutual accommodation and trade-offs) occur at many interstitial points, and there is competition, mostly concealed, to further ambitions and concerns held individually or shared with others. Societies with these characteristics might be called *mono-organisational*,[65] and the communist countries (except for Yugoslavia in recent years) display these characteristics in the 'purest' form yet known, although they have been approached in varying degrees by several Western countries at war, by Nazi Germany, Fascist Italy, and by several 'modernising' single-party states.

There are two main sets of factors making for differences among communist systems and for changes over time. The first relates to the level and character of socio-economic development. The mono-organisational system, while suited to the drive for a limited set of priority goals, such as external defence, internal security, basic industrialisation, and space research, seems difficult to adapt, at least under present technological conditions, to attain general levels of efficiency in a complex, sophisticated, industrialised society. The organisation experiences increasing difficulty coping with the rapidly multiplying demands for information, decision and coordination, causing pressures for the decentralising and autonomisation of structures and for expanding and legitimising 'market' elements in the system. The same pressures may tend to reactivate democratic elements in the communist tradition, which previously had been trimmed and channelled to serve the mobilisational and legitimising needs of the mono-organisational system. The predominant response of communist regimes to these pressures has been to make only minor concessions, while attempting to shore up the mono-organisational system: only in Yugoslavia and in Czechoslovakia in 1968 have there been more far-reaching attempts to adapt the system to changed conditions.

The other set of factors relates to leadership. Included here are differences in the backgrounds, personalities, and ideas of top leaders and the men around them.[66] At least as important, but relatively neglected, is the pattern of relationships among the top leaders themselves.[67] The traditional labels for political systems (absolute monarchy, constitutional monarchy, oligarchy and so forth), while ignoring important socio-political determinants, properly stress the importance of the internal structure of leadership for the operation of the whole system. The main variable here has been the degree of concentration or personalisation of leadership – that is, location on a personal rule-collective rule continuum. The tendency of communist mono-organisational systems to personal rule is often exaggerated. In the USSR there have been substantial periods when leadership has been less personalised than is normally the case, for example, in the United States or Britain. Dictatorship in such systems is due less to their proneness to personal as against collective leadership patterns than to the lack of built-in constraints on the top leadership, however structured, so that more personal rule amounts to dictatorship and more collective rule amounts to oligarchy. Changes in leadership structure have important consequences for the system at large; in particular, arbitrary police terror and a ritualised ideology focusing on the leader cult, while useful supports for a personal dictatorship, will need drastic modification under an oligarchy. One weakness of most 'totalitarian' models is their failure to distinguish communist leadership structures (and the by-products of these structures), which vary over place and time, from the basic (mono-organisational)

features of most communist societies.[68]   Nonetheless, while
dictatorship is not essential to mono-organisational systems, less
concentrated leadership structures probably afford more favourable
conditions for the modification of these systems through such
processes as decentralisation, autonomisation, marketisation, and
democratisation.[69]

Notes and References

1   Notable here was the appearance of new editions of the two classics
of totalitarian theory, namely Carl J. Friedrich and Zbigniew K.
Brzezinski, *Totalitarian Dictatorship and Autocracy*, 2nd edn., rev. by
Carl J. Friedrich (Cambridge, Mass.), 1965, and Hannah Arendt, *The
Origins of Totalitarianism*, 3rd edn. (New York), 1966 – this being a
reissue of the 2nd revised edition which appeared in 1958.   See also
Raymond Aron, *Democracy and Totalitarianism: A Theory of
Political Regimes*, trans.   Valence Ionescu (New York), 1969; Z. K.
Brzezinski, *Ideology and Power in Soviet Politics*, 2nd rev. edn.
(New York), 1967; A. James Gregor, *Contemporary Radical
Ideologies: Totalitarian Thought in the Twentieth Century*, (New
York), 1968; A. James Gregor, *The Ideology of Fascism: The
Rationale of Totalitarianism*, (New York), 1969; Alberto Aquarone,
L'Organizzazione dello Stato Totalitario, (Turin), 1965; Paul T.
Mason, *Totalitarianism – Temporary Madness or Permanent
Danger?*, (Boston), 1967; Eleonore Sterling, *Der Unvollkommene
Staat: Studien ueber Diktatur und Demokratie*, (Frankfurt), 1965;
Paul Hollander, 'Observations on Bureaucracy, Totalitarianism, and
the Comparative Study of Communism', *Slavic Review*, vol.XXVI
(June 1967), pp.302–7; Roy D. Laird, 'Some Characteristics of the
Soviet Leadership System; A Maturing Totalitarian System?',
Midwest Journal of Political Science, vol.X (February 1966), pp.29–38;
Patrick O'Brien, 'On the Adequacy of the Concept of
Totalitarianism', *Studies in Comparative Communism*, vol.III
(January 1970), pp.55–60; Boris Meissner, 'Totalitarian Rule and
Social Change', *Problems of Communism*, vol.XV (November–
December 1966), pp.56–61; and Leonard Schapiro, 'Reflections on the
Changing Role of the Party in the Totalitarian Polity', ibid., vol.II
(April 1969), pp.1–13. Schapiro's *Totalitarianism* was listed to appear
in 1971 in the series 'Key Concepts in Political Science', but it was not
yet available when this review was written.   Of the many articles
critically evaluating the uses of the concept of totalitarianism, see
especially Herbert J. Spiro's entry, 'Totalitarianism', in *International*

Encyclopedia of the Social Sciences, 2nd edn., vol.XVI, pp.106–13; Herbert J. Spiro and Benjamin R. Barber, 'Counter-Ideological Uses of "Totalitarianism"', *Politics and Society*, vol.I (November 1970), pp.3–21; Frederic J. Fleron, Jr., 'Soviet Area Studies and the Social Sciences: Some Methodological Studies in Communist Studies', *Soviet Studies*, vol.XIX (January 1968), pp.314–39; and a review article by Robert Burrowes, 'Totalitarianism: The Revised Standard Version', *World Politics*, vol.XXI (January 1969), pp.272–94.

2 Friedrich, Curtis, and Barber, pp.125, 126. This volume originated in a discussion at the 1967 Annual Meeting of the American Political Science Association. Friedrich describes his paper as 'an extension of the changed concept of totalitarianism involved' in the revised edition of *Totalitarian Dictatorship and Autocracy*.

3 Ibid., p.126. Later, having invoked the role of modern technique to distinguish 'totalitarian dictatorship' from earlier systems aiming at total control over their subjects' lives, Friedrich offers a second, streamlined definition: 'a system of autocratic rule for realising totalist intentions under modern technical and political conditions' (p.136).

4 The third trait in the syndrome was originally 'a system of terroristic police control'. See *Totalitarian Dictatorship and Autocracy*, 1st edn., Chapters 1, 4.

5 Friedrich, Curtis, and Barber, pp.63–6.

6 Ibid., pp.137–8.

7 Ibid., pp.104–5.

8 Ibid., pp.150–1.

9 Ibid., pp.144–5.

10 For example, 'Lenin refused to permit any non-Bolshevik group to exist, except, for a short time, the Left Social Revolutionaries' (ibid., p.89); 'At the twenty-third party congress in 1966, Brezhnev announced the withdrawal of the party cadres from the direct administration of the economy and their return to the role of overseers' (p.91); 'While in power, Khrushchev proposed the compulsory retirement of a certain proportion of officials: one third of the deputies to the Supreme Soviet were to be replaced and one quarter of the members of the Soviet Presidium and the Central Committee were to retire after each election, though the decisions on the persons to be chosen for retirement were to be made by the party secretary' (pp.101–2).

11 Ibid., pp.63–93, 108–12.

12 Ibid., pp.93, 112. One wonders also how Curtis would defend his view that totalitarianism 'still possesses utility for analysis of the Chinese regime and those regimes adhering to the Chinese position in the Sino-Soviet dispute' (p.112).

13 Ibid., p.130.

14 Ibid., p.144.

15 Herbert Marcuse, 'Repressive Tolerance', in *A Critique of Pure Tolerance*, (Boston), 1965.

16 Friedrich, Curtis, and Barber, pp.132 ff.

17 Ibid., p.131.

18 Ibid., p.103.

19 Ibid., p.19.

20 Ibid., p.24.

21 Ibid., p.26.

22 Ibid., p.30.

23 Ibid., pp.34–6.

24 Buchheim, p.21.

25 Friedrich, Curtis, and Barber, pp.134-35. Friedrich has subsequently reviewed Buchheim's book elsewhere. See *Political Science Quarterly*, vol.LXXXVI (March 1971, pp.170–1.

26 Friedrich, Curtis, and Barber, p.8.

27 Ibid., pp.44, 134: evidently their rendering; Buchheim's translator offers a more acceptable version: 'the creeping assault on man' (Buchheim, p.14).

28 Buchheim, p.11.

29 Ibid., p.21.

30 Many of these insights are expressed in aphoristic terms, some translating quite effectively across the culture-gap: for example, 'Whenever humanism takes no cognizance of the limits set for mankind, it leads to the same ends as anti-humanism, which denies human freedom' (p.30); 'It will not take long for someone who has learned to silence his conscience for the sake of historical necessity to comprehend how he can lend his personal everyday aims the desired ideological interpretation' (p.48).

31 See Skilling and Griffiths, pp.401–2.

32 H. Gordon Skilling, 'Group Conflict and Political Change', in Chalmers Johnson, pp.215–34.

33 Cf. Peter Ludz, *Parteielite im Wandel*, (Cologne), 1968. Paul Hollander cites 'absence of legitimate and significant pluralism' as one of the five features of communist systems that justify retention of the totalitarian model ('Observations on Democracy', PO 305). Frederic J. Fleron, Jr. rejects 'the oversimplified totalitarian-pluralistic dichotomy' in favour of a typology along a monocratic (political offices monopolised by professional career politicians)-pluralistic axis; but totalitarianism is admitted as a modern type of monocratic polity with 'unlimited power over all aspects of people's lives' – that is, it and pluralism are mutually exclusive. See his, 'Toward a Reconceptualisation of Political Change in the Soviet Union: The Soviet Leadership System', *Comparative Politics*, vol.I (January 1969), p.237.

34 As early as 1957 Dankwart A. Rustow was able to write: 'With some significant modifications, the sociologically oriented group theory of politics has been successfully applied to the interaction of such forces as the army, party, the managerial élite, and the secret police in a totalitarian system.' See Rustow, 'New Horizons for Comparative Politics', *World Politics*, vol.IX (July 1957), p.531.

35 The findings of the 'Kremlinological' phase of the study of Soviet politics are masterfully interpreted by Robert Conquest in *Power and Policy in the USSR*, (London), 1961; see also Roger Pethybridge, *A Key to Soviet Politics: The Crisis of the Anti-Party Group*, (London), 1962. On a more general level, Shils wrote as early as 1956 that 'incapacity on the one side, evasiveness, creativity and the necessity of improvisation on the other, introduce into totalitarian regimes, which would deny its validity, a good deal of pluralism'. See Edward A. Shils, *The Torment of Secrecy*, (Glencoe), 1956, p.154.

36 H. Gordon Skilling, 'Interest Groups and Communist Politics', *World Politics*, vol.XVIII (April 1966), pp.435–51.

37 Philip D. Stewart offers a useful analysis of some of this work in his article, 'Soviet Interest Groups and the Policy Process: The Repeal of Production Education', *World Politics*, vol.XXII (October 1969), pp.29–32. For negative assessments, see Andrew C. Janos, 'Group Politics in Communist Society: A Second Look at the Pluralistic Model', in Samuel P. Huntington and Clement H. Moore, eds, *Authoritarian Politics in Modern Society: The Dynamics of*

Established One-Party Systems, (New York), 1970, pp.437–50, and Paul Shoup, 'Comparing Communist Nations: Prospects for an Empirical Approach', *American Political Science Review*, vol.LXII (March 1968), pp.201–2. See also David Lane, 'Socialist Pluralism', *Political Studies*, vol.XVI (January 1968), p.104; T.H. Rigby, 'New Trends in the Study of Soviet Politics', *Politics*, (Sydney), vol.V (May 1970), pp.7–9; Klaus von Beyme, 'Gesellschaftliche Organisationen und Interessenpluralismus in der Sowjetunion', in Richard Loewenthal and Boris Meissner, eds, *Sowjetische Innenpolitik: Triebkraefte und Tendenzen*, (Cologne), 1968; Martin Jaenicke, 'Monopolismus und Pluralismus im Kommunistichen Herrschaftssystem', *Zeitschrift für Politik*, vol.XVI (June 1967), pp.150–61; and Sidney I. Ploss, 'Interest Groups', in Allen Kassof, ed., *Prospects for Soviet Society*, (New York), 1968, pp.76–103. For case studies see especially Peter H. Juviler and Henry W. Morton, eds, *Soviet Policy-Making: Studies of Communism in Translation*, (New York), 1967; Alexander Dallin and Alan F. Westin, eds, *Politics in the Soviet Union: 7 Cases*, (New York), 1966; Joel J. Schwartz and William R. Keech, 'Group Influence and the Policy Process in the Soviet Union', *American Political Science Review*, vol.LXII (September 1968), pp.840–51; Philip D. Stewart, 'Soviet Interest Groups and the Policy Process'; and Milton C. Lodge, *Soviet Elite Attitudes since Stalin*, (Columbus), 1969.

38 Skilling and Griffiths, p.17.

39 Ibid., p.29.

40 Ibid., p.35.

41 It would be a useful exercise to test this approach against the cases dealt with in the literature referred to in note 37. An outstanding example of tendency analysis is Grey Hodnett's articles, 'What's in a Nation?', *Problems of Communism*, vol.XVII (September–October 1967), pp.2–15.

42 Skilling and Griffiths, pp.87–91.

43 For further elaboration of this viewpoint, see Rigby, 'New Trends in the Study of Soviet Politics', pp.7–9.

44 Stewart, 'Soviet Interest Groups'.

45 See, for instance, Stewart, *Political Power in the Soviet Union*, pp.34–36, 128–33, 189–93.

46 See R.V. Burks' account of the workshop in *Newsletter on Comparative Studies in Communism*, vol.II (June 1969), pp.2–11.

47 For a useful stocktaking of the earlier stages of this bridge-building enterprise, see Frederic Fleron, Jr, ed., *Communist Studies and the Social Sciences: Essays on Methodology and Empirical Theory*, (Chicago), 1969. See also Rigby, 'New Trends'.

48 Johnson, p.349.

49 Ibid., p.117. For Johnson's comments on the defects of the totalitarian model for analysing change, see p.3.

50 Wendell L. Willkie, *One World*, (New York), 1943, p.83. Willkie described Stalin's reaction to this suggestion as follows: 'He threw his head back and laughed and laughed. Nothing I said to him, or heard anyone else say to him, through two long evenings, seemed to amuse him so much'. Who will have the last laugh?

51 Herman F. Achminow, *Die Macht im Hintergrund: Totengräber des Kommunismus*, (Grenchen), 1950. More precisely, it is the *technical intelligentsia* who are the gravediggers. For the subsequent development of Achminow's views, see his *Die Totengräber des Kommunismus: Eine Soziologie der bolschewistischen Revolution*, (Stuttgart), 1964.

52 Johnson, p.22.

53 Ibid., p.115.

54 One point on which Dallin and Breslauer (following Apter) diverge from Johnson is in the stress they place on the paralysing effect of terror on communications (p.199), which Johnson tends to discount (p.22).

55 Ibid., p.186.

56 Ibid., p.189.

57 Ibid., p.231.

58 See, for example, pp.17, 34, 110, 196, 200.

59 Farrell, p.26.

60 For further explication of Fleron's concept of cooptation, see Frederic J. Fleron, Jr., 'Toward a Reconceptualisation of Political Change in the Soviet Union: The Political Leadership System', *Comparative Politics*, vol.I (January 1969), pp.236–44; and 'Cooptation as a Mechanism of Social Change', *Polity*, vol.II (Winter 1969), pp.176–201. It should be stressed that Fleron avoids identifying his 'coopted' and 'recruited' officials as reified groups, although the unwary reader might be forgiven for being misled by some of his

formulations and so falling into this trap. The further labelling of 'recruited' officials as 'professional politicians' seems to sharpen the dichotomy beyond the point of usefulness. The hypothesis that 'coopted' officials afford 'virtual representation' to specialist élites remains to be demonstrated, as Fleron points out (Farrell, p.139). Fleron rightly argues that institutional affiliation cannot be assumed necessarily to determine political alignments in the Soviet leadership; it would be rash to conclude, however, that early career experience and the attitudes and contacts then formed are necessarily liable to prove more influential than current institutional roles in actual conflict situations, as the case of Malenkov in 1953–54 illustrates. Furthermore, while the political effects of changes in 'élite' characteristics may be largely unintended, it may be useful in seeking to identify these effects to take into account the genesis of these changes in personnel policy and attendant political circumstances. For instance, while Stalin in the 1930s seems to have been no less concerned than Khrushchev in the 1950s to bring into the party apparatus men with specialist training and experience, in the former case the purges (and later the war), by greatly accelerating apparatus turnover, made for such transfers at earlier career stages than during the more stable 1950s.

61 Substantial data on élite composition appeared in the main post-war text-books, namely Julian Towster, *Political Power in the U.S.S.R. 1917–1947*, (New York), 1948, and especially Merle Fainsod, *How Russia Is Ruled*, (Cambridge, Mass.), 1953. Other early analyses include Boris Meissner, 'Das Generations-problem im Kreml', *Der Monat*, (Berlin), June 1953; T.H. Rigby, 'The Selection of Leading Personnel in the Soviet State and Communist Party' (PhD. dissertation, University of London), 1954; and John A. Armstrong, *The Soviet Bureaucratic Elite: A Case Study of the Ukrainian Apparatus*, (New York), 1959.

62 See George Fischer, *The Soviet System and Modern Society*, (New York), 1968; Severyn Bialer, 'How Russians Rule Russia', *Problems of Communism*, vol.XIII, September–October 1964, pp.45–52; Michael P. Gehlen and Michael McBride, 'The Soviet Central Committee: An Élite Analysis', *American Political Science Review*, vol.LXII (December 1968), pp.1232–41; Grey Hodnett, 'The Obkom First Secretaries', *Slavic Review*, vol.XXIV (December 1965), pp.636–52; Peter Frank, 'The CPSU Obkom First Secretary: A Profile', *British Journal of Political Science*, vol.I (April 1971), pp.174–90; Jerry Hough, 'The Soviet Elite', Part I, 'Groups and Individuals', *Problems of Communism*, vol.XVI (January–February 1967), pp.28–35, and

Part II, 'In Whose Hands the Future?', ibid., vol.XVI (March–April 1967), pp.18–25; Borys Lewytzskyi, 'Generations in Conflict', ibid., vol.XVI (January–February 1967), pp.36–40; John W. Lewis, *Leadership in Communist China*, (Ithaca), 1963; John W. Lewis, ed., *Party Leadership and Revolutionary Power in China*, (Cambridge), 1970; Doak Barnett, *Chinese Communist Politics in Action*, (Seattle), 1969. See further Carl Beck and J. Thomas McKechnie, *Political Elites: A Select Computerized Bibliography*, (Cambridge, Mass.), 1968. Much useful information about relevant research projects, conferences, publications and dissertations is reported in *Newsletter on Comparative Studies in Communism*.

63 Cf. the doubts and caveats expressed by Barghoorn (Farrell, p.77) and Fleron (pp.108–23). For further discussion of the problems of relating élite data to political decision-making, see ibid., pp.339–40.

64 See Jeremy R. Azrael, *Managerial Power and Soviet Politics*, (Cambridge, Mass.), 1966.

65 This is a more precise term than 'organisational societies', as proposed in an earlier article (T.H. Rigby, 'Traditional, Market and Organizational Societies and the U.S.S.R.', *World Politics*, vol.XVI (July 1964), pp.539–57 (this volume, Chapter 3), and clearly distinguishes such societies from other modern societies in which organisations are the most characteristic structures, but which lack close organisational coordination and integration and allot a far larger role to markets. The characterisation of communist systems suggested here has much in common with Alfred G. Meyer's account of the Soviet system as 'bureaucracy writ large' (see his *Soviet Political System: An Interpretation*, (New York), 1965). While 'organisation' and 'bureaucracy' are substantially overlapping concepts, the latter tends to bear associations which may prove misleading in this context. See also Roy D. Laird, *The Soviet Paradigm: An Experiment in Creating a Monohierarchical Polity*, (New York), 1970, which presents a similar approach, although in my view the Soviet polity is mono-organisational but multihierarchical.

66 Apart from 'Elite' studies, discussed above, the substantial literature on 'Kremlin' politics is of course also relevant here. One important variable, namely the psychopathology of 'totalitarian' dictators, is given interesting treatment in Robert C. Tucker, 'The Dictator and Totalitarianism', *World Politics*, vol.XVII (July 1965), pp.555–83.

67 For a relevant discussion of this aspect of a different set of systems, using as a point of departure Max Weber's typology of *Herrschaft*, see

Guenther Roth, 'Personal Rulership, Patrimonialism, and Empire-Building in the New States', *World Politics*, vol.XX (January 1968), pp.194–206.

68 This is epitomised by the term 'totalitarian dictatorship', by which Friedrich and Brzezinski identified their system-type. More recently Friedrich has increasingly dissociated the two concepts, tending to treat dictatorial rule as aberrant. See Friedrich, Curtis, and Barber, p.131, and Farrell, p.26.

69 For a rather cumbersome and only partly successful attempt to explore this relationship, see T.H. Rigby, 'The Deconcentration of Power in the U.S.S.R. 1953–1964' in J.D.B. Miller and T.H. Rigby, eds, *The Disintegrating Monolith: Pluralist Trends in the Communist World*, (Canberra), 1965, pp.17–45.

7 Political Legitimacy under Mono-organisational Socialism*

The expectation of political authorities that people will comply with their demands is typically based not only on such considerations as the latter's fear of punishment, hope of reward, habit or apathy, but also on the notion that they have the right to make such demands. This notion both inheres, explicitly or implicitly, in the claims of the authorities, and is reciprocated, to a greater or lesser extent, in the minds of those of whom compliance is demanded. This is what we mean by the 'legitimacy' of political power and authority, a concept of ancient pedigree whose modern usage we owe largely to Max Weber. Both the term and the phenomenon have given rise to much argument, and some of the matters at issue will be touched on in what follows, but this account will suffice to launch our discussion.[1]

The grounds on which claims to legitimacy may be made are varied, Max Weber's three 'pure types' of legal (rational), traditional, and charismatic legitimacy offering only one of several possible typologies. It will be immediately obvious that while 'legitimacy' as understood here has in common with 'legality' that

---

*'Introduction: Political Legitimacy, Weber, and Communist Mono-organisational Systems', in T.H. Rigby and Ferenc Fehér, eds, *Political Legitimation in Communist States*, (Macmillan, London), 1983, pp.1–26. References here to other chapters refer to chapters in that book.

both refer to claims held to be validly asserted and binding on those to whom they are addressed, the two concepts are not identical: legitimacy may be based on legality, but it may be based on grounds of a completely different order. To be sure, the legitimacy–legality distinction is at odds with some earlier understandings of legitimacy, and is still contested by some contemporary writers.[2] It is arguable that we should find a different term for the phenomenon we are dealing with here, but since most relevant discussion of it is now conducted, as Wilhelm Hennis has aptly put it, 'under the spell of Max Weber'[3] only greater confusion would be caused by our doing so.

It would be utterly misleading, of course, to suggest that this phenomenon was quite unknown to theorists and practitioners of politics before Weber drew attention to it. Aspects of it have been considered from various angles by writers from Plato and Aristotle on, and an extensive literature exists within intellectual traditions other than the empirically-oriented political science and political sociology with which I am mainly concerned here, discussing it in terms of such concepts as 'consent', 'authority', 'political obligation', 'compliance' and 'obedience', etc., and representing such diverse disciplines as history, political philosophy, jurisprudence, anthropology and sociology.[4]

Throughout history, usurpers have perceived the importance of legitimating their rule, and established rulers of maintaining the symbols, rituals and beliefs in which their legitimacy is enshrined, while contenders for power and for conflicting concepts of rule have sought to build up support and control of institutional resources by pressing alternative formulas of legitimacy. The matter was well understood over three millennia ago by Pharaoh Amenhotep IV, in the early years of whose reign (at least according to one reading of the evidence) the long-standing power struggle between the imperial household and the Thebes establishment came to a head. The latter's dominance over priestly and administrative appointments and therewith their great political and economic power was centred on the temple of the imperial sun-god Amon, whose cult had been vital to the Pharoah's authority. Amenhotep challenged this dominance at its focus by promoting the new cult of the life-giving sun-disc Aton and asserting his direct relationship with the god through changing his name to Akhenaton and propagating a corresponding new iconography. The ensuing struggle, largely played out as a competition between the rival cults and their conflicting concepts of legitimacy, ended in the victory of the Pharaoh, who then proceeded to purge the bureaucracy and shift the political system of the empire decisively, if briefly, in the direction of a personal despotism. It requires no great straining of the imagination, incidentally, to perceive parallels here with certain aspects of Soviet political history in the 1920s and 1930s, analysed in this volume by Graeme Gill.

More familiar examples of the interplay between structures of power and legitimating doctrines are the care taken by the Emperor Augustus to conceal his essentially monarchical revolution in Roman government behind the outward forms of the Republic, the elaboration of concepts of the divine right of kings as the feudal order gave way to royal absolutism in early modern Europe, and the subsequent development of the doctrine of popular sovereignty as the growth of commercial and then industrial capitalism brought ever wider social groups to assert a say in government. In Europe in the nineteenth-century, and more widely in the twentieth, national myths and symbols have proved a potent force in legitimating political authority in new states. Myths have likewise been fostered by power-seeking radical movements of Right and Left as well as forming a legitimating 'resource' competed for in the normal politics of democratic communities.[5]

These few examples remind us of the diversity of legitimating formulas,[6] which vary vastly in form, complexity and content, in the nature of their appeal to reason, belief or feeling, and in the extent and manner in which they tie into wider belief-systems. Nor as a rule does the political system of a complex society operate with only one legitimating doctrine, or on only one level of legitimation. Overtly, as Georg Brunner shows in Chapter 2, the claims to legitimacy of communist regimes rest on quite elaborate rational argumentation embedded in a systematic world view. However, this 'overt' legitimation is supplemented by other, more or less 'covert' forms of legitimation, as Maria Markus argues in Chapter 5, and the most significant of these are explored by several contributors to this volume.

There are two extreme views on the role of Marxist–Leninist doctrines in the political legitimation of communist countries. The first sees this official ideology as the dominant social force, determining both the content of policies and the structure of power, with the communist party figuring as a kind of priesthood thoroughly indoctrinated in 'Marxism–Leninism' and in turn indoctrinating the population at large, and *thereby* 'mobilising' them in pursuit of the party's communist programme. The second view regards the official ideology as a mere smokescreen, or at best a source of *ex post facto* justification of policies determined on purely pragmatic grounds, and considers that neither it nor any other beliefs play any significant part in securing the compliance of the population, which is a consequence simply of fear, of coercion exercised by the political police and militia, by judges armed with arbitrary powers, backed by the internal security troops and the regular army. Thus, in the first view, legitimating beliefs explain everything, while in the second they explain nothing.

Such notions in their raw form have rarely been held by close observers of communist systems, though some *combination* of the two, seeing these systems as based on a blend of ideology and terror (or naked power), has had a considerable currency, underlying in particular some earlier conceptions of communist 'totalitarianism'. Such a picture is not to be dismissed too lightly, since it is scarcely open to dispute that communist systems *are* dominated by a single highly centralised party, which tolerates no opposition, which directs all the institutions of society, and which had its origins in Marxist–Leninist doctrines and continues to justify all its actions in terms of these doctrines. Yet one conclusion that emerges from this volume, I believe, is that this two-dimensional view is also inadequate, that the reality of political legitimation in communist countries is considerably more complex.

It is time to turn to a closer examination of Weber's analysis of political legitimacy, since this provides the starting point for the consideration of political legitimation in communist countries which I shall be offering later in this chapter and some familiarity with it is also assumed in several other chapters in this book. Weber discusses legitimacy in two contexts: in relation to normative social 'orders' or arrangements (*Ordnungen*) and in relation to systems of rule (*Herrschaft* – often translated 'domination' and sometimes 'authority'). These discussions are not as mutually consistent as they might be expected to be (since a system of rule is after all a species of 'order' as well as a sub-system of a total social 'order')[7] but their contradictions are not very pertinent to my argument and need not detain us here.

The 'legitimacy' of an 'order' resides in its participants believing its demands, 'no matter to what actual extent', to be properly binding upon them, whether or not they in fact comply with these demands and whatever other motives they may have if they do so comply.[8] It is important to recognise that Weber is very far from explaining the effectiveness of a system of rule or other 'order' simply in terms of its legitimacy.

Naturally, the legitimacy of a system of authority may be treated sociologically only as the probability that to a relevant degree the appropriate attitudes will exist, and the corresponding practical conduct ensure. It is by no means true that every case of submissiveness to persons in positions of power is primarily (or even at all) oriented to this belief. Loyalty may be hypocritically simulated by individuals or by whole groups on purely opportunistic grounds, or carried out in practice for reasons of material self-interest. Or people may submit from individual weakness and helplessness because there is no acceptable alternative.[9]

If this is so, why does Weber accord such centrality to the discussion of legitimation in his analysis of political systems? The continuation of the same paragraph provides the answer.

But these considerations are not decisive for the classification of types of imperative coordination [that is, rule]. What is important is the fact that in a given case the particular claim to legitimacy is to a significant degree and according to its type *treated* [my italics] as 'valid'; that this fact confirms the position of the persons claiming authority and that it helps to determine the choice of means of its exercise.[10]

It is in the elaboration of these last points, and specifically in the claim that there is a substantial degree of congruence between types of legitimacy claims and structures and methods of rule, that Weber's most original and valuable contribution to the sociology of power lies. It is true that the reasons for this congruence are not fully clarified by Weber and the causal relationship he suggests remains problematical. Nevertheless a strong tendency to such congruence is in my view empirically observable and an exploration of its ramifications can provide invaluable insights into the character of socio-political systems, not least those of the communist countries.

Weber's typology of legitimate rule (*legitime Herrschaft* – 'legitimate authority' in the translation from which my quotations are taken) is well known, but it will be useful here to recall its main propositions. He distinguishes three 'pure types' (which in practice may occur in various 'combinations, mixtures, adaptations and modifications') in terms of the three main grounds which the validity of legitimacy claims may be based, namely:

1. rational grounds – resting on a belief in the 'legality' of patterns of normative rules and the right of those elevated to authority under such rules to issue commands (legal authority);

2. traditional grounds – resting on an established belief in the sanctity of immemorial traditions and the legitimacy of the status of those exercising authority under them (traditional authority); or finally,

3.   charismatic grounds – resting on devotion to the specific and exceptional sanctity, heroism or exemplary character of an individual person, and of the normative patterns or order revealed or ordained by him (charismatic authority).[11]

The terms on which people may consider they have an obligation to obey their ruler's commands differ according to the type of legitimation. In the case of legal rule it is the legally established order rather than the *persons* of those holding office under it that is owed obedience. In a system of traditional rule, by contrast, obedience 'is a matter of personal loyalty within the area of accustomed obligations'. Under charismatic rule obedience is likewise personalised, based however not on the leader's occupancy of a traditionally sanctioned position but on a personal trust in him and his extraordinary capacities.[12]

Furthermore, each type of legitimate rule is served by a distinctive type of 'administrative staff'. In a legal system this is a 'bureaucracy' of appointive, salaried officials, selected on the basis of educational qualifications, and making careers within a hierarchy of offices each charged with a legally defined sphere of competence.[13] Their distinctive mode of operation is the application of intentionally established abstract rules to particular cases.[14] A traditional ruler recruits his administrative staff either from within his household (kinsmen, slaves, clients etc.) or from others in a relation of personal fealty or dependence ('vassals', favourites, etc.); they are usually directly supported within the ruler's household, and are charged with an arbitrary and shifting range of responsibilities. The traditionally–prescribed limits within which the ruler and his staff are free to command vary greatly as between different sub-types ('patrimonialism', 'sultanism', 'feudalism' etc.).[15] The administrative staff of a charismatic ruler or leader consists of 'followers' or 'disciples', 'summoned' by the leader on the basis of their charismatic qualification, and bound 'in an emotional form of communal relationship', supported typically by voluntary gifts and operating without formal hierarchy and formal rules.[16] Charismatic rule being of its nature revolutionary and therefore transitory, it is subject to 'routinisation' as the charismatic community seeks to stabilise and perpetuate its existence through adopting regular organisational structures and as its administrative staff 'seek and achieve the creation of individual positions and the corresponding economic advantages for [its] members'. Thus charismatic rule is transformed in either a rational (legal) or traditional direction, but may leave a residue in the form of 'hereditary charisma' or a 'charisma of office'.[17]

While the applicability of this typology to communist systems of rule may not be immediately obvious, I propose to argue shortly that it provides a starting point for grasping the character and significance of political legitimation under these systems. First, however, we will need to identify and try to resolve certain problems implicit in Weber's analysis.

This analysis has provoked a considerable critical literature. Much comment has focused on Weber's methodology and the logical status of his operative concepts: the difficulties involved in his attempt to create a value-free *Verstehen* sociology, in the construction and use of 'ideal-types', and so on. This class of problems must be put to one side in the present discussion, but our attention is claimed by certain others which relate to the *content* of his concepts and their applicability to social and historical reality.

We have already noted that the detailed discussion of legitimacy outlined above relates to what Weber calls *'legitime Herrschaft'*. This earthy German word, evoking images of the *paterfamilias*, the 'lord and master', the *dominus*, owes its currency in modern German scholarship and quasi scholarly discourse primarily to Weber's appropriation and adaptation of it to his analytical purposes.[18] The difficulty of rendering it adequately in English speaks to the culture-specific colouration of Weber's terminology, despite his aspirations to 'value-freedom'. Sternberger will allow only 'dominion'; I employ 'rule', a modern approximation to this archaic term, but something is lost.[19] The *Herr* (lord) or *Herrscher* (ruler) gives the orders: he is the boss (the Russian *khozyain* catches something of it). In choosing 'rule' as his central analytical term for the exercise of legitimate political power rather, for instance, than leadership, authority, government, etc., Weber immediately focuses on one kind of relationship within the political system, namely the command–obedience relationship, while marginalising others. In so doing he displays a view of the salient and the normal which seems to reflect a *particular* socio-political reality, namely the authoritarian–bureaucratic order of post-Restoration Europe – an order still largely intact in the Germany of Weber's day; and this despite Weber's highly critical attitude towards it. The effect is sometimes to play down if not to obscure what is most salient and normal in *other* socio-political systems, both historical and contemporary.

In traditional systems, rulers do indeed issue commands, but this is a less distinctive aspect of their role than that of maintaining, defending, implementing and interpreting *customary* obligations and expectations, in which the content of what is demanded is often determined more by precedent than by the ruler's deliberate choice.

In the case of modern Western systems, the decisions of political leaders do indeed come down to the citizen in the form of enforceable 'commands', but again 'command' scarcely catches the distinctive role of these leaders – which is why we rarely speak of them as our 'rulers' unless with a strong dash of irony or theatrical indignation. The leader's role is much more one of presiding over (albeit while seeking to steer and orchestrate) an institutionalised process of reaching compromise *agreement* on competing and often conflicting aspirations and claims. While elsewhere in his work Weber deals at length, and with great perception and sophistication, with both custom and agreement as modes of structuring social action and culture, these central features respectively of traditional and modern Western political systems recede into the background in his ideal-types of traditional and legal rule. It is for such reasons that I have argued elsewhere for a typology of socio-political systems in which custom, contract and command figure as alternative structuring principles.[20] Weber's concentration on legitimate *rule* defined so as to focus attention on the command–obedience relationship leads him to adopt some curious positions. For instance, when the corporations of medieval towns come into conflict with their local lords or princes he sees them as exercising 'non-legitimate domination' even when they are defending rights and privileges hallowed by tradition.[21] Even more striking is Weber's oft-noted failure to discuss modern 'bourgeois' democracy in the context of his analysis of the rational–legal system, and its relegation to an appendix to his treatment of the routinisation of charisma. The reason is that the central feature of democracy as he sees it is simply the people's choice of those who will rule them. This is epitomised in a comment addressed by Weber to Roberto Michels in 1908: 'Any thought...that forms of "democracy" however ingeniously elaborated can eliminate the *Herrschaft* of men over men is a utopia.'[22] But it is agreements or contracts that form the essential building blocks out of which both the institutional arrangements and substantive political outcomes of a 'bourgeois' democratic order are constructed, just as customs are the essential building blocks of the institutional arrangements and political outcomes of a traditional order.

If, then, it was not in the liberal democracies of his day that Weber saw the 'pure type of rational–legal rule with bureaucratic administrative staff' historically most closely approximated, where was it? The answer, as has frequently been noted, is of course the bureaucratic *Rechtsstaat*, and specifically that of Wilhelmine Germany. And the latter, despite its residue of traditional *Herrschaft* focused on the Kaiser's person, and despite its incipient parliamentary democracy, did indeed elevate the bureaucratically-administered and law-bound command–obedience relationship to the dominant political reality. It was a reality that Weber contemplated not without profound anxiety both as to the future of Western man generally and the fate of his native land in particular. For on the one hand while it represented the ultimate development of a distinctive Western type of rationality it also involved a spiritually impoverishing 'disenchantment of the world'. And on the other Weber doubted whether the purely bureaucratic order of this 'authority state' (*Obrigkeitstaat*) would be adequate to Germany's political needs, a doubt that came to a head as the tide of war turned against Germany in 1918, a fact which Weber attributed to the advantages accruing to the Western democracies from having a 'working parliament' (rather than a mere 'parliament of the ruled') which subjected the bureaucracy to political direction under a charismatically-coloured political leadership enjoying the institutionalised consent and support of the people. But he had no patience with 'democracies without leaders' (*führerlose Demokratien*) which sought to reduce *Herrschaft* to a minimum, and in his growing pessimism he found his one hope in a new form of charismatic rule which he termed 'plebiscitary leader-democracy' (*plebiszitäre Führerdemokratie*).[23]

History has vested these views with several levels of irony. Firstly and most obviously, when Germany did indeed acquire, and all too soon, its *Führer*, it proved to be one from whom Weber would certainly have recoiled and who brought disaster upon his fatherland. Secondly, bureaucratically-structured command–obedience *Herrschaft* has turned out not to be the wave of the future in Germany, whose political development over the past century, if we ignore the brief interlude of the 'Thousand-Year Reich' and (for the present) the GDR, has been marked by the growing dominance of those institutionalised processes for reaching agreement or accommodation of competing claims which characterise the democratic, 'market' polities of the industrialised West generally – even if 'bureaucratisation' has proceeded apace in the constituent public and private subsystems of these societies. And the final irony is that the apotheosis of bureaucratically-structured command–obedience *Herrschaft* did appear, and within a very few years of Weber's death, not in Germany, and not even on the soil of the Western rational–legal order at all, but, of all places, in Russia.

In explaining this last proposition I shall be repeating and developing arguments recently published in *Authority, Power and Policy in the USSR*,[24] a procedure prompted less by an overdeveloped scholarly narcissism than by the underdeveloped state of our topic. For this volume is the first ever to focus on political legitimation in the communist countries and its contributors must perforce attempt the ungainly task of pulling themselves up by their own bootstraps. It is not that nothing has been written about political legitimation since Weber. Indeed after years of relative neglect it has received a greatly increased scholarly attention over the last decade or so, mainly in response to the alleged 'legitimacy crisis' in the 'capitalist' democracies in the later 1960s and early 1970s. As early as 1971 McWilliams was able to write that '"legitimacy" is a new master word in political science'[25] and in 1975 discussion of it took up the whole conference programme of the German Political Science Association. Some of this recent literature contains insights of more general applicability that will reward consideration by the student of communist politics, but for the most part it is preoccupied with specific aspects of Western politics and precious little has been written directly on the communist countries.[26] This latter neglect is striking, as Peter Graf Kielmannsegg has pointed out, when one considers that the legitimacy of communist regimes in the eyes of their subjects is on the face of it at least as questionable as that of Western regimes in the eyes of theirs.[27]

There are three main points I would like to argue in summarising my own position:

1. The Soviet type of socio-political order consists of a complex pattern of command structures (or 'bureaucracies') bound together into a single all-embracing structure by the communist party machine: it is a mono-organisational society.

2. The predominant orientation of these command structures is towards goal achievement, rather than towards the application of rules, which Weber correctly identifies as the predominant orientation of the public bureaucracies of Western 'capitalist' societies.

3. Consonant with this, the legitimacy claimed for the commands issuing from this system, and for those holding office under it, is framed in terms of 'goal–rationality' rather than the formal–legal rationality of Western 'capitalist' systems.

There is little that need be said in elaboration of my first point. Apart from the family and, to a degree, the churches, all officially tolerated social units in the USSR and other communist systems modelled on it take the form of hierarchically-operating organisations transmitting centrally-formulated commands ultimately to the operative levels throughout the country. The party integrates these into a single structure partly through the controlling and coordinating role exercised by its apparatus at each level, and partly through ensuring that party members subject to party instruction and discipline are in charge of all significant units of 'non-party' organisations. These features characterise not only formally 'bureaucratic' bodies but also organisations which are professedly and formally democratic or associational in structure, such as the soviets and trade unions. 'Elections' constitute not a choice between alternative candidates and their policies, but rather a coerced ritual of legitimating intent but little legitimating force. Politics, in the sense of competition between ambitions, interests and values, denied an open, institutionalised arena, flourishes covertly in the 'informal organisation' of the system.

My second and third points call for some explication. This is not the place to review the extensive critical literature on Weber's 'ideal-type' of bureaucracy but there is one aspect of the latter which has received little attention but which is of crucial importance to my argument, namely the view that bureaucracies are primarily oriented towards the application of abstract rules to particular cases. This is certainly true of many modern bureaucracies, such as welfare, customs or licensing agencies, but it is misleading with respect to others, notably military and industrial bureaucracies: for in these the primary orientation is towards the achievement of specific assigned tasks rather than the application of rules.[28] On this basis it is essential to distinguish between what might be termed 'rule-applying bureaucracies' and 'task-achieving bureaucracies'.

Now despite the increasing intrusion of the Western 'capitalist' state into task-achievement activities, the predominant mode of its bureaucracy, at least in peacetime, is still the rule-applying mode. The reason is that the state does not set out systematically to prescribe the goals and specific tasks of the constituent units of society, but rather, while engaging in substantial steering, controlling and redistributive activities, primarily to provide a stable framework within which those units may pursue their autonomously-generated goals. Accordingly the central role in the political system is played by institutions concerned with facilitating these autonomously-generated goals and directing the inevitable competition and disagreement into channels where accommodations may be reached and destructive conflict avoided. Consonant with this, the legitimacy claims of the political system, of those holding office under it and of the latter's commands, are validated in terms of freedom within an impersonal legal order and government by agreement and resting on consent.

Not so in the communist system. Here the political authorities *do* set out not only to prescribe the goals and specific tasks of the constituent units of society but indeed directly to manage their implementation through official bureaucracies. Though some essentially rule-applying bureaucracies are present, the predominant bureaucratic mode is the task-achievement mode. Accordingly the central role in the political system is played by institutions concerned with formulating the goals and tasks of the constituent units of society and supervising their execution. Consonant with this, the legitimacy claims of the political system, of those holding office under it, and of the latter's commands, are validated in terms of the final goal ('communism') from which the partial and intermediate goals set by the leadership are allegedly derived and to which individual goals should be subordinated. The details are spelled out by Georg Brunner in Chapter 2.

Both cases incorporate a kind of rationality, but whereas in the former this relates to the appropriateness of the formal laws and rules to the political process and the social order, in the latter it relates to the appropriateness of the means used (the machinery and specific commands) to the goals set. Hence the terms 'formal–legal rationality' and 'goal rationality'.

The legitimation of authority in goal-rational terms is, of course, not unfamiliar in Western societies: it is characteristic, say, of an industrial undertaking or a military force in action. What is peculiar to communist systems is the organisational integration and centralised *management* of the whole society as a single 'enterprise' in which authority is legitimated in goal-rational terms. Something like this was aspired to, but most imperfectly achieved, in Fascist Italy and Nazi Germany, and it was also approximated in certain Western countries, notably Britain, during the Second World War. In communist societies the structural and ideological features of a country totally mobilised for war have been converted into a permanent, 'normal' condition. The 'war', however, in which they engaged, is the 'struggle for communism'. 'Our Goal is Communism!' proclaims the enormous banner in the machine-shop, and indeed it is in terms of this goal that the Politburo justifies its Five-Year Plan guidelines, that Gosplan spells these out into annual and quarterly plans for the industry concerned, that the ministry running it translates into specific targets for the particular plant, and the latter's management sets the tasks of individual workshops and workers.

Let us be very clear what is meant by the 'goal rationality' of such a system. It does not mean that it is necessarily well designed to achieve the goals it proclaims, but simply that the validity of its demands for compliance is *claimed* to be based on a rational relationship between the ultimate goal of communism and the specific tasks assigned to social units and individuals, and the dominant rationale for evaluating social action is the achievement of prescribed tasks. The 'rationality' of the system does not inhere in the results of the commands issuing from it, but in the structure of the argument for justifying these commands. There is no mystery here. On the one hand the 'rational–legal' justification for demanding compliance with the laws passed by Western governments is also not invalidated by the unreasonableness of the objectives claimed for such laws or their failure to achieve the intended results.[29] On the other hand all hierarchical organisations, and not just the 'mono-organisational' systems of communist societies, may suffer a disjunction between proclaimed goals and actual results, because such goals are intrinsically unreasonable, because of 'goal displacement' as commands are transmitted 'down the line', or because of the hypocrisy or sheer inefficiency of their office-holders. That Nazi Germany failed to win the Second World War or the United States the war in Vietnam may be due to a variety of reasons, but neither the failures nor their reasons disprove the goal-rational legitimation of commands issued in the waging of these wars.

No complex society can function without the predictability flowing from an elaborate system of enforceable laws, and the mono-organisational societies of 'real socialism' are no exception. But the higher legitimacy of task-achievement criteria over rule-compliance criteria in official evaluation of performance is apparent in every facet of these societies. If industrial managers break the law in an effort to achieve their plan targets, they are likely to escape punishment if they succeed but may well suffer it if they fail. When in 1962 the editors of *Novy mir* published Solzhenitsyn's *One Day in the Life of Ivan Denisovich* it was not because they had a legal right to do so but because Khrushchev specifically authorised it with current political purposes in mind. What may be reported and not reported in the newspapers is determined not by law but by the current Propaganda Department guidelines embodying the 'tasks' of the press. The political police enjoy wide legal powers and since 1953 are expected to operate generally within the limits of these powers, but they are authorised to resort to extra-legal methods where necessary to the effective performance of their tasks of combating unorthodox views and actions. While the doctrine of the 'dictatorship of the proletariat', described as 'power unlimited by any laws', is no longer said to apply in Soviet-type societies, the priority of goal over law in legitimating political behaviour is still proclaimed not only in propaganda intended for internal party use but even in national constitutions, as when for instance they state (in Article 39 of the 1978 Soviet Constitution) that 'enjoyment by citizens of their rights and freedoms must not be to the detriment of the interests of society or the state'. This flows logically from the teleological definition of the Soviet state in the preamble to the Constitution as 'the basic instrument for defending the gains of the revolution and for building socialism and communism'.

From the preceding analysis it should be plain why I place such emphasis on certain Weberian concepts in seeking to understand the character of political legitimation in communist countries. First and foremost is the view that the focus of legitimation in any system of rule is a particular kind of command–obedience relationship, of *Herrschaft*. I have mentioned reasons for questioning Weber's universalisation of this focus and specifically its application both to traditional political systems and to modern Western systems. But there can be no doubts as to its centrality in Soviet-type systems, where the whole socio-political order consists of a complex but integrated system of hierarchical command–structures or 'bureaucracies'. It is this system of *Herrschaft* that is hallowed by such legitimating doctrines and formulas as the leading and directing role of the Communist Party, 'democratic centralism', 'socialism' understood as a totally state-owned and centrally managed economy, etc. As Georg Brunner shows below, while Soviet-type systems also seek ancillary legitimation through purportedly popular representative bodies, these are made to serve both in doctrine and practice to *reinforce* rather than to qualify the primary legitimation of 'bureaucratically'-organised command-obedience *Herrschaft*.

Secondly there is Weber's stress on the congruence between the dominant principle of legitimation and the character of the 'administrative staff', their relationship to the 'ruler' – mode of selection, organisational structure, powers and mode of operation. In Soviet-type systems these consist of career officials, appointed by, and responsible to, their hierarchical superiors, and organised and operating according to 'bureaucratic' principles. As I have argued, it is necessary to qualify Weber's analysis of bureaucracy in order to bring out this relationship fully – hence my use of quotation marks above. The 'administrative staff' through which Soviet-type systems are ruled consists of *task-oriented* rather than rule-oriented bureaucracies, just as the primary legitimating doctrines and formulas of these systems are *goal-oriented* rather than rule-oriented, and the tasks assigned to particular administrative units and officials and those under their command are held to be derived from the goal of the system as a whole. And here I must stress again that what is important in this connection is that it is *treated* as valid. A further aspect noted by Weber is equally important and highly relevant to Soviet-type systems: namely that even in cases where the system of rule is so assured of dominance that its claim to legitimacy plays little or no part in the relationship between rulers and subjects, the mode of legitimation retains its significance as the basis for the relation of authority between rulers and administrative staff and for the structure of rule.[30]

The approach outlined above focuses on those aspects of political legitimation in communist systems which seem to me most basic and distinctive to those systems. It is, of course, only a partial view, and others would argue that the emphasis should be placed elsewhere. As Weber himself noted, not only may different modes and principles of legitimation operate at different times, levels, and sections in a particular society, they may also co-legitimate individual social acts.[31] I have argued elsewhere the significance of rational–legal, charismatic and traditional legitimation as adjuncts to the dominant goal-rational legitimation of the Soviet system.[32] In Chapter 6 Graeme Gill examines more closely the character of charismatic legitimation in communist systems, through a comparative analysis of the cases of Stalin and Mao. In Chapter 3 Agnes Heller presents strong arguments for a periodisation of political legitimation in the Soviet Union which identifies different modes of legitimation as dominant in different phases; in this view the charismatic legitimation that prevailed in the Stalin period has more recently been supplanted by a form of traditional legitimation.

My own approach differs sharply from the frequently encountered view of political legitimacy which more or less equates it with positive popular acceptance or support.[33] Nevertheless the presence or absence of 'legitimacy' in this sense, which may rest on nothing more than popular evaluation of a government or regime as in general efficacious or benign, may indeed become a question of acute importance for a political system, and this appears to have been the case in communist Europe in recent years. This dimension is explored in Chapter 4 where Ferenc Fehér develops the concept of paternalism as the now dominant mode of legitimation in these countries.[34] Another and complementary element in popular acceptance clearly relevant to the communist countries is that of familiarity; with time an imposed or revolutionary system of rule may come gradually to seem the normal order of things and people's life strategies become increasingly intertwined with the expectations arising from it. One way of conceptualising this process is to assimilate it to a model of traditional legitimation, as Agnes Heller does in Chapter 3. Alternatively we may follow Weber in viewing it as an incomplete 'functional equivalent' to legitimacy,[35] or again as a stage of 'pre-legitimacy'.[36]

The conclusion we should draw from these considerations is not that we ought all to agree on a single usage of the term 'political legitimation' and declare all other usages illegitimate. It is rather the more modest one that different usages serve to illuminate different aspects of the political system, but we must be clear how we are using it and what aspects we are seeking to illuminate. Not only may the content of legitimating doctrines, symbols, beliefs etc. differ in different contexts but so may their functions. An important distinction here is that between the functions of legitimation within the ruling group itself, with respect to the relations between the latter and the 'administrative staff', and with respect to the relations between both of these and the population at large. It is this last that tends to be at the focus of attention in studies of political legitimation, including most of those in this book. My own approach, by contrast, brings the functions of 'goal-rational' legitimation for the position and character of the 'administrative staff' and the organisation of power to the centre of the stage. On the same level, Stoppino draws attention to the function of legitimating beliefs in promoting cohesion between the diverse individuals and groups constituting the power-holders in a system by providing principles and rules of conflict resolution among them.[37] Nor should we overlook the obvious point that whether or not a political system enjoys legitimacy at the mass level may exercise a profound influence on the character and style of the ruling group itself. For Ferrero this was the prime significance of legitimating principles, which were 'capable of immunizing [power] against the most terrible evil from which it can suffer – the fear of its subjects'.[38] The relevance of this perspective for political legitimation in communist systems scarcely needs stressing. No less relevant, however, is the consideration that the very need which regimes experience for legitimacy prompts them to evolve *ex post facto* justifications for their power, in the form of beliefs which in Stoppino's terms are merely 'ideological', since they are not a basis but a consequence of this power, and thus constitute a 'false legitimacy'.[39] As Ferrero puts it, 'a legitimate government has no need of propaganda'.[40]

And here, in conclusion, we broach a further dimension of our subject, to which, alas, space does not permit me to devote the attention its importance warrants: namely, the significance for the legitimacy of a regime that its policies and actions be seen to conform with the basic values and beliefs of the society concerned. The view that they *should* so conform has been an important strain in European political thought and practice ever since the Middle Ages, when it was held that a prince with a legitimate title to rule might lose that legitimacy by governing 'tyrannically'.[41] Historically the value concerned has usually been discussed in terms of 'divine law' or 'natural law', and even Weber took the view that 'natural law is the sole form of legitimation that remains to us, once religious revelation and the sacred authority of tradition have lost their force'.[42] Normative political theory has in consequence produced, and continues to produce, a rich literature on the subject, and some might see it therefore as beyond the more empirical concerns of this volume.

But of course scholars in several branches of social science also have their ways of studying beliefs and values and while most would applaud Raymond Polin's assertion that 'a norm of legitimacy is a fact of civilization, incomprehensible independently of the civilization to which it belongs', few would follow him in the view that 'a view of legitimacy implies a system of values and the philosophy of this system. It is itself a certain philosophy'.[43] The beliefs and values identified by the political anthropologist or political scientist are too rough-hewn to be dignified by the term 'philosophy' and if they form a system then it is more an ecological than a logical one. One approach to organising the information that comes to us from various research disciplines about values and beliefs relevant to the political system of a society (and we must remember that beliefs have a cognitive as well as a normative aspect) is through the concept of 'political culture', and substantial beginnings have been made in applying this approach to communist systems.[44] This literature makes rewarding reading for the student of political legitimation in communist Europe.[45]

Considered dynamically, the view that the legitimacy of a regime depends importantly on its performance conforming or not conforming to the beliefs and values of its subjects opens up several possibilities. One, that a regime may begin to act in such a way as to violate these beliefs and values and thereby lose legitimacy, we have already noted. Then there are two ways in which an originally 'illegitimate'[46] regime may acquire legitimacy, firstly by the regime itself increasingly conforming its actions to established social beliefs and attitudes, and secondly by new beliefs and attitudes supportive of the regime's legitimacy taking root in the society. Both these processes have been observable in greater or lesser degree in the countries of communist Europe, as is noted by several contributors to this volume. But there is a further possibility: that social values and expectations, accepted views of what is 'normal' and proper, the 'social construction of reality', may themselves change – and sometimes quite rapidly – in ways that 'delegitimate' a regime that fails to adapt its own performance to these changes.[47] This was clearly an important element in the recent 'legitimacy crisis' in Western countries, and there is no reason to believe that communist countries are exempt from it, despite the vast efforts of their regimes to monitor, mould and remould the minds and hearts of their peoples. Here the unintended consequences of education, urbanisation, and technological change may not only generate 'undesirable' indigenous changes in social beliefs and values but render society more open and receptive to beliefs and values current in the non-communist world, primarily those of 'bourgeois' origin; and Eurocommunism may prove, in some countries at least, a significant channel in this respect, as Robert F. Miller shows in Chapter 8. So far, therefore, as the conformity between social values and beliefs and regime performance is concerned, we may well see in future years something of a race between legitimating and delegitimating tendencies.

Notes and References

1   The best brief introduction is Dolf Sternberger's entry 'Legitimacy' in *International Encyclopedia of the Social Sciences*, 2nd edn., (New York), vol.9 (1968), pp.244–8. See also the same author's 'Typologie de la légitimité' (in English) *Annales de Philosophie Politique*, vol.VII (1967), pp.87–96; C.J. Friedrich, 'Die Legitimität in politischer Perspektive', *Politische Vierteljahresschrft*, (1960), pp.119–32 and Robert A. Dahl, *Modern Political Analysis*, (Englewood Cliffs, NJ), (1964), pp.19–20. Until recently structural–functional and 'systems' approaches have dominated the treatment of legitimacy in American 'mainstream' political science. The seminal influence here was Talcott Parsons, through ideas developed in his *Structure of Social Action*, (New York), 1937, Talcott Parsons, Edward A. Shils (eds) *et al.*, *Toward a General Theory of Action*, (Cambridge, Mass.), 1951 and later articles. The proposition that political systems are supported by congruent norms and values inculcated in their

citizens by early 'socialisation' was given prominence by such works as Gabriel Almond and Sidney Verba, *The Civic Culture: Political Attitudes and Democracy in Five Nations*, (Princeton), 1963 and Gabriel Almond and Bingham Powell, *Comparative Politics: A Developmental Approach*, (Boston), 1966. An important correlate was the concept of 'political culture' developed by Almond, Verba, Lucian Pye, Harry Eckstein and others. The assumptions and methods displayed in this stream of writing have not gone unchallenged; see, e.g., Brian M. Barry, *Sociologists, Economists and Democracy*, (London), 1970, Chapter 3. The view of legitimacy as a 'support' of the political system acquired greater explicitness and elaboration in the work of David Easton, especially in his *Framework for Political Analysis*, (Englewood Cliffs, NJ), 1965, and *A Systems Analysis of Political Life*, (New York), 1965.

2   For the Romans *legitimum imperium* and *legitima potestas* seem to have meant no more than legally constituted powers. In the Christian Middle Ages concepts of legitimacy evolved that combined notions of the conformity of both title to and exercise of power to law and tradition *and* the consent of the governed. Later the development of natural rights and social contract theories raised the question to a new level, but it took the French revolutionary era with its challenge to the legitimacy of traditional rulers and regimes to render it a major practical concern of political theory. In his *Die Legitimation einer usupierten Staatsgewalt*, (Heidelberg), 1863, Chapter 1, Siegfried Brie identified four major theories of legitimacy, namely the 'legitimist theory', the 'theory of the inalienable sovereignty of the people', the 'possession theory' and the 'theory of the passage of time'. On the continent, however, the influence of *Rechtsstaat* concepts and 'positivist' theories of law encouraged a widespread identification of legitimacy with legality. The issue acquired its somewhat embarrassing *locus classicus* in Carl Schmitt's *Legalität und Legitimität*, (Munich), 1932 and continues to command attention, e.g. it is discussed by several contributors to *L'idée de Légitimité*, (vol.7 of *Annales de Philosophie Politique*, Paris, 1967) and to the special issue (*Sonderheft 7*) on legitimacy of the *Politische Vierteljahresschrift*, (1976), vol.17. There appears to be no book-length study of the history of ideas of political legitimacy in English, but readers of German are referred to Thomas Würtenberger's valuable *Die Legitimität staatlicher Herrschaft. Eine staatsrechtlich-politische Begriffsgeschichte*, (Berlin), 1973.

3 Wilhelm Hennis, 'Legitimität-zu einer Kategorie der bürgerlicher Gesellschaft', *Politische Vierteljahresschrift*, vol.17 (1976), p.13.

4 Here one can merely recommend some samples of the relevant literature in various disciplines: P.H. Partridge, *Consent and Consensus*, (London), 1971; Bertrand de Jouvenal, *Sovereignty: An Enquiry into the Public Will*, trans. by J.F. Huntington, (Cambridge), 1977 esp. Chapter 12; Carl J. Friedrich, ed., *Authority*, (Cambridge, Mass.), 1958; Leonard Krieger, 'The Idea of Authority in the West', *American Historical Review*, vol.82 (1977), pp.249–70; Carl J. Friedrich, *Tradition and Authority*, (London), 1972; Clarke E. Cochran, 'Authority and Community: The Contributions of Carl Friedrich, Yves R. Simon, and Michael Polanyi', *American Political Science Review*, vol.LXXI (1977), pp.546–58; J. Roland Pennock and John W. Chapman, eds, *Political and Legal Obligation*, (New York), 1970; Carole Pateman, *The Problem of Political Obligation. A Critical Analysis of Liberal Theory*, (Chichester), 1979; H.L.A. Hart, *The Concept of Law*, (Oxford), 1961 esp. Chapter VIII; Henry Orenstein, 'Asymmetrical Reciprocity: A Contribution to the Theory of Political Legitimacy', *Current Anthropology*, vol.21 (1980), pp.69–91; Amitai Etzioni, *A Comparative Analysis of Complex Organizations.   On Power, Involvement, and Their Correlates*, (New York), 1961; Peter L. Berger and Thomas Luckmann, *The Social Construction of Reality: A Treatise in the Sociology of Knowledge*, (Penguin Books, Harmondsworth), 1967.

5 See Henry Tudor, *Political Myth*, (London), 1972, Chapters 4 and 5. For a case study raising important theoretical issues, see Anthony P. Cohen, *The Management of Myths.   The Politics of Legitimation in a Newfoundland Community*, (Manchester), 1975.

6 Cf. Mosca's discussion of 'political formulas', but note that for him these serve to legitimate the power of a *social group*, which he terms the 'political class'.   See, e.g. Gaetano Mosca, *The Ruling Class. Elementi di Scienza Politica*, ed. and rev. by Arthur Livingston, trans. by Hannah D. Kahn, (New York), 1939, pp.70–1.

7 See Friedrich, 'Die Legitimität in politischer Perspektive', pp.124–6. Cf. Martin E. Spencer, 'Weber on legitimate norms and authority', *British Journal of Sociology*, vol.22 (1970), pp.123–34, Martin Albrow, 'Weber on legitimate norms and authority: a comment on Martin E. Spencer's account', ibid., vol.23, p.483–7, and John Scott, 'Power and Authority: a comment on Spencer and Martin', ibid., vol.24 (1973), pp.102-7.

8 Max Weber, *The Theory of Social and Economic Organisation*, trans. by A.M. Henderson and Talcott Parsons, ed. with an Introduction by Talcott Parsons, (New York), 1947, pp.124–5 (referred to hereinafter as Weber, *Theory*). This is a translation of Part 1 of Weber's *Wirtschaft und Gesellschaft*, which originally appeared posthumously as Volume III of the collaborative work *Grundriss der Sozialökonomik*, (2nd edn. Tübingen), 1925. An alternative translation of sections of *Wirtschaft und Gesellschaft* is available in *From Max Weber: Essays in Sociology*, trans., ed. and with an Introduction by H.H. Gerth and C. Wright Mills, (London), 1947, Part II. The most complete translation, however, is to be found in Max Weber, *Economy and Society: An outline of Interpretive Sociology*, Guenther Roth and Claus Wittich, eds, (Berkeley etc.) 3 vols, 1968. There is a brief presentation of Weber's typology of legitimacy in his article 'Die drei reinen Typen der legitimen Herrschaft', *Preussische Jahrbücher*, vol.187, pp.1–12; this is reprinted as an appendix in Johannes Winckelmann, *Legitimität und Legalität in Max Weber's Herrschaftssoziologie* (Tübingen), 1952.

9 Weber, *Theory*, p.326. Cf. Hart, pp.198–9.

10 Ibid., pp.236–7.

11 Ibid., p.328. The 'rational legitimacy' proposed by Rogowski is a quite distinct concept from Weber's ideal type of rational (legal) legitimacy; it posits that the legitimacy (support) accorded a government depends on rational choice exercised by its subjects. See Ronald Rogowski, *Rational Legitimacy: A Theory of Political Support*, (Princeton), 1974.

12 Weber, *Theory*, p.328.

13 Ibid., pp.333–4.

14 Ibid., p.330.

15 Ibid., p.342ff.

16 Ibid., pp.359.

17 Ibid., pp.363–73; Weber, 'Die drei reinen Typen der Legitimen Herrschaft', Winckelmann, pp.117–19.

18 The following paragraphs owe much to Dolf Sternberger, 'Max Weber's Lehre von der Legitimität: eine kritische Betrachtung', in W. Röhricht, ed., *Macht und Ohnmacht des Politischen. Festschrift für Michael Freund*, (Cologne), 1967 and to Otto Brunner, 'Bemerkungen zu den Begriffen "Herrschaft" und "Legitimität"', in *Festschrift für Hans Sedlmayr*, (Munich), 1962. They have greatly

benefited, moreover, from the valuable criticism of Professor B.D. Beddie, who, however, would not necessarily endorse all the propositions and formulations they contain.

19 See Sternberger, p.123. As noted, some writers translate *Herrschaft* as 'authority'. The difficulty here is that authority is often understood as *'legitimate* power' or *'legitimate* rule', whereas *Herrschaft* as used by Weber needs the adjective added to make it legitimate. Accordingly Henderson and Parsons appropriately render *legitime Herrschaft* as 'authority', but for *Herrschaft* unqualified they use the awkward and misleading term (borrowed from N.S. Timasheff) 'imperative control', on which see Sternberger, p.123. Other writers, notably Gerth and Mills and Reinhard Bendix (*Max Weber, An Intellectual Portrait*, New York, 1962) prefer 'domination'. This is less problematic, but carries psychological overtones lacking in *Herrschaft*. Carl Friedrich has also argued for 'rule'; see his 'Political Leadership and Charismatic Power', *Journal of Politics*, vol.23 (1961), p.9.

20 T.H. Rigby, 'Max Weber's Typology of Authority: A Difficulty and Some Suggestions', *The Australian and New Zealand Journal of Sociology*, vol.2 (1966), pp.2–15.

21 Cf. O. Brunner, pp.128–9, Sternberger, pp.122–3.

22 Quoted Sternberger, p.125.

23 See Wolfgang Mommsen, *The Age of Bureaucracy. Perspectives on the Political Sociology of Max Weber*, (Oxford), 1974, Chapters IV and V. The same author's *Max Weber und die deutsche Politik 1890–1920* is an outstanding study of the evolution of Weber's thinking in relation to political developments in his country.

24 T.H. Rigby, 'A Conceptual Approach to Authority, Power and Policy in the Soviet Union', Chapter 2 in T.H. Rigby, Archie Brown and Peter Reddaway, eds, *Authority, Power and Policy in the USSR*, (London), 1980.

25 Wilson C. McWilliams, 'On Political Illegitimacy', *Public Policy*, (Summer), 1971, p.429.

26 Some recent writings on political legitimacy were directly provoked by the political turbulence beginning in the late 1960s and in the United States specifically in reaction to the Vietnam War and the Watergate scandal, others were more indirect responses to the atmosphere engendered by these developments, and others again represent the continuation of pre-existing lines of political research

and thought and many would probably have appeared even without the 'legitimacy crisis'. Noteworthy examples of the first category are John H. Schaar, 'Legitimacy in the Modern State', in Philip Green and Sanford Levinson, eds, *Power and Community: Dissenting Essays in Political Science,* (New York), 1970, pp.276–327; Wilson McWilliams, op.cit., and Arthur J. Vidich, 'Political Legitimacy in Bureaucratic Society: An Analysis of Watergate', *Social Research,* vol.42 (1975), pp.778–811. Of particular importance is Jürgen Habermas, *Legitimätionsprobleme in Spätkapitalismus,* (Suhrkamp, 1973; English translation, entitled *Legitimation Crisis,* London, 1976). This complex and many-layered essay in 'critical theory', with its distinctive blend of empirically-oriented and normatively-based argument, cannot be summed up in a few words; for exposition and critical evaluation, see *inter alia* L.J. Ray, 'Habermas, Legitimation and the State', *Journal for the Theory of Social Behaviour,* vol.8 (1978), pp.149–63; see also Richard Löwenthal, 'Gesellschaftliche Umwandlung und demokratische Legitimität. Zu Jürgen Habermas' Analyse der Krisentendenzen im "Spätkapitalismus"', *Neue Rundschau,* vol.86 (1975), pp.549–73, Werner Becker, 'Die missverstandene Demokratie. Über die Ideologie der Legitimitätkrise', ibid., no.5, pp.357–75, and the papers presented at the 1975 conference of the German Political Science Association, including a summary by Habermas of his own position, in *Politische Vierteljahresschrift,* Sonderheft 7, 1976. An alternative approach to the character of political legitimation in contemporary Western society, though one of which Habermas himself makes critical use, is presented by Niklas Luhmann in his *Legitimation durch Verfahren,* (Neuwied) 1969, 2nd edn. 1975. This important work, unfortunately not available in English, essays a systems-theoretical and social-psychological underpinning to the proposition that the operational procedures of the political and legal order themselves generate the legitimation of this order. An earlier discussion of political legitimation from a systems theory standpoint was offered by David Easton, in his *A Systems Analysis of Political Life,* esp. Chapters 18 and 19.. In this context, see also Karl W. Deutsch, *The Nerves of Government. Models of Political Communication and Control,* (New York), 1963, 2nd edn. 1966 especially Chapter 9; Richard M. Merelman, 'Learning and Legitimacy', *American Political Science Review,* vol.60 (1966), pp.548–61; Claus Mueller, *The Politics of Communication: A Study in the Political Sociology of Language, Socialization, and Legitimation,* (New York), 1973; and Edward N. Muller, 'Correlates and Consequences of Beliefs in the Legitimacy of Regime Structures', *Midwest Journal of Political Science,* vol.14

(1970), pp.392–412. Other authors following Muller in using survey data to test hypotheses about political legitimacy are J. Fraser, 'Validating a Measure of National Political Legitimacy', *American Journal of Political Science*, vol.18 (1974), pp.117–34, and Bert Useem and Michael Useem, 'Government Legitimacy and Political Stability', *Social Forces*, vol.57 (1979), pp.840–52. The 'comparative government'–'political development' strand of 'mainstream' American political science has also produced relevant discussions of legitimacy, notably Lucian W. Pye, 'The Legitimacy Crisis', Chapter 4 in Leonard Binder *et al.*, *Crises and Sequences in Political Development*, (Princeton), 1971, pp.135–58, and Paul R. Dettman, 'Leaders and Structures in "Third World" Politics. Contrasting Approaches to Legitimacy', *Comparative Politics*, vol.6 (1973), pp.245–69; see also Gwyn Harries-Jenkins and Jacques van Doorn, *The Military and the Problem of Legitimacy*, (Beverly Hills), 1976. Weber's analysis and particularly his 'ideal-types' are discussed with greater or lesser penetration by many of these authors; of special interest in this regard is an exchange in the pages of the *British Journal of Sociology*; Martin E. Spencer, 'Weber on Legitimate Norms and Authority', *British Journal of Sociology*, vol.21 (1970), pp.123–34, Martin Albrow, 'Weber on Legitimate Norms and Authority; A comment on Martin E. Spencer's Account', ibid., vol.23 (1972), pp.483–7, and John Scott, 'Power and Authority: A Comment on Spencer and Martin', ibid., vol.24 (1973), pp.101–16. An important new work, pertinent to many of the matters discussed here, is J.G. Merquior, *Rousseau and Weber: Two Studies in the Theory of Legitimacy*, (London), 1980. Useful and stimulating reviews of the 'state of the problem' are Peter Graf Kielmansegg, 'Legitimität als analytische Kategorie', *Politische Vierteljahresschrift*, vol.12 (1971), pp.367–401, Peter G. Stillman, 'The Concept of Legitimacy', *Polity*, vol.7 (1974), pp.32–56, and Günther Maluschke, 'Zur Legitimität politischer Institutionen und politischen Handelns', *Zeitschrift für Politik*, vol.23 (1976), pp.366–67; see also Uriel Rosenthal, *Political Order. Rewards, Punishments and Political Stability*, (Alphen), 1978, Chapter 7. These sources discuss many of the publications cited above as well as other relevant literature which there has been insufficient space to mention. Richard Löwenthal offers a valuable consideration of legitimation in communist countries in his 'The Ruling Party in a Mature Society', Chapter 4 in Mark G. Field, ed., *Social Consequences of Modernization in Communist Societies*, (Baltimore and London), 1976, esp. pp.100–8. Two collections of special interest, in containing essays on both 'capitalist' and communist states are Peter Graf

Kielmansegg and Ulrich Matz, eds, *Die Rechtfertigung politischer Herrschaft*, (Freiburg-München), 1978 and Bogdan Denitch, ed., *Legitimation of Regimes. International Frameworks of Analysis*, (Beverly Hills), 1979, esp. Chapter 3 by Joseph Rothschild, 'Political Legitimacy in Contemporary Europe'; Chapter 9 by Peter C. Ludz, 'Legitimacy in a Divided Nation: The Case of the German Democratic Republic', and Chapter 10 by David Lane, 'Soviet Industrial Workers: The Lack of a Legitimation Crisis?'. The only book-length study on a communist country appears to be Bogdan Denis Denitch, *The Legitimation of a Revolution. The Yugoslav Case*, (New Haven and London), 1976, though this study does not deal extensively with theoretical issues. Alfred G. Meyer's 'Political Change through Civil Disobedience in the USSR and Eastern Europe', Chapter 17 in Pennock and Chapman, op.cit., is largely about legitimacy, though the term is hardly used. Jerome M. Gilison's *British and Soviet Politics. Legitimacy and Convergence*, (London), 1972 presents an alternative approach to those represented in this book. Finally, for a thoughtful discussion of one important aspect, see Thomas A. Baylis, *The Technical Intelligentsia and the East German Elite. Legitimacy and Social Change in Mature Communism*, (London), 1974.

27 Kielmansegg and Matz, p.19.

28 One can indeed discern the seeds of such a distinction in Weber, and at one point he wrote specifically that 'it is perfectly true that "matter of factness" and "expertness" [characteristic of bureaucracies] are not necessarily identical with the rule of general and abstract norms'. See Weber, *Economy and Society*... Roth and Wittich, eds, vol.3, p.978. However he does not appear to have developed this perception in a systematic way and the rule-applying aspect is salient in his most influential discussions of bureaucracy.

29 If, as is often argued, there are grounds for refusing to comply with such laws, these grounds must invoke principles of legitimacy *other than* rational–legal principles.

30 Weber, *Theory*, p.327. Cf Hume: 'The sultan of Egypt or the Emperor of Rome might drive his harmless subjects like brute beasts against their sentiments and inclination. But he must, at least, have led his *mamelukes* or *praetorian bands*, like men, by their opinion', (Charles W. Hendel, ed., *David Hume's Political Essays*, (New York), 1953 p.24).

31 Weber, *Theory*, p.125.

32 Rigby, 'A Conceptual Approach to Authority, Power and Policy in the Soviet Union', in Rigby, Brown and Reddaway, op.cit.

33 See discussion in Rosenthal, op.cit., Chapter 7. While writers such as Easton and Almond evidently did not intend 'support' to be understood simply in a commonsense way, the distinction is not always easy to maintain, e.g. in research based on questionnaire surveys, and is in practice often ignored. It is revealing that even such a writer as Rogowski, who rejects 'mainstream' understandings of political legitimacy, nevertheless identifies it with support. Cf. also Ted Robert Gurr, *Why Men Rebel*, (Princeton), 1970, pp.183–92. For a useful analysis of the distinction between legitimacy and support, see Renate Mayntz, 'Legitimacy and the Directive Capacity of the Political System', Chapter 10 in Leon N. Lindberg *et al.*, *Stress and Contradiction in Modern Capitalism: Public Policy and the Theory of the State*, (Lexington), 1975.

34 Fehér's concept of paternalism has a good deal in common with George W. Breslauer's 'image' of 'welfare-state authoritarianism', as presented in his *Images of the Soviet Future: A Critical Review and Synthesis*, (Berkeley), 1978. Alfred G. Meyer also discusses the 'paternalism' of communist systems, although he gives the concept a slightly different content; see Pennock and Chapman, op.cit., p.422ff.

35 Weber writes: 'An order which is adhered to from motives of pure expediency is generally much less stable than one upheld on a purely customary basis through the fact that the corresponding behaviour has become habitual. *The latter is much the most common type of subjective attitude.* But even this type of order is in turn much less stable than an order which enjoys the prestige of being considered binding, or, as it may be expressed, of "legitimacy"', (*Theory*, p.125, my emphasis).

36 The term is taken from Ferrero, whose extensive discussion of 'pre-legitimacy' has considerable relevance to our topic. He quotes with approval Talleyrand's view that 'A legitimate government, be it monarchical or republican, hereditary or elective, aristocratic or democratic, is always the one whose existence, form and mode of action have been strengthened and sanctioned over a long period of years, I might even say over a period of centuries'. For this reason, he argues, legitimacy 'is preceded by a preparatory condition, which may be called prelegitimacy. Prelegitimacy is legitimacy still in its cradle. Every government began by being a government that had not yet won, but was attempting to win, universal acceptance and had a

good chance of succeeding; it became legitimate the day it succeeded in conciliating the opposition aroused by its advent', (Guglielmo Ferrero, *The Principles of Power, The Great Crises of History,* trans. Theodore R. Jaeckel (New York), 1942, pp.138–9). The view that a 'usurped power' can acquire legitimacy with the passage of time has a long pedigree that goes back to the political theory of the middle ages (see Würtenberger, Chapter 1), and it retained some currency in the generation in which Ferrero grew up. 'L'autorité du temps porte avec elle le préjugé de la légitimité', wrote Sismondi. This 'Verjährungstheorie' is critically discussed by Siegfried Brie in his *Die Legitimation einer usupierten Staatsgewalt,* pp.33–45.

37 See Mario Stoppino, 'Appunti sul concetto di autorità, *Politico,* vol.34 (1969), p.438. Frederick C. Teiwes has illustrated this function in his paper, 'The Legitimacy of the Leader in China: Mao, Hua and the Shifting Bases of Authority', California Regional Seminar on China, Berkeley, March 1980.

38 Ferrero, p.135.

39 Stoppino, pp.44–6.

40 Ferrero, p.200.

41 E.g. by John of Salisbury and Thomas Aquinas. See Walter Ullmann, *A History of Political Thought: The Middle Ages,* (Harmondsworth), 1965, p.123, Oscar Jászi and John D. Lewis, *Against the Tyrant. The Tradition and Theory of Tyrannicide,* (Glencoe), 1957, Chapter II, Würtenberger, Chapter 1.

42 Max Rheinstein, ed., *Max Weber on Law in Economy and Society,* trans. Max Rheinstein and Edward Shils, (Cambridge, Mass.), 1954, p.288. Cf. Reinhard Bendix, *Max Weber. An Intellectual Portrait,* (New York), 1962, p.420.

43 Raymond Polin, 'Analyse philosophique de l'idée de légitimité', *Annales de Philosophie Politique,* vol.VII (1967), p.26.

44 See Archie Brown and Jack Gray, eds, *Political Culture and Political Change in Communist States,* (London), 1977; Stephen White, *Political Culture and Soviet Politics,* (London), 1979; Robert C. Tucker, 'Culture, Political Culture and Communist Society', *Political Science Quarterly,* vol.88 (1973), pp.173–90; Archie Brown, *Soviet Politics and Political Science,* (London), 1974, Chapter 4; Lucien W. Pye, *The Spirit of Chinese Politics: A Psychocultural Study of the Authority Crisis in Political Development,* (Cambridge, Mass.), 1968; Richard H. Solomon, *Mao's Revolution and the Chinese Political*

Culture, (Berkeley), 1971; Richard R. Fagen, *The Transformation of Political Culture in Cuba*, (Stanford), 1969.

45 See especially Brown and Gray, pp.23, 42–5, 49, 56, 72, 138, 154 and White, pp.189–90.

46 Irving Horowitz has argued that 'illegitimacy' may be the 'norm' in certain countries; see I.L. Horowitz, J. de Castro and J. Gerassi, eds, *Latin American Radicalism: A Documentary Report on Left and Nationalist Movements*, (New York and London) 1969, pp.3–29 and Irving Louis Horowitz, 'The Norm of Illegitimacy', in Denitch, *Legitimation of Regimes*, Chapter 2. Some would argue that this is indeed the case with communist countries, and Peter Ludz has gone further and suggested that 'legitimacy is not a primary goal of ruling Communist parties' (ibid., p.173) arguing this from the case of the East German regime. It is not difficult to see grounds for considering the one-dimensional legitimacy–illegitimacy dichotomy (or continuum) as empirically simplistic and analytically insufficiently discriminating. Rose, distinguishing between independently varying 'support' and 'compliance' as bases of a regime's 'authority' has devised a nine-cell matrix ranging from 'fully legitimate' to 'repudiated' regimes, which may change in any one of four directions: towards legitimation, isolation, coercion or repudiation. See Richard Rose, 'Dynamic Tendencies in the Authority of Regimes', *World Politics*, vol.XXI (1969), pp.604–28. This schema and a number of particular propositions in Rose's articles may be found suggestive, although the few references it makes to communist states are of limited interest and his approach leads to some odd moves, such as including regimes destroyed by foreign invasion in the category of 'repudiated' regimes. Cf. also Lipset's discussion of the interplay between 'effectiveness' and 'legitimacy' in determining the 'stability' of a regime; see Seymour Martin Lipset, *Political Man. The Social Bases of Politics*, (New York), 1960, pp.77–83.

47 'Delegitimation' is a rather neglected term that would often be more accurate than the overworked 'legitimacy crisis'; Branko Horvat has recently used it, though not in relation to political systems; see his 'The Delegitimation of Old and the Legitimation of New Social Relations in Late Capitalist Societies', Chapter 5 in Denitch, *Legitimation of Regimes*.

8 Security and Modernisation in Tsarist Russia and the USSR*

The primary and only universal functions of the state are to see to the internal order of a society and its protection against external attack. Even primitive societies usually invest certain members or categories of members with special powers and responsibilities for the exercise of these functions. However, it is only in the relatively large and complex societies of more recent ages that substantial groups of members have been set aside and equipped to devote themselves primarily to these tasks. These groups constitute the framework of the state. The most distinctive feature of the state is that, whatever methods it employs for the attainment of its objects, these are ultimately backed by the sanction of force, and its effectiveness requires that in the last resort *its* force shall prevail.

States vary in a great number of ways, of which the most important are these:

1. How much they engage in rule-*making*, as distinct from the interpretation and enforcing of existing rules.

2. The extent to which their power to issue enforceable commands is limited within rules they are not free to alter by themselves.

3. The extent and nature of their dependence on kinship, caste, property-owning and functional groups within their society.

---

*'Security and Modernisation', *Survey* , no.64 (July 1967).

4.   What functions, other than their two primary ones, they engage in. There are few social functions, whether in the field of economic production and distribution, in welfare or in the socialisation of members, which some state somewhere has not taken on.

From the standpoint adopted here, the Soviet state includes both the 'party' and the 'government'. This is of course at variance with both communist doctrine and Soviet constitutional theory, which are concerned to draw a sharp distinction between the party and the state. Even in theory, however, this distinction is blurred by the constitutional provision that the party maintains a 'guiding nucleus' in all state bodies (as well as in other social organisms), and by the view of Soviet administrative lawyers that decisions of party bodies, while not 'constituting law', nonetheless 'possess the force of law'. In practice, the involvement of full-time party officials in the decision-making process is one of the Soviet state's most obvious and best-documented features, and the most important matters of state have usually been decided in a party body formally lying outside the structure of the state, namely the Political Bureau (in 1952–66 the Presidium) of the Central Committee.

In terms of the variables listed above, the Soviet state is characterised by the following features:

(a)   Its powers of decision-making (framing and changing rules and issuing commands) are extremely broad, being limited in only minor degrees by existing rules or by dependence on functional or other social groups.

(b)   The range of social functions in which it directly engages is likewise extremely broad. Most social institutions in the USSR are *state* institutions (in our sense). This can be properly appreciated only when we take account of the functions of the CPSU as a branch of the state.

Why did the Soviet state acquire these features? Was it due to the attempt to remake society in conformity with an abstract ideal, or was it rather due to the internal and external circumstances in which this attempt was made? How far did it result from the organisational principles and traditions of Bolshevism, and how far from the personal psychology of Lenin and Stalin? These questions all direct our attention to important proximate causes which (along with others) should find a part in any systematic account of the development of the Soviet state. Yet behind each of them stands another question. Why was it *Russia* that set out to 'build communism'? Why were Russia's circumstances at this time such as to foster the results we have noted? Why did Bolshevism develop such organisational principles and traditions? Why did men like Lenin and Stalin come to the top in Russia?

The tsarist state emerged between the fifteenth and seventeenth centuries as a response to the internal disorder and external menace afflicting the vast, culturally homogeneous but sparsely settled and vulnerable Great Russian territories. It was an eminently successful response, which explains the persistence of its basic elements until the early twentieth century. It owed this success largely to an unusual harnessing-together of the forces of ethnocentric conservatism with those of bold and sometimes revolutionary innovation. Yet there was always a tension between these forces, a tension which several times threatened and ultimately encompassed the collapse of the system. The communist regime, which aimed to abolish this tension, soon found that it could not survive and flourish without pursuing policies which revived it. Hence the recurrence throughout the Soviet period of patterns familiar from the tsarist past.

The Making of Tsarism

The emergence of Tsarism was part of a European trend from loose, decentralised political systems to centralised monarchies. Without examining here the reasons for this trend, it is worth considering some of the similarities and differences between the forms it took in Russia and in western Europe.

Everywhere it involved the replacement of local and functional autonomies by the universal jurisdiction of the monarch, of an essentially military ruling group organised on a semi-contractual lord–vassal basis by an essentially bureaucratic ruling group linked to the monarch on a master–servant basis, of a church separate from and coordinate with the state by a church more or less integrated with and subordinate to the state. Everywhere princes and kings figured as innovators, riding roughshod over established patterns and privileges even while claiming to protect the ancient ways, and hallowing their innovations by claims of divine right.

In much of western Europe, substantial autonomies survived the rise of absolutism, often serving as a base for new groups (especially commercial) in their efforts to influence, share, or challenge the power of the monarch and his aristo-bureaucracy. Moreover, the Reformation and the emergence of vernacular cultures transformed but did not destroy the international culture of western Christendom.

Russia's geography and international environment, however, meant that a centralised monarchy could be created there only by a *tour de force* utterly destructive of entrenched privileges and liberties and conducive to extreme forms of those basic features of the new monarchies that we have just noted.[1] The innovatory achievements of the princes of Moscow went beyond the creation of a new state to the creation of a new social order to maintain it. A class of serfs was fashioned to support the new aristo-bureaucracy which was needed to hold the state together and defend its borders. The old quasi-feudal aristocracy was 'liquidated as a class'. This whole process, moreover, manifested an unusually high level of consciousness. There were no institutional or legal survivals around which new liberties could accrete, providing commercial, land-owning, or other strata with a point of leverage against the absolute power of the monarch. The alliance of church and state to provide a bulwark against infidel and heretic reached its climax in the duumvirate and confrontation of Alexei Mikhailovich and the Patriarch Nikon, and the latter's defeat crippled the church and prepared it for reduction to the role of a state instrumentality.

In creating a centralised state where there had been none before, the Muscovites borrowed heavily, ideologically, institutionally and technically, especially from Byzantium and the Tatars. The resultant amalgam, however, which identified the cause of true Christianity with the Russian state and people, and which elevated the prince not just to *a* king by divine right, but to *the* Caesar by divine right, possessed a xenophobic and messianic quality highly functional for the coherence and independence of the state, but profoundly resistant to further innovation. Moscow's xenophobic ideological exclusivism militated not only against useful foreign borrowings, but also against smooth internal evolution, as was shown by the disastrous reaction to Nikon's reforms, the result of a 'know-nothing' traditionalism reinforced by an officially-inspired Latinophobia.

Security, Modernisation, and the State

Thus Russia conducted her social and political revolution in the sixteenth and seventeenth centuries effectively isolated from those profound material and intellectual changes which in Europe laid the foundations of the modern world. Not that Russia was entirely unaware of the fruits of these changes. They were present as a useful but mistrusted and dangerously irritating foreign body in the Russian social organism itself, in the form of Polonised Ukrainian grammar school teachers, Scottish soldiers, German craftsmen, and English physicians. Muscovy at the end of seventeenth century was riven by profound contradictions, between prematurely frozen ideology and institutions on the one hand, and the need for modernisation on the other. For the institutions and ideology which had arisen as a revolutionary solution to Russia's need for internal and external security, now threatened that security by hindering spontaneous internal evolution and fruitful foreign influence, so allowing Russia to fall dangerously behind its rapidly modernising neighbours.

If this analysis is correct, it is not too hard to see why these contradictions required a revolution from above to resolve them. For the system inhibited the spontaneous development which might have generated a modernising élite, and condemned political struggle to the sterile channels of court intrigue and Razin-type *jacqueries*. Nor should it surprise us that this pattern was to become a recurrent one in Russian history, for the solution obviously contained within itself the seeds from which the problem would be reborn. Peter preserved the basic elements of the tsarist system – the absolute monarch served by an aristo-bureaucracy commanding a bonded peasantry – but sought to orient it towards technical modernisation, by administrative rationalisation to render the system responsive to his initiatives, by purging the security and ideological machines of conservative opposition, and by technical training and attempts to open careers in the bureaucracy to men of talent and technical qualifications. In so doing, however, he raised to an even higher level that concentration of the power of creative social initiative at the apex of the state machine, that inhibition of spontaneous evolution, which had made a Peter necessary. Furthermore, the attempt to create a modernising élite from above, dictated as it was by the needs of external security, was destined to undermine the internal coherence and security of Russia itself. For not only did it greatly deepen the existing cleavage between the élite and the masses, it also opened up divisions within the élite itself. Peter had sought only to equip his servants with Western techniques, but it was inevitable that some of them should be infected by the social and intellectual values of the societies that produced these techniques, and become thereby alienated from Russia's own political and social order. The path from Peter's first 'exchange students' in artillery and navigation to the revolutionary intelligentsia of the nineteenth century is a familiar one, as is the reaction of the bulk of the aristo-bureaucracy into ultraconservatism. What is less often appreciated is the paradoxical character this gave to the process of modernisation in Russia.

The impatience with Russian backwardness and the orientation towards radical change which Peter had attempted to build into his aristo-bureaucracy now became the monopoly of a counter-élite regarded by the former as a dangerous threat to stability and order. For most of the time, when their primary concern was precisely for stability and order, successive monarchs were bound to value the conservative, ethnocentric inertia of the aristo-bureaucratic class. Yet it was the monarch who alone had the power to initiate major social change, and when the need for change was forced on his attention (usually as a result of war) he was 'objectively' bound to ally himself with the system's critics and to 'betray' its supporters. It was the monarch's Janus-like role as defender of order and fountainhead of modernisation that explains the reign of an Alexander I, which begins as a conspiracy of reformers and ends as the tyranny of Arakcheev, or that of Alexander II, whose first acts are greeted by the counter-élite as the triumph of virtue and by the bulk of the aristo-bureaucracy with dismay, yet who lives to earn the execration of the counter-élite and death at their hands.

The hypertrophy of the tsarist state, by origin a response to the needs of internal order and external protection, both induced and in turn was reinforced by its monopoly of modernising initiative. It aided modernisation by permitting the imposition of radical changes, but hindered it by inhibiting unauthorised borrowing from abroad and spontaneous social evolution. It made for macro-innovation but held back micro-innovation. It could achieve the abolition of serfdom but not the spread of productive farming methods, the creation of a new civil service but not the evolution of institutions representing particular interests. The inadequacy of this modernisation-by-delayed-but-massive-response became increasingly apparent as the pace of technical and social change quickened in the West in the the nineteenth and early twentieth centuries. As in the seventeenth century, the new techniques, to the extent they were found in Russia, were increasingly the fruits of foreign enterprise. Technical and social backwardness led to military defeats which threatened not only the credibility of tsarism as Russia's protector but also the ability of the regime to impose discipline on the masses. Hence the accelerated growth and desperation of the critical counter-élite, the deepening conservative reaction in the bulk of the aristo-bureaucracy, the zig-zag from concession to suppression that led straight to 1917.

The Bolsheviks Repeat the Pattern

October 1917 brought to power a section of the counter-élite, a section which manifested in extreme form its disdain for the state and promotion of innovation at the expense of stability and order. For the Bolsheviks sought to refashion society in such a way that the state – that is, social authority backed by force – would be redundant. For a transitional period, indeed, the state would be necessary to protect the revolution against its internal and external enemies and to build the new society, but no special qualifications would be needed by the proletarians and other members of the masses who were to man it. The Bolsheviks themselves, organised as a consciously disciplined party, would show the way, while the masses, perceiving it to be in their best interests, would freely accept their guidance, and could be relied on to discipline those of their number too stupid or selfish to see where their best interests lay.

The Bolsheviks emerged from the Civil War with their Utopianism of ends intact, but disabused of their Utopianism of means. Establishment of the Soviet regime had been a *tour de force* which, like the establishment of the tsarist regime some centuries earlier, had led to an extreme hypertrophy of the state. Problems of external protection and internal order took priority over all other concerns, and authority backed by force permeated all areas of social life. Far from 'any housewife' being capable of performing the functions of the state, these called for expertise, for experience, for the professional. Far from the masses freely accepting Bolshevik guidance, their cooperation had to be ruthlessly compelled, and other parties offering alternative policies forcibly suppressed. Far from conscious discipline sufficing to ensure the coherence of the party itself, groups of communists critical of the leadership were made liable to expulsion and the membership was subjected to a massive purge.

Even giving maximum weight to the Civil War in explaining this hypertrophy of the state and its concomitant paralysis of spontaneous social response and innovation, however, we have not fully explained why the 'building of socialism' in Russia should have proved so similar a 'revolution from above' to all the major social reorganisations of the tsarist era. Here subjective factors clearly reinforced objective ones: the Bolshevik leaders *could not conceive it otherwise*. And their inability to conceive radical social change other than as a programme consciously willed and administratively implemented they owed not to Marxism, but to the Russian political culture that had nurtured them. It was not their adherence to specific forms of conspiratorial organisation that made the Leninists the most Russian (and most successful) of all Russian Marxist groups, but rather their constant stressing of 'consciousness' against 'spontaneity', and their identification of spontaneity with chaos, inertia, aimlessness, formlessness.

In the triumph of 'consciousness' over 'spontaneity' no factor was of more fateful importance than the integration of the party in the state. This was not an immediate consequence of the taking of power, nor did it follow with inevitable logic from Bolshevik ideas. It was rather an evolution that took many years to complete, though the decisive step was the decision to create a full-time party apparatus in 1919. There is much that remains unclear about this decision and about the subsequent rapid evolution of the party apparatus as a key organ of rule directing and supervising the machinery of government. What can be said is that the decision reflected a widespread concern at the withering of the internal political life of the party and its lack of influence on the day-to-day work of government; that no-one seems to have proposed any alternative way of reviving the party than by endowing it with a full-time officialdom; and that the assertion of party influence was seen as requiring this officialdom to function primarily as a chain of command directed from the centre, superimposed on the organs of the state and freely disposing of party members. As Lenin was to put it in a note dictated a year before his death, 'for the worker and peasant state – a state constructed on completely new principles – in order to get it functioning properly, it was demanded and is still demanded now, that the members of the party be concentrated in it in a most hierarchical framework'.[2]

To non-communists it has always seemed obvious that to entrust the life of local party organisations to officials whose tenure was conditional on their securing quick and efficient fulfilment of commands from above was to deliver the *coup de grâce* to those democratic internal processes and that vigorous and critical discussion, beliefs in which the Bolsheviks had imbibed from the traditions of European Marxism. The Bolsheviks themselves, however, who regarded it as an elementary 'rotten liberal' error to 'make a fetish' of outward political forms, were genuinely dismayed when the bureaucracy they had created began to behave bureaucratically. The careerism, the red tape, the nepotism, the crippling of initiative and smothering of criticism – these could be due only to habits carried over from tsarism, to permitting officials to lose touch with the workers, to allowing self-seekers into office.

The remedies were to punish offenders more surely and severely, to appoint more workers, to turn them out to grass occasionally. This meant streamlining the party's Central Control Commission and the Commissariat of Worker–Peasant Inspection, and reforming the party's personnel machinery. In thus seeking an essentially bureaucratic solution to the evils of bureaucracy, the Bolsheviks revealed a blind spot that they have never lost. They had no difficulty in identifying the evils of bureaucracy, but failed to recognise bureaucracy as one particular form of structuring social action, consisting essentially of a hierachy of command, and possessing its own characteristic vices and virtues. And here again we see the influence of Russian political experience, which knew no effective method of structuring social action other than through a hierarchy of command, and therefore took it for granted.

As for democratic processes in party and government, these were desirable, but not essential, so long as the right policies were being carried out. Indeed in the Civil War, as in the underground, concern with democratic processes was usually seen as a hindrance to effective action. Of course this was unfortunate, and of course it would be repaired with victory. Hence the programmes of 'reviving the soviets' and of inculcating 'workers' democracy' in the party, which received such prominence in the early and mid 1920s though increasingly coloured with hypocrisy, were in large part, and especially at the beginning, sincerely conceived and promoted. If these programmes remained stillborn, it was not only because their realisation depended on the efforts of established officials and cliques who had a vested interest in preventing opposition emerging in their bailiwicks, but also because everyone concerned recognised that democracy must be limited within the bounds of 'correct' policies. Never questioning that democracy *for* the people must prevail over democracy *by* the people, the good Bolshevik took alarm whenever electors, soviets, party rank-and-file, or committee members failed to act as recommended by their officials. This could only mean that they were misled or inadequately informed and indoctrinated, or alternatively that the recommendations were incorrect. It was the responsibility of higher echelons to establish which was the case and take corrective action. There is no evidence that the Bolsheviks of the 1920s ever realised that if people were not allowed to err, and there was held to be a 'correct' solution to all significant problems, then the operation of democratic processes must be limited to trivia. And this is another blind spot that their successors have never lost.

Political Struggle and Opposition

It is in the context of these two blind spots that we should consider
the history of political struggle and opposition within the Soviet
regime. The 'Left Communists' of 1918 consisted of a number of
prominent party members who opposed the decisions taken on
certain important issues, especially the Brest–Litovsk Treaty, and
thereupon withdrew from positions of authority so as not to be
involved in their implementation. Since, however, they showed
sufficient Bolshevik discipline to abstain from working for the
reversal of the policies they opposed, and indeed sought no
continuing identity as a group offering alternative policies to the
leadership, they represented no challenge to basic Leninist principles
and were soon readmitted to leading positions.

The 'Workers Opposition' and 'Democratic Centralists' of 1920–21
were of an entirely different order. The bureaucratisation of the
party after 1919 and its integration in the state meant that the critical
discussion of current political and social issues, a function heretofore
accepted as proper for party members, was increasingly limited to
groups lying outside the mainstream of the active day-to-day life of
the party, who were increasingly alienated from the busy officials of
the party apparatus who merely 'had a job to do'. Unlike the Left
Communists, the Workers Opposition and Democratic Centralists
sought a continuing identity as groups criticising the incumbent
leadership, proposing alternative policies, and advocating radical
changes in existing political arrangements. We should note,
however, that though these groups desired changes going further
than the leadership were prepared to accept, directed towards
combating bureaucratisation and rendering the machine more
responsive to the party rank-and-file and the workers, they had no
clearer realisation than did the leadership that the root of these
problems lay in the crucial bureaucratic functions with which the
party was now endowed.

The trade union discussion on the eve of the Tenth Congress in
1921, in which different groups within the leadership as well as the
major opposition groups publicly debated an important policy issue
and competed for support in party elections, suggested that even
within the framework of the one-party state devices might be found
for diluting the concentration of social initiative at the apex of the
bureaucratic hierarchy and for institutionalising the representation
of different opinions and interests. Yet was there ever a chance that
such discussions would become accepted as a normal and regular

feature of Soviet political life? Certainly it was the wave of peasant violence and industrial unrest culminating in the Kronstadt revolt that swung the Tenth Congress delegates behind the Politburo proposal to ban 'factionalism' and dissolve existing 'factional' groups. But one can also detect a widespread feeling that there was something unhealthy or dangerous about the behaviour and processes that emerged in the trade union discussion, quite apart from any threat they might involve of disunity in the face of new dangers to the regime, and this indicated the formidable obstacles entrenched in the Bolshevik tradition that any trend to institutionalise these processes and behaviour would have encountered.

The events of 1921 repeated a pattern so frequently associated with spells of relative liberalisation in Russia, when a flurry of apprehension about external or internal security has prompted a reassertion of close bureaucratic control, which has proved fatally easy simply because non-bureaucratic politics have such weak roots in Russian life.

The decision of the Tenth Congress in effect outlawed all informal political association and communication in Russia. Even before this, the party secretariat had forbidden unauthorised lateral communication between party committees and officials, as well as vertical communication between the party groups working at different echelons in non-party bodies. Meanwhile, as we have noted, political expression and activity in the soviets, party committees, and other pseudo-democratic institutions were restricted to what their officials recognised as conforming to current national policies. So, except in so far as party-approved editors chose to publish divergent views, all political communication, association, and initiative in Russia were henceforth concentrated in the bureaucracy and focused on the formal hierarchical channels of the party.

The drift to absolute rule by an oligarchy of leaders institutionalised in the Politburo and directing the various bureaucratic hierarchies was now complete. The crucial importance of the party machine in the structure of their power obviously opened the possibility of this oligarchy being converted to a dictatorship of whichever oligarch exercised primary responsibility for the party machine. The general acceptance in the party of the principle of collective leadership represented by the Politburo was, however, a severe obstacle to the establishment of a dictatorship of the General Secretary. Though Stalin was ultimately to achieve this, it required patient effort over several years, and an indirect strategy which consisted of using the machine to install supporters in the party congress and Central Committee, and then using the formal rights of these bodies to adjudicate in disputes within the Politburo and to change its membership; and meanwhile securing his rear by building up a preponderant influence in the armed forces and police. Once he had achieved this, the key positions in the government, including that of Chairman of the Council of People's Commissars, the one formal post in the regime held by Lenin, were his to dispose of at will, without his ever having to struggle openly for them.

It was in 1919–21 that the basic structure of the Soviet political system was forged. Through all the profound changes in Soviet society since then, the structure of power has remained essentially unchanged. After 1921, as was to become immediately apparent, opposition could take only two forms: illegal opposition, and opposition organised in sections of the bureaucracy and enjoying protection within the supreme leadership.

Those who refused to conform to the Tenth Congress decisions soon found themselves outside the party, and if they still wanted to try to influence events, could do so only through such clandestine organisations as the 'Workers Group' and 'Workers Truth', which were quite 'properly' dealt with by the political police. Since in principle *no* utterance or association between individuals had a right to existence unless authorised by the bureaucracy as 'in accordance with the interests of the working people and with the aim of strengthening the socialist system', as the 1936 Constitution was later to put it, it now became a question of administrative discretion in which unauthorised utterances constituted 'counter-revolutionary propaganda' and in which unauthorised associations constituted 'counter-revolutionary organisation'. There is a great practical difference between punishing the unauthorised activities of the Workers Group leader Miasnikov or the writers Siniavsky and Daniel, and the prophylactic terror of Stalin, but the latter was no more against the principles of Soviet communism than the Papal Inquisition was against the principles of medieval Catholicism. If it was required by the interests of the revolution, it was 'correct'. It was wrong only if ill-judged – for instance if it caused *unnecessary* suffering, or even, as Khrushchev was later to claim, harmed the revolution by destroying valuable personnel and paralysing initiative.

The extent and character of intra-bureaucratic opposition has depended, of course, on the way power is held at the top. At periods when no individual has strongly dominated the leadership, as for instance in 1922–29, 1953–57 or since 1964, personal rivalries or divergent views within the leadership might find expression in semi-autonomous and occasionally contradictory decision-making in different sections of the bureaucracy, jurisdictional struggles between them, and manoeuvres to redistribute control over them. In these circumstances, divergences might overflow from the corridors of power to find partial expression in the press or at meetings of the pseudo-democratic institutions of party or government. In contrast to the situation before 1921, however, this could now happen only if and in so far as it was contrived through the bureaucratic machinery. It was the one-ninth of the iceberg that lay above the surface of intra-bureaucratic struggle. Of course the nature of political struggle under a divided leadership is greatly affected by the individuals and issues involved and the contingent circumstances. Obviously a struggle between such giants as Trotsky, Stalin, and Bukharin, articulated in terms of whether a socialist society can be created in Russia, and if so, how, is bound to seem, and indeed to *be*, grander than the struggle between such epigones as Malenkov, Molotov, and Khrushchev, articulated in terms of how much should be invested in the manufacture of consumer goods and whether or not to open up marginal lands to grain cultivation. But the forms and limitations of these struggles and the manner of their resolution remain basically unchanged.

When one individual dominates, political struggle has been concentrated on competition for office, for the ear and goodwill of the boss, for efficient fulfilment of tasks assigned to the apparatus under one's supervision, for the appointment of adherents to positions where they can enhance one's own programmes and reputation at the expense of one's rivals. Again, of course, individuals, issues and circumstances are important. Rudzutak, Ordzhonikidze and Kirov, surrounding the Stalin of 1932, were bound to behave rather differently from Malenkov, Beria and Khrushchev, surrounding the Stalin of 1952, let alone Kirichenko, Kozlov and Brezhnev, surrounding the Khrushchev of 1959. Yet again the rules of the game were basically the same. Obviously, too, individual power is a matter of degree. It took Stalin nearly a decade of personal power to place himself completely beyond the need to consider the views and interests of his entourage, and neither Lenin nor Khrushchev ever achieved that position. Clearly complete personal control over the political police is a vital factor in the boss's relations with his entourage. There is much force in the view of 'socialist legality' as an obstacle to 'the cult of personality', tautological though this statement may be in terms of the ordinary Soviet uses of these euphemisms. In all periods of individual dominance, however, irrespective of how tyrannically or moderately that power is exercised, open opposition to the boss has suffered from that lack of institutional basis that has frustrated political opposition in general ever since 1921. Such opposition could take only clandestine conspiratorial forms, like the unsuccessful conspiracy to replace Stalin by Kirov in 1934, the unsuccessful conspiracy to remove Khrushchev in 1957, and the successful conspiracy to remove him in 1964. And the unsuccessful conspiracies, like all unauthorised political initiatives, were *ipso facto* identifiable as counter-revolutionary crimes, and whether or not they were punished as such became a matter merely of political judgement and expediency.

Security and Modernisation since 1917

A complex dialectical relationship between demands for security and for modernisation has been the mainspring of Soviet political and social history no less than of pre-revolutionary Russia. Though dedicated to totally refashioning society, the Soviet regime has been from the beginning so preoccupied with problems of internal and external security that in practice only those changes that appear to enhance that security have been allowed to go forward.

As in tsarist Russia, the impulse to radical social or political change or to programmes of modernisation has often been closely linked with particular problems of security. The institutions of War Communism owed as much to the striving for maximum mobilisation as to revolutionary Utopianism. The resistance of the *boyars* under Ivan IV and of the *kulaks* under Stalin was aroused by innovations affecting their interests, and the solution to the security problem so caused was in both cases the revolutionary one of their 'liquidation as a class'.[3]

Stalin's forced industrialisation in the 1930s, and all the institutional and social consequences that flowed therefrom, were stimulated by considerations of external security no less than were the revolutionary innovations of Peter the Great. 'To slacken the tempo would mean falling behind', said Stalin in his famous speech to industrial executives in 1931, 'and those who fall behind get beaten.... One feature of the history of old Russia was the continual beatings she suffered for falling behind, for her backwardness.... Do you want our socialist fatherland to be beaten and lose its independence? If you do not want this you must put an end to its backwardness in the shortest possible time and develop genuine Bolshevik tempo in building up its socialist system of economy.'[4]

But if the demands of security have sometimes reinforced or even provoked radical innovation, they have also sometimes been responsible for obstructing or even reversing it. It was largely in the interests of internal order, discipline, and control that the Bolsheviks abandoned War Communism and partially revived capitalism in the 1920s, and that they later threw their support behind Russian nationalism at the expense of 'cosmopolitanism', and behind old-fashioned patterns in family life, education, the arts, etc., at the expense of 'progressivism' and 'modernism'. Security considerations certainly played a part in the early 1930s, in 1953–54, and perhaps too in 1964–65, when elements of peasant enterprise recently under attack were granted a reprieve. It was solely in the interests of security that the campaign against religion was moderated after the outbreak of war in 1941. How many innovations in science (for example, cybernetics) or economic life (for example, Liberman's proposals in 1962) were held up by fear of the unknown consequences of disturbing established dogma or procedure? One is reminded of the many excellent projects of reform which were shelved by successive tsarist governments out of apprehension for the potential disturbance to stability and order.

But it is not only in canalising change that security has interacted with innovation in Soviet Russia in ways reminiscent of the pre-revolutionary past. As we have already noted, the hypertrophy of the state was in both cases the product of the needs of internal order and external defence, and of the will to initiate and control radical change. Once this hypertrophied state was a fact, however, any initiative from below seemed like a bid to diminish it and therefore a threat to security, and the consequent paralysis of spontaneous change meant the constant accumulation of pools of backwardness which only intervention from the summit could then eliminate. As a consequence Soviet Russia, like tsarist Russia, has been macro-revolutionary but micro-conservative. The Moscow metro coexists with the *izba*, moon-probes with the abacus. This phenomenon was first noted by Lenin, one of the acutest observers of the emergent Soviet society. 'Our present way of life', he wrote in 1922, 'combines to a striking degree features of the desperately bold with timidity of thought before the most minor changes.'[5]

A further similarity was the combination of a messianic universalism with a marked ethnocentrism. The credentials of the Soviet regime, as of early tsarism, rested heavily on the claim to incarnate History's (God's) supreme purposes for humanity. Very soon these purposes were being identified with the interests of the Russian state, and the more fortuitous and superficial, as well as the more entrenched and profound, features of Russian life and character were being hallowed by association. Conversely, foreign ways were perceived not only as curious or distasteful, but as coloured with falseness or iniquity. Russians were encouraged to see their country as a bulwark against Western wickedness under Nicholas I no less than under Brezhnev. These official attitudes were superimposed upon ingrained Russian responses, which combined a certain tolerance and willingness to learn from the foreigner with assimilationist assumptions. The results sometimes verged on the absurd: the arch-xenophobe Dostoevsky proclaiming the 'pan-humanity' of the Russians, Khrushchev befriending the Americans and helping himself to their techniques – but all on the assumption that *their* grandchildren would live under *his* social system.

The final parallel we should note between the interaction of national security and national renovation in tsarist and communist Russia is its effect of dividing the élite. In the style of Peter the Great, the Soviet leaders sought to create from the party membership and the new technical intelligentsia an élite trained and dedicated to modernisation. Like their eighteenth century predecessors, however, the Soviet élite, required to serve as bureaucrats in a milieu where every unauthorised action smelt of treason and every unauthorised utterance smelt of heresy, quickly fell into habits of conformism and conservatism, limiting their innovatory efforts to approved channels. There have always been individuals, however, who have internalised the modernising ethos, are thereby more or less alienated from the timid, conservative bureaucracy, and are too disturbed by the country's pools of backwardness to limit their reforming impulse within approved official programmes. These constitute the Soviet counter-élite. The pre-revolutionary counter-élite, though centred in the intelligentsia, had wider ramifications in the educated public (*obshchestvo*), making of the latter in the late tsarist period a *political* force peacefully, though critically, coexisting with the state. Although officially dissolved in a 'new socialist intelligentsia', consisting of the 20 million or so held to be 'engaged in mental work', an intelligentsia defined in the old sense by attitudes rather than by education or employment, placing social, intellectual, or aesthetic values above official relationships, has never wholly disappeared. Moreover, *this* intelligentsia has continued to exert an influence in wider sections of the educated public, making Soviet public opinion (*obshchestvennost*), despite massive efforts to domesticate it to the party, a separate factor to be taken into account by political leaders.

Of course this comparison must be heavily qualified. The vastly improved machinery of control, repression, and indoctrination deployed by the Soviet bureaucratic élite has made organisation and communication far more difficult for the Soviet counter-élite than for their precursors in tsarist times. The role of illegal groups and publications, such as existed throughout the nineteenth century, has been insignificant since the 1920s, and of course there has been nothing resembling the open opposition parties and newspapers of 1905–17. Yet the importance of the counter-élite should not be identified with *organised* opposition. It could indeed be argued that its greatest influence in tsarist Russia was exerted through amorphous though pervasive personal channels, and through esoteric content and implied values contained in permitted publications. Indeed, the downfall of tsarism itself was not the work of any organisation of the counter-élite, though its influence over many decades, both in preparing 'society' and the 'masses' for the possibility of change, and in undermining the assurance of the bureaucracy, was clearly an essential factor. The unorganised character of the Soviet counter-élite, then, is no measure of its potential influence. Though minimal at the height of Stalin's dictatorship, this influence has been a continuing factor in Soviet political life. It was an important (though certainly not decisive) ingredient in the context of attitudes and ideas in which the leadership struggles of the 1920s were fought. Since 1953, the reaction against Stalinism has significantly revived its influence.

For that curious ambivalence of the political leadership towards the counter-élite which we observed under tsarism has been reactivated in post-Stalin Russia by attempts to overcome areas of backwardness in Soviet life and to renovate obsolescent processes and institutions. Insofar as existing patterns are seen by the leadership as effective to their ends, the counter-élite, with their suggestions and criticisms, are merely trouble-makers. But insofar as such patterns are seen as *ineffective* the counter-élite, enjoying by bureaucratic default a monopoly of innovatory zeal and creativity, must serve as a source of ideas. Moreover, as the bureaucratic élite, set in conformist postures and upset by the conversion of old heresies into new dogma, proves resistant to decreed change, and other leaders seek to capitalise on this resistance, the innovating leader is driven to court the counter-élite and to throw its support into the balance. A clear illustration of the ambivalent relationship between the innovating leader and the counter-élite can be found in Khrushchev's dealings with Soviet scientists, economists, and artists.

Borkenau's characterisation of the old intelligentsia as those members of Russian society who had fallen under the spell of European civilisation, though one-sided, contains a truth that retains its importance today. In post-Stalin Russia, the problem of the counter-élite is in large part the problem of Western influence. All bursts of modernisation in Russia since Peter the Great have been prompted, directly or indirectly, by the challenge of the technologically advanced West, and it is the West, therefore, that has provided the standards and models of modernisation. But it is as true in the 1950s and 1960s as it was in the eighteenth century that a generation cannot be brought up to admire and emulate foreign technique without some of its number coming to admire and emulate other aspects of the culture that has produced it. You cannot import foreign technical ideas wholesale without risking some ideological contraband. Thus the *petit maître* of the 1750s and the dandy of the 1820s are matched by the *stiliaga* of the 1950s and the beatlomane of the 1960s, while Catherine's young guard officers with their Voltaire are matched by Brezhnev's economics graduates with their Rostow. For most Russians, Western contraband has always served simply as titillating exotica to be discarded when inconvenient; wherever the attitudes of the counter-élite are found, however, it serves as a constant stimulus to dissatisfaction and source of ideas for change. It is this Westernising posture of the counter-élite, confronted by the ethnocentric–universalist posture of the bureaucratic élite, today no less than a century ago, that explains the depth and sharpness of their mutual antagonism. It is hard to see in this a threat to the political or social order: the bureaucracy is well in control and likely to stay so. But it is a built-in weakness, distorting the formation of rational solutions of internal and foreign problems.

The Future

Social changes in the Soviet Union during the coming decade could affect the patterns not just of the past half-century, but of the past half-millennium. For that concentration of social initiative at the apex of a hypertrophied state, which has lasted since Muscovite times, now hangs in the balance.

The existing socio-political order in Russia has amply demonstrated its efficacy for macro-innovation. It has proved the possibility of a non-capitalist method of industrialisation, provided the material and organisational basis to defeat the Nazi invasion, mounted one of the world's two major space programmes, and attained world standards in selected areas of production and intellectual life. These are impressive achievements by any standards, and a legitimate object of Soviet pride.

But Soviet society has now entered the phase when it is micro-innovation, not macro-innovation, that is pressingly required. Within the framework of an advanced industrial order there remain vast swamps of backwardness, inefficiency, and *nekulturnost'*. Crash programmes and administrative reorganisations have demonstrated, most recently in Khrushchev's repeated attempts to overcome the defects of industry and agriculture, their complete inadequacy to deal with problems on this level. But these problems *must* be dealt with, if the claims of the Soviet regime to have established a higher social order, and the sacrifices involved in so doing, are to be vindicated before their own people and the world. And with increased cultural contacts since 1953 (necessary to avoid isolation from revolutionary technological developments abroad) enough people, both in Russia and the West, *do know* that the quality of Soviet life still compares abominably in so many respects. This question has acquired increasing urgency as the nuclear stalemate and the reaction from Chinese 'bast-shoes communism' have led Soviet politicians and ideologists to concentrate more and more on the provision of a better life, which all peoples will insist on emulating, as the goal of their international mission.

It seems abundantly clear that this goal cannot be reached unless Soviet leaders are prepared to allow the command hierarchy to be supplemented or supplanted by other methods of structuring social action in large areas of national life. There is an enormous scope for self-regulating social mechanisms generating their own immediate tasks in terms of broad basic goals (which may be politically determined or influenced), and with built-in feedback to keep them efficient and on the right path. Such mechanisms already predominate in one area, namely science. What are the prospects for their extension to others, especially the economy?

On the ideological level, the obstacles seem formidable, but not necessarily decisive. On the face of it, the commitment to communism as a stateless society would appear to *favour* self-regulatory mechanisms. However, official discussion and pronouncements over recent years on the transition to communism and the nature of communist society have tended to habituate Soviet people to the indefinite perpetuation of the command hierarchy as the normal framework of social action. True, people will receive from society 'according to their needs' and 'self-administration' is to replace government by paid officials. But the determination of needs will not be left to the whim of the individual, and self-administration will be channelled through a plethora of nationally coordinated public organisations. Communism, in fact, will be a superlatively organised, planned, and disciplined society. Certainly, people will be so conditioned to conform their personal desires and impulses to the needs of society that no special apparatus of repression will be needed, but there will always be individuals who refuse to conform, and society must preserve the right, and the means, of compelling them. For a very long time to come, the party will need to retain and indeed to increase its supervising and coordinating role, even under communism.

Meanwhile we have the example of those many voluntary organisations – from street committees and sanitary brigades to voluntary militia and comradely courts – which have come to supplement official institutions in the performance of certain social functions, and which are held to manifest, in embryo, the outlines of the future communist society. These have so far shown no signs of developing action patterns enabling them to function other than as auxiliaries of the great command hierarchies of party, government and trade unions; far from their signifying a narrowing of the coercive order (which we have identified as the state) they have simply rendered its action more pervasive and arbitrary.

Existing doctrine on communist society, then, will need to be substantially revised if a large expansion of self-regulating mechanisms of social action is to become possible in the next few years. The domination of the Soviet ideological establishment by old party hands, unaccustomed to the idea of pursuing social objectives except through programmes administered by command hierarchies, will make this revision difficult. Already, however, theoreticians grappling with the problem of accommodating recent intellectual and social developments – particularly cybernetics and the market elements now present in the Soviet and other communist economies – have demonstrated the possibility of a conceptual framework within which such a revision could occur.[6] Moreover, it would not be surprising if maturer consideration did not reveal much of the theorising about communism over the past decade to have been coloured by that hastiness, superficiality and subjectivity which are now recognised as characteristic of the Khrushchev era.

Until recently, the introduction of self-regulating (market) processes in the economy has been unthinkable simply because the market was identified with capitalism. Hence, of course, the great importance of Yugoslavia's demonstration of the possibility (and efficacy) of a *socialist* market; and the fact that this was pioneered *not* in the West, but in what might be regarded as in some degree an extension of Russia's historical mission, greatly reduces the ideological and psychological obstacles to accepting its relevance for the USSR. Moreover, as market elements spread rapidly in other east European economies, there will be political advantages for the Soviet Union, given the present state of communist international relations, in keeping pace with and if possible giving a lead to this process.[7]

A more fundamental obstacle than specific ideological tenets to the growth of self-regulating mechanisms in Soviet society is that preference for 'consciousness' to 'spontaneity' which is so central to Leninism and which strikes so many answering chords in Russian political culture. An assumption that still runs through nearly all political discussion in the Soviet Union is that there is a 'correct' solution to all problems, which may be perceived by those combining practical experience with correct theory, who furthermore have an obligation to guide others in the application of this correct solution and prevent them from erring. And there is a second assumption – which remains widespread despite decades of seeking to harness individual material incentives to plan fulfilment – that, unless closely guided and controlled by those equipped with correct theory, effort directed towards immediate individual or group ends will tend towards social chaos and defeat the larger ends of society.

This largely accounts for the fact that mathematical techniques making for improved economic planning and administration have been taken up so wholeheartedly, and 'economic methods' (that is, market-oriented techniques) so half-heartedly, in recent years; and why the 1965 economic reform, while cautiously increasing the scope of 'economic methods' of coordinating economical effort, placed its main emphasis on a counter-revolution in economic *administration* restoring the highly centralised system evolved under Stalin. On the other hand, one might argue that since the question of economic methods poses so directly the issue of consciousness versus spontaneity, the recognition of their propriety in principle marks a revolutionary step forward in Russian social thinking.

The attachment of Soviet communists to 'consciousness' has always derived much strength from its identification with science. Its application in practice, however, has usually shown greater affinities with religious than with scientific ways of thinking. It has tended to produce solutions made in the light of irrelevant external considerations, while the relevant facts are shunned, are unknown, or unknowable. Thus much of the 'consciousness' in Soviet life has always been 'false consciousness'. With the rapid extension of *genuinely* scientific habits of thought, however, 'false consciousness' is bound to be eroded. In the Soviet Union today, it is now recognised that to impose 'truths' and guidelines deduced from Marxist–Leninist theory on the work of scientists is to condemn them to sterility, that those immediately involved must feel free to make choices that may turn out to be wrong, and that scientific truth can be approached only by the constant critical testing of currently accepted theory. The Soviet Union will have a right to regard itself as a truly scientific society when the same is acknowledged to apply to economic activity, the social sciences, and other areas of life. Here, of course, we are in the realm of long-term trends, but science *is* the most prestigious activity in the Soviet Union today, it *must* proceed largely by self-regulating processes, and its likely influence on the patterns of social action in the Soviet Union therefore seems clear.

The most formidable potential obstacle to the spread of self-regulating mechanisms in Soviet society, however, is the implications this would have for the role of the party. Since 1919 the party apparatus has reserved for itself responsibility for major decisions arising in the day-to-day activities of all social institutions and organisations, and exercised constant supervision over these activities, probing, calling to account, and demanding corrections. Though this has had certain unfortunate consequences for the party, there was clearly much to be said for maintaining some such machinery of overall supervision and coordination so long as the regime was seeking to run the whole range of social activities through a system of command hierarchies. Such constant external intervention, however, is of course deadly to the proper functioning of any self-regulating mechanism – and this applies no less in the arts and the economy than in science – which presupposes autonomously-interacting participants orienting their decisions systematically and unequivocally towards the 'market'. It is obviously not enough that the party exercise its day-to-day supervising and controlling function without resorting to 'petty tutelage' and 'supplanting' of managements, government officials, etc. – which it has been constantly but vainly enjoined to do ever since 1921. If the CPSU is to have a chance of achieving its world mission, self-regulating patterns of social action will have to be given the same scope in the economy and elsewhere as already in the natural sciences, and this means that the party must be prepared to confine itself to defining the overall scale and direction of effort, abstaining from *any* attempt to exercise day-to-day supervision and control endowed with 'the force of law'. It means, in other words, a reversal of that process of integration with the state that began in

1919. The party would remain master of the state, by continuing to determine the main lines of policy and to monopolise key posts, but would abdicate its responsibility for controlling the detailed execution of policy. This could lead to a renaissance of the political, as distinct from the administrative, role of the party; detached from bureaucratic preoccupations, it could maintain a constant critical and objective scrutiny of social developments, engage in creative forward thinking, canvass and appraise policy alternatives, explore theoretical issues free of the tyranny of political pragmatism, and apply itself more effectively to the political and ideological education of the public. Any trend to disengage the party from the state, however, would undoubtedly encounter resistance from members of the party apparatus, who would see in it a threat to their status, influence, and career prospects. This would therefore demand of the political leadership great clarity and unity of purpose, firmness and tact, in reallotting priorities and jurisdictions and redeploying personnel. One need scarcely mention the possible effects of power considerations in the leadership, in facilitating, obstructing, or distorting such changes.

Space has permitted mention of only a few of the major questions relating to the possible growth of self-regulating mechanisms in Soviet society. In particular, I have not discussed the likely effects of such developments on what were referred to earlier as the pseudo-democratic institutions of the party and the state. Enough has been said, however, to indicate their revolutionary implications for that complex dialectical tangle between the hypertrophied state and its concern for security and for innovation, which has been advanced here as basic to Russian politics since Muscovite times. These developments would at last begin to unravel the tangle, large areas of social life would be freed from subjection to the coercive order (the state), a constant self-generating renovation would render redundant the process of innovation-by-massive-but-delayed-response, the split within the Soviet élite would be healed, and relations with the West, freed of that love-hate involvement resulting from previous patterns of modernisation, would become more normal.

Notes and References

1   Cf. G.L. Yaney, 'Law, Society and the Domestic Regime in Russia in Historical Perspective', *American Political Science Review*, June

1965. Mr Yaney's paper was largely responsible for stimulating the train of thought that has issued in the present article.

2 'What are we to do with Rabkrin?', *Sochineniya*, vol.45, p.444.

3 It seems possible, as has recently been argued, that the mass collectivisation of 1929–30 was not premeditated by Stalin, that he believed his existing administrative machinery strong enough even without collectivisation to extract the surplus from the peasantry necessary to support the Five-Year Plan, and that the massive effort to reestablish order when peasant resistance proved more formidable than was expected both made possible the mass formation of *kolkhozes* and required this as ideological cover. See O.A. Narkiewicz, 'Stalin, War Communism and Collectivization', *Soviet Studies*, July 1966. In much the same way, serfdom was not premeditated as an essential support for the tsar's new service nobility, but the unwillingness of the peasants to serve the new nobility prompted Ivan IV and his successors to revoke the peasants' 'right of departure' in the octave of St George's Day, thus creating the essential elements of serfdom. In both cases, when obstacles were encountered to changes initiated by the state, the state did not shrink from even more revolutionary changes in order to impose its innovations.

4 Stalin, *Problems of Leninism*, (Moscow), 1945, pp.355–56. Stalin was later to treat the defeat of Nazism as a vindication of his imposed socialism (in his 1946 election speech) in much the same way as Peter, and later historians, saw his final victory over the Swedes at Tilsit as the crowning achievement of his innovatory zeal.

5 Lenin, *Sochineniya*, vol.45, p.400.

6 See especially Iu. Levada, 'Kiberneticheskie metody i sotsiologiia', *Kommunist*, no.14 (1965).

7 The importance of the experience of negotiation and compromise in communist international relations, particularly among the Comecon countries, in habituating the Soviet leaders to decision-making other than by command hierarchy, is discussed in my paper 'The Deconcentration of Power in the USSR, 1953–1964', in J.D.B. Miller and T.H. Rigby, eds., *The Disintegrating Monolith: Pluralist Trends in World Communism*, (ANU, Canberra), 1965.

9 Gorbachev and the Crisis of Mono-organisational Socialism

That the Soviet system is changing, and changing more or less radically, nobody can now seriously doubt. But is it changing into a *different* system? At the dawn of the 1990s it seems very probable but we still cannot say for sure. We can, however, chart the main directions and extent of change, and perceive the contours of the most likely possible outcomes. The best starting point is the preliminary question: why should Gorbachev and his Politburo colleagues, the quintessential products, operators, beneficiaries and guardians of the Soviet system of mono-organisational socialism, have taken it on themselves to change it?

The Slide into Crisis

When in 1985 the new General Secretary Mikhail Gorbachev stated that the USSR was in a 'pre-crisis situation' Soviet public communications were as yet little touched by the emergent policy of *glasnost'* (openness) and still dominated by the traditional monotone dogmatism, half-truths and veiled hints. His words, therefore, left no doubt that the alarm bells were being struck, that the leadership had decided that things were going profoundly wrong, and that they even perceived a threat to the very existence of Soviet society.

As to what was going wrong, and how, there is now fairly general agreement, and it will suffice to outline it here briefly. Up to the early 1970s, although the Soviet Union continued in important respects to lag well behind the most advanced capitalist democracies, its leaders still had some grounds for believing their system would ultimately prove superior. Their economic growth rate remained relatively high, the technological gap still appeared to be narrowing, and the system seemed capable of satisfying simultaneously the three basic goals of matching the West militarily, steadily raising mass living standards, and continuing a fairly rapid expansion of the USSR's industrial, energy and other resource base. Meanwhile the Western economies, beginning with the 'first oil shock' of 1973, seemed in deep trouble, thus giving a new dimension to the 'legitimacy crisis' that began in the 1960s, and Western resolve and confidence were further shaken by the American defeat in Vietnam. Against this background, the Brezhnev regime's strategy of 'steady as she goes' seems unsurprising and hardly irrational. Khrushchev's structural innovations, notably the regional councils of national economy (*sovnarkhozy*) and the separate regional party committees for industry and agriculture, were scrapped. The public airing of proposals for more radical reforms, especially those looking to decentralisation and the greater use of market mechanisms, ceased. The 1965 reorganisation of the economic administration amounted in practice to a restoration of the pre-Khrushchev system inherited from Stalin, its modest decentralising provisions remaining a dead letter. Ideological conformity was reinforced and a long and bitter struggle ensued between the authorities and those encouraged by the changes of the Khrushchev era to seek greater freedom, democracy and protection of rights, a struggle which the authorities seemed to have virtually won by the end of the 1970s. On the other hand, the 'normal' citizen who displayed the requisite public conformity enjoyed considerable *de facto* toleration of his or her peccadilloes, and this matched a general ethos of 'don't rock the boat' and 'something for everyone' in the formulation and implementation of public policies.

If the general confidence of the Brezhnev regime in the virtues of their system fostered conservatism at home, it encouraged a cautiously forward policy abroad: maintaining discipline in the Soviet bloc (Czechoslovakia 1968 and the 'Brezhnev doctrine'); seeking reduction of inter-bloc tensions while driving for parity (some would argue superiority) in all major components of the East-West military balance; and extending Soviet influence in a whole series of new quasi-communist regimes in Third World countries (Ethiopia, Angola, Nicaragua, Afghanistan, and so on.).

Well before Brezhnev's death in 1982, however, it was becoming apparent that the 'system confidence' underpinning Soviet domestic and foreign policies was ill-grounded. The slow decline in the economic growth rate accelerated during the 1970s and, by the early 1980s, growth had virtually ceased, it now being abundantly clear, moreover, that this was not due to temporary, conjunctural factors like a capitalist recession. Although it was partly attributable to the exhaustion of fresh supplies of cheap labour and energy and to the obsolescence of much of the country's industrial and infrastructural capital stock, underlying this was something more alarming: the bureaucratic command economy, effective though it had been in the earlier stages of modernisation, and still remained so in selected high priority areas such as defence and the space program, was proving increasingly inefficient as the economy grew in size and complexity. And meanwhile the Western capitalist economies, instead of being plunged into terminal decline by the troubles of the mid 1970s, had been jolted into a new phase of revolutionary technological change. The 'technology gap', after narrowing for decades, was widening again at a startling rate, especially in the vital area of communication technology. The situation in agriculture was scarcely more encouraging. The party-controlled collective and state farms, which had once served the regime well in extracting cheap food from the peasantry to feed the growing industrial labour force, were now proving quite incapable of meeting the increasing food needs of the population, and the Soviet leadership began resorting to large scale food imports from capitalist countries in order to alleviate mass dissatisfaction.

Meanwhile deteriorating economic performance was accompanied by a range of deepening social and moral pathologies: corruption was becoming ever more widespread and blatant, reaching even into Brezhnev's family circle; there was an alarming growth of alcoholism and crime; the mortality rate among infants and working-aged men rose markedly; and outward conformity scarcely concealed the spread of cynicism regarding official dogmas and values.

The Soviet gerontocracy of the early 1980s was initially unable to confront these problems, and even went out of their way to conceal the evidence of their existence. Yuri Andropov, during his brief general secretaryship (November 1982–February 1984), began tentatively to acknowledge them, and to respond with a campaign for discipline and order, but his successor Konstantin Chernenko revived the smug complacency prevailing under his late patron Brezhnev. Meanwhile the drift into crisis continued, with the deepening economic and social decline assuming a new and menacing aspect in the light of international developments. The 'third industrial revolution' continued apace in the West, the NATO alliance had mustered the resolution and political support (perhaps contrary to Soviet hopes) to match Brezhnev's military build-up, while the Soviet army was bogged down in Afghanistan and the Soviet forward policy in the Third World was in tatters. On top of all this, President Reagan's Strategic Defence Initiative (SDI) faced the Soviet Union with the prospect of a new challenge which it could prove economically and technologically incapable of meeting.

The crisis which the Soviet socio-political order entered in the 1980s reflects a pattern in Russian historical development whose roots, as we saw in Chapter 8, can be traced back to Muscovite times. Its very existence threatened by a combination of external enemies, internal disorder, and economic and technological backwardness, Russia throws up a new absolute ruler who carries out a political, social, economic and cultural revolution from above, which provides effective new supports for external defence, domestic consolidation and order, and forced-pace modernisation. But the very structures and attitudes that make this possible also erect obstacles to spontaneous, self-generating evolutionary development and to fruitful external influences, thus inducing a further slide into relative backwardness, which ultimately begins to imperil the essential functions and rationale of these very structures and attitudes, namely the maintenance of external security and internal peace. This evokes a new absolutism, and the cycle is repeated.

Lenin's 'proletarian dictatorship' had succeeded in carrying through a social transformation of unprecedented scope and depth while restoring and raising to new heights the integrity, security and standing of the Russian state. In the process it congealed into a historically new socio-political order, mono-organisational socialism, an order which within a half century had spread to more than a dozen countries embracing a third of the world's population. By this time, however, the conflict between security and progress built into mono-organisational socialism was already manifest, and was entering a phase in which the hindrance of progress was undermining the very basis of security itself. Some awareness of this was apparent at the end of the Khrushchev era, and was provoking, as we have seen, ideas of more or less radical change in the existing order. The fact that substantial actual change was delayed for a further quarter century was a measure both of the conservatism of the Soviet political élite, and of the inertia built into the foundations of mono-organisational socialism.

A New Revolution from Above?

When on Chernenko's death in March 1985 the Politburo chose their youngest and most vigorous member as General Secretary, they thereby displayed a belated readiness to break with the ethos of 'steady as she goes' and, one is tempted to add, to acquiesce in such more or less radical measures as were needed in order to halt the slide into crisis. One should not overstate the point. Alternatives to Mikhail Gorbachev were available but they were relatively unattractive. It was he, moreover, who had run the Central Committee Secretariat under Chernenko and chaired the Politburo's meetings during the latter's prolonged illness, performing 'brilliantly' in this role, according to Andrei Gromyko, who nominated him as General Secretary on behalf of the Politburo.[1] And this had come as the culmination of long years of exemplary service in the standard leadership roles of regional first secretary and Central Committee secretary. All this must have been reassuring to his predominantly conservative Politburo colleagues, but Gorbachev had also revealed himself as a genuine reformer, most clearly and vigorously in a speech delivered at an ideological conference in the Central Committee in December 1984. In this speech, he urged the need, *inter alia*, for real *glasnost'* in public communications and for a *perestroika* (restructuring) of the economic system, the latter to involve the development of 'commodity–money relations' (that is, market mechanisms).[2] The ruling oligarchy, then, were duly warned, and they would scarcely have accepted him as General Secretary had the majority been unwilling to go along with a policy approach radically at variance with that which had prevailed over the previous two decades. To be sure, 'going along' probably entailed attitudes ranging from warm approval to anxious and qualified acquiescence. Nor had Gorbachev's record given reason for doubt that he would act otherwise than with caution and deliberation, let alone place in jeopardy the foundations of the socio-political order.

For nearly two years such expectations seemed thoroughly justified by the actual measures, social, economic and political, initiated by the General Secretary. First in order of impact was a drive for order and discipline, which picked up and pursued with far greater intensity a cluster of campaigns initiated by Andropov and quietly shelved under Chernenko: campaigns against corruption, which led to the arrest of many high officials and the dismissal of thousands of police (militia) officers; against alcohol abuse, involving both harsher penalties for public drunkenness and restrictions on production and retail outlets; and against slacking and slapdash performance in the workplace (thus violating the tacit social compact of the Brezhnev era, 'you pretend to pay us, and we pretend to work'). Prominent among the economic measures was a drive for acceleration (*uskorenie*) of the growth in output and efficiency, and increased capital investment, especially in the machine-building industry. While scholars were now licensed to explore ideas of more radical, market-oriented reform, actual proposals aired in authoritative contexts, including the Twenty-seventh CPSU Congress in February 1986, amounted to little more than administrative devolution and tying rewards more strictly to performance. True, a law authorising individual and family labour activity was adopted in November 1986, but this was designed essentially to legitimate (and tax) segments of the entrenched shadow economy, and it was preceded by a harsh measure against unearned income and overshadowed by the establishment of a new state quality control agency (*Gospriyomka*), whose rejection of much sub-standard production was to arouse widespread resentment among the industrial workforce and management.

In the political sphere there were considerable changes of personnel, both at the centre and in the provinces,[3] but the structures and the way they operated remained almost wholly unaltered. Furthermore, traditional controls over the media, the arts and intellectual life generally remained in place, albeit with some loosening of the reins in the course of 1986, comparable with what was experienced in certain phases of the Khrushchev period. There was a gradual increase in *glasnost'*, chiefly in the way of reporting negative events (natural disasters, train and plane crashes, public disturbances, and so on) and negative conditions (such as crime, drug-addiction, increased morbidity) as well as revelations about the Soviet past, especially under Stalin. But there had certainly been no breakthrough to freedom of information, or of public communication and expression.

The initial phase of Gorbachev's primacy, which lasted for nearly two years, is therefore best characterised as one of *revitalising* the mono-organisational system. Then, in 1987 there was a dramatic shift towards *changing* that system. It is still unclear whether Gorbachev had intended this all along but needed first to substantially consolidate his personal power and authority, or whether it was the blocking of his efforts at economic reform by entrenched party and government bureaucrats that convinced him he would have to change the way the political system operated, if he was ever to overcome their resistance. Both explanations may be partly true, allied perhaps with the influence of reform-minded officials, scholars and advisors.[4] In any case, from the middle of 1986 he began publicly to advocate the restructuring of the political system, and specifically of the party, as an essential prerequisite for social and economic progress,[5] and in January 1987, at a contentious (hence thrice postponed) plenum of the Central Committee he moved from words to action. His report envisaged wide-ranging democratisation of all political structures, and specifically genuine, contested elections, including those within the party itself.[6] It was now evident that the area of policy consensus within the leadership had narrowed, that a polarisation of reform-oriented and conservative forces both in the ruling oligarchy and broader sections of the élite was in train, and that radical reform measures could not yet command a majority either within the Politburo or the full Central Committee, despite a number of leadership changes in favour of Gorbachev's supporters. An immediate illustration of this was that certain of Gorbachev's proposals, including the key one of contested elections of party officials, were omitted from the Central Committee resolution. In such situations it is not only the strength of one's supporters in decision-making bodies that matters, but also control of the executive machinery, and in this instance the fact that the Central Committee department responsible for party personnel and organisational matters was now in the hands of Gorbachev's ally G.P. Razumovsky may help to account for the fact that contested party elections actually began to be introduced at the next round of local conferences later in the year.[7] Thus, while radical measures could be, and frequently were, weakened or even brought to nothing in the process of implementation, the reverse could also occur. Experience over the next few years was to show that the former was more likely to happen in the case of economic reforms, while the latter was more likely with political reforms.

The Turn to Freedom and Democracy

It is impossible in the space of a single chapter to trace in detail the events and measures which effected such deep changes in Soviet society between 1987 and 1989, but it is important to attempt some overview and to identify the forces and processes involved. It is widely held that the central element in Gorbachev's strategy was to unleash forces for reform within the political community, and especially among the intelligentsia, and to use these to overcome the inertia of the official apparatuses (for historical parallels, see pp.191 and 204). The General Secretary revealed his hand as early as June

1986, when he convened a group of leading writers and appealed for their support in reforming society against the resistance of 'the managerial stratum' in the ministries and party apparatus, 'which does not want to give up its privileges'.[8] The strategy had three main components: radically widening the freedom of public expression; easing the entrenched *de facto* prohibition of unofficial association; and investing the long empty democratic forms of party and state with genuine democratic content, specifically with respect to electoral choice and public policy debate. While there were many within both the Soviet public and the Western sovietological community who initially discounted these measures as either cosmetic in intent or doomed to ineffectiveness by the power of the apparatus, it was generally agreed by 1989 that they had effected a major transformation in the character of Soviet public life.

The central factor in the freeing of public expression was of course the sharp diminution in bureaucratic control and direction of the mass circulation and specialised press, publishing houses, radio, television, theatre, cinema and classroom, which had been exercised through party propaganda department officials, agencies of the Ministry of Culture, the *nomenklatura* system of personnel selection, the workplace party committees, the Komsomol, the state censorship network (*Glavlit*), the KGB, and the 'creative' unions (of writers, cinema workers, and the like), each disposing of its own battery of privileges to confer and sanctions to impose. While the diminution of bureaucratic control and direction did not mean their total abrogation,[9] by the beginning of the 1990s the Soviet Union enjoyed a relatively high level of freedom of expression in public situations, both institutionalised and informal, a major ingredient of which was relative freedom *from* enforced cant and mendacity. This freedom of expression, new to the experience of the overwhelming majority of Soviet people, brought a profound change in the amount and quality of information and ideas available to them about their own country, its history and its present condition, and about the outside world. Culture in all its manifestations – the arts, entertainment, journalism and scholarship – was largely unshackled.[10]

The character and dynamics of this 'cultural revolution' are sometimes obscured by simplistic images of Soviet 'totalitarianism'. In fact its roots go right back to 1953, when the powers and resources of the political police were sharply reduced in the wake of Stalin's death. Denied the licence to practise prophylactic arrests and arbitrary punishments on a large scale, they concentrated on maintaining their saturation surveillance capacities while limiting arrests to cases where convictions could be secured by politically guided courts under the generously worded 'state crimes' provisions of the criminal code. This had the consequence of leaving a substantial 'private' sphere within which citizens could pursue with relative impunity a range of activities unwelcome to the authorities: from rock music to avant-garde art and from passing on uncensored manuscripts to listening to Western radio broadcasts. There thus emerged under Khrushchev, and flourished under Brezhnev, a 'second' or 'shadow culture' to match the 'shadow economy' and 'shadow polity' discussed in earlier chapters. As in the latter cases, the boundaries of this shadow culture were variably set, patrolled and enforced in line with changing regime priorities, and those men and women, numbering for most of this period in their thousands, who transgressed these boundaries out of uncompromising commitment, miscalculation or ill-luck, were despatched to labour camps or other forms of detention.

Tens of millions of Soviet citizens participated, in one way or another, in this shadow culture, and their participation was characteristically savoured not in isolation but in the company of family members and close friends. It has been said of the three decades that separated the death of Stalin from the death of Brezhnev that the Soviet people then acquired 'not freedom of speech, but freedom of talk', or alternatively 'freedom of speech in one kitchen'. There was a literal as well as a metaphorical truth to the latter phrase, as it was indeed during this period that the bulk of the urban population gained the privacy that came from moving from 'communal' to one-family apartments. Many people thus became accustomed not only to enjoying other sources of information, ideas and opinions alongside the official ones, but also to communicating these within trusted circles of their relations and intimates. It was indeed a mighty leap from this private *glasnost'* to the public *glasnost'* of the late 1980s, but without the former as a jumping-off point that leap would have been out of the question.

The sharply enhanced freedom of association under Gorbachev has a similar prehistory. One important background factor was the ubiquitous 'informal organisation' which, as we have repeatedly stressed in this book, has been a basic component of the mono-organisational system since its origins, manifesting itself, *inter alia*, in the plethora of local cliques and patronage groupings which cut across formal structural boundaries and operate according to unofficial norms and procedures supplementing and, in some cases measure subverting the official ones. An 'informal organisation' exists, of course, in all large-scale organisational structures. Its extraordinary importance in the Soviet mono-organisational system is explained, we have argued, by the latter's vast, societal-wide ramifications and by the absence of legitimate unofficial structures through which citizens can pursue their personal and group interests and concerns, such associations as purport to serve these purposes having long since been converted into bureaucratic organisations directed by the Communist Party. It would be mistaken, however, to think that no unofficial groupings exist under mono-organisational socialism other than those cliques and clienteles spawned by, and symbiotic with, the formal bureaucratic structures. Even at the height of Stalin's terroristic dictatorship the image of Soviet society as one of totally atomised individuals facing an all-powerful apparatus was misleadingly simplistic. It is true that nearly all forms of association for non-official purposes were effectively suppressed, and that (as a corollary) by far the largest and most ramified sphere of non-official association was the criminal world.[11] But kinship and friendship solidarities survived the years of terror, albeit scarred and tattered, and, in the post-Stalin generation, they gathered the requisite strength to serve as the chief bearers of that 'shadow culture' referred to above.

Now, however, a new factor emerged, the 'dissident movement', a congeries of informal circles dedicated to the pursuit of officially neglected or suppressed interests and causes. Such circles were made possible by the post-Stalin curbs on the powers of the political police, but cast in a posture of dissent and opposition by the hostility of the authorities, and forced by the denial of legal avenues to employ methods which made them vulnerable to police harassment and arrest. Although the ranks of active dissenters probably never exceeded a few thousand, there were perhaps hundreds of thousands of citizens, especially among the professional strata, including members of élite families, who were more or less directly influenced by them, and many millions of others who learnt of their ideas and activities, often with interest and sympathy, from Western radio broadcasts.[12]

In the first stages of Gorbachev's general secretaryship, there was little change in the official treatment of dissidents, and new arrests continued to swell the ranks of those languishing in camps and prisons for their over-zealous advocacy of human rights, ethnic, religious or other causes. As in the case of the 'shadow culture', it was in 1986 that a new approach emerged, to be dramatically launched by Gorbachev's telephone call to Academician Sakharov in his Gorki exile, inviting him to return to active public life in Moscow. Hundreds of 'prisoners of conscience' were released from detention, and the kinds of non-violent activities for which most had been sentenced ceased to attract punishment. Unofficial clubs and associations for the pursuit of shared interests and concerns, treated since the 1920s as subversive of the established order, now began to be praised as a positive factor in the cause of *glasnost'* and *perestroika*.

Apart from political dissidents, a far larger category of what may be called 'behavioural non-conformists' also benefited from this turn to relative tolerance of unofficial association. These were mostly student and working youth, amongst whom the first experiments in self-organised activities outside the stultifying structures of the Komsomol, trade union and factory club go back to the Khrushchev years, when a Soviet non-conformist youth culture emerged, largely imitative, in its dress, music, dances and other fads, of the youth culture of the West. The repressive conservatism of the mid 1960s to mid 1980s, which drove political non-conformity into open opposition, pushed some of this youthful behavioural conformity into anti-social, sometimes violent channels, epitomised by the gangs of swastika-wearing Nazis. With the new tolerance after 1986 these pathological strands of the youth-culture lost in salience.[13]

The years 1987 and 1988 saw a vast proliferation of unofficial 'clubs', 'associations', 'funds' and so on of all kinds, popularly labelled 'the informals' (*neformaly*). The term was misleading insofar as alongside the numerous spontaneous, unstructured and often ephemeral groups, there were others that were quick to acquire more or less formal structures and procedures. They remained 'informal', however, in the important sense that they stood outside the structures of the mono-organisational system, and were therefore, in the eyes of many people, deserving of a qualified tolerance at best.[14] Already by the end of 1987 there were said to be over 30,000 such unofficial groups[15] and by early 1989 their number had doubled to 60,000.[16] Meanwhile a public opinion poll indicated that some 50 per cent of Soviet young people were members of one or more such groups.[17] Precise breakdowns are unavailable, but an analysis of some 2,000 unofficial groups identified in Moscow showed that about three quarters of them were oriented towards leisure activities, while the remaining 500 or so consisted of 'organisations most varied in form which strive to some degree or other to influence the domestic or foreign policy of the state'.[18]

It was this latter category of unofficial organisations that embodied the breakthrough to relative freedom of association made possible by Gorbachev's policies. By 1989 the authorities were allowing some thousands of organised groups spread throughout the USSR to engage in active criticism of aspects of the Soviet social and political order and to agitate and work for changes. While younger people predominated, all age groups were represented. The leading members, mostly in their twenties or thirties, but including some veteran dissenters of the Brezhnev era, tended to be academics drawn from the humanities and social sciences. Attempts by the authorities in 1987–88 to 'co-opt' and control them through the Komsomol and other official organisations proved a dismal failure. The causes to which they were dedicated included civil rights and freedoms, democratic reform, protecting the natural environment and cultural heritage, health, housing and other social issues, nationality interests and religious freedom. Although their rights to publish were for the most part dubious at best, many of them gained access to printing facilities of one kind or another to produce their leaflets, news-sheets and pamphlets. *Samizdat* was now thus substantially tolerated, and practised widely. Likewise, unofficial public gatherings, processions and demonstrations, harshly suppressed rarities up to 1986, now became commonplace, although subject to new local regulations hastily adopted in 1988, which provided for stiff fines or imprisonment.

Freedom of association, like freedom of expression, was far from absolute. Some unofficial organisations, such as the anti-communist Democratic Union, were harassed by the KGB. Some meetings and demonstrations were dispersed by the militia. Some groups had their printing facilities confiscated. The sufferers were for the most part radical liberal–democratic critics of the Soviet system who threatened to acquire substantial influence. Nor were the newly tolerated unofficial groups necessarily democratic and progressive. Conservatives and chauvinists quickly learned to exploit the new-won freedom of association as they did the heightened freedom of expression, the xenophobic Russian nationalist organisation *Pamyat'* (Memory) being but the most notorious example.

Whereas in Russia proper the most influential unofficial organisations were concerned with general issues of political and social reform, in the non-Russian republics those focusing on national causes quickly came to the fore. The question of national rights vis-à-vis Moscow was usually salient even when the immediate issue was one, say, of industrial pollution or religious freedom. The same applied to the republic-based Popular Fronts for the Support of Perestroika, versions of which emerged in most republics in the wake of the Estonian Popular Front, formed in 1987. At the other extreme there were open and militant national-issue organisations, the most spectacular example of which was the Karabakh Committee formed clandestinely by a handful of

Armenians in 1985, and which developed by 1988 into a mass movement.[19]

The third element in Gorbachev's strategy to unleash spontaneous political forces and to mobilise them in support of his restructuring policies was 'democratisation'. The very use of this term embodies a remarkable confession, in the light of the claims over many decades that the Soviet political system was the most democratic of all time. It was now ever more openly conceded that the democratic forms of party and state, with respect both to the choice of representatives and leaders and the making of public policy decisions, had long been an empty pretence. Yet, as I argued in Chapter 2, democratic sentiment had been a genuine element in the early Bolshevik tradition, and even more so in the original soviets. It was the relentless deployment of massive coercive, organisational and propaganda resources to establish and safeguard communist rule and push through radical social changes in the name of 'building socialism' that had emptied the democratic forms of content and reduced them to a façade for bureaucratic absolutism. Such hypocrisy, however, can help to sustain the very values it traduces, and I have long been intrigued and encouraged by the unmistakeable evidence that these apparently moribund forms could take on new life in circumstances where the apparatus's coercive, organisational and propaganda pressures were eased.[20] In past times the leadership has soon taken alarm and hastened to reinforce the pressures, perceiving the spectacle of spontaneous, undirected political activity as a threat to the bureaucratic controls on which their own power and indeed the whole social order rested. But to Gorbachev and his supporters it seemed precisely what was needed to give them the power to transform that social order.

Nevertheless, throughout 1987 and 1988 the democratisation of formal political institutions lagged well behind the democratisation of public expression and public association. A small minority of district and city party secretaries were chosen in contested elections in 1987 and a considerably larger proportion in 1988, but it was only in 1989 that the first contested elections at regional and republic levels began to be reported.[21] Even then the potential threat to the *nomenklatura* system of bureaucratic selection of officials, with all its implications for the structure of power and privilege in the USSR, seems to have been substantially offset by resorting to more sophisticated procedures.[22] Meanwhile in the elections to the local soviets in June 1987, the first timid steps were taken to permit voters an element of choice in a small proportion of electorates.

It was the elections to the newly established Congress of People's Deputies of the USSR in March 1989 that saw the first major breakthrough to democracy of choice. One third of the 2250 deputies were nominated by the CPSU, the Komsomol, trade unions, Academy of Sciences and other official 'social organisations' (a significant number turning out to be 'liberals'), but the 1500 one-member local constituencies (in two equal categories, one based on population and the other on quotas for union and autonomous republics and other national divisions) were contested by a total of 2901 candidates. It is true that conservative local bosses in over a quarter of the electorates succeeded in manipulating the procedures for nominating and registering candidates to protect their favoured sons (and a few daughters) from having to compete with alternative candidates, and in many other electorates in keeping the names of more radical nominees off the ballot-papers. Nevertheless the election campaign evoked a sharp intensification and maturation of the qualified freedom of expression and association that had been growing over the preceding three years. Unofficial clubs and associations played a prominent part both in nominating candidates and campaigning for them, making vigorous use of their new-won opportunities for holding public meetings and demonstrations, distributing *samizdat* electoral material, and for access to the official media. The result was that something like a fifth of the successful candidates were persons active in liberal or radical causes, while a number of the local party bosses and other apparatus nominees standing uncontested suffered the humiliation of winning less than the 50 per cent of positive votes needed to gain election.

The incipient democratisation of the policy-making process had two dimensions. On the one hand the ever freer flow of information and opinion flooding the media, coupled with the public pressure applied by unofficial organisations, began to act both as a constraint on and a goad to decision-making at the centre as well as at the republic and local levels. On the other hand the formal representative bodies of party and state, relegated for decades to the role of perfunctorily legitimating executive decisions, began to assume a role in debating and deciding policy issues. How far and how fast this process went in the party it is difficult to evaluate, and the subject awaits serious scholarly investigation. Certainly press reports of party congresses and conferences and the meetings of full party committees at different levels revealed an increasing diversity of opinion and sharper criticism of existing conditions. At the centre this trend is apparent in the changed content and style of speeches of delegates to the Nineteenth CPSU Conference in June 1988 as compared with the Twenty-seventh Congress in March 1986. There is similar evidence from the reports of Central Committee plenums, however partial and sanitised the press versions of these may be.[23] There have been earlier, ephemeral phases in the post-Stalin politics of the USSR in which the Central Committee has shown signs of assuming a 'parliamentary' role vis-à-vis the ruling Politburo, and the entrenchment of such a role is one possible consequence of Gorbachev's democratisation program. However, at the beginning of 1990 there was no conclusive evidence of this at the centre or in the relations of party bureaus and full committees at lower levels.

Indeed the apparent tendencies in this direction were overtaken in 1989 by the unfolding of another central element in Gorbachev's political program, summed up by the revived revolutionary slogan, 'All Power to the Soviets!' The key policy decisions on this were adopted at the Nineteenth Party Conference in mid 1988. They envisaged the conversion of the soviets into 'genuinely working organs', the establishment of their effective control over the executive machinery from top to bottom, and the restriction of the party's role to overall policy development.[24] Sceptics pointed out the echoes of traditional hypocritical rhetoric, and doubts were reinforced by the decision to empower the new Congress of People's Deputies to choose the members of the Supreme Soviet, instead of their being elected directly by the population.

Once the first session of the Congress opened in May 1989, however, it became immediately obvious that the Gorbachev leadership was genuinely aiming at major changes in the role and operation of these institutions. The two week session, replete with the clash of ideas, personalities and interests, with arresting revelations, and with spontaneous outbursts and passionate debate, galvanised the tens of millions of Soviet people who watched it on television.[25] While the session made few major decisions, its cathartic and educational impact on Soviet political life was enormous. The 450-strong Supreme Soviet elected by the Congress, while predominantly conservative in orientation, included, like the Congress itself, a substantial minority of liberal and radical deputies. The same applied to Congress standing commissions, which continued working between sessions, and most importantly to its Constitutional Commission. The Congress came back for a second, less dramatic session in December. The Supreme Soviet, for its part, sat for two months in its first session and resumed for a similar period after the summer recess. The Soviet Union now had, for the first time in its history, a working parliament. It dealt with a considerable body of important legislation in its commissions and plenary meetings and, while disappointing radicals with its predominantly conservative tenor and docility towards the party and government leadership, its decisions reflected the influence of a variety of interests, opinions and professional expertise; occasionally it stood up to the leadership, most notably in refusing endorsement to certain of their ministerial nominees.

At the beginning of 1990 the Soviet Union, despite its continued exclusion of formal opposition parties, displayed the rudiments of a democratic polity, and the impending elections to the local and republic soviets promised to reinforce these substantially. By now, however, a range of problems had assumed such threatening proportions that the whole reform process was clearly in jeopardy.

The Crisis Matures

Five years after Gorbachev's election as General Secretary the crisis of Soviet mono-organisational socialism, far from being resolved, continued to deepen. The situation was replete with irony and paradox. As Gorbachev's grip on the leadership had strengthened, his capacity to control political developments had declined. As his popularity soared abroad, it faded at home. The changes which reduced the menace of international conflict also laid the country open to domestic disorder. Radical political reforms not only far outran the economic transformation they were intended to foster, they simultaneously engendered new obstacles to such a transformation.

Gorbachev's personal prominence and authority notwithstanding, the oligarchical character of supreme power persisted. The oligarchy's composition, however, underwent many changes, the net effect of which was to strengthen Gorbachev's predominance.[26] Its core group, the full (voting) members of the Politburo, consisted of twelve men as it emerged from its initial phase of consolidation at the time of the Twenty-seventh Congress. As we see from Table 9.1, only six of them were left by the beginning of 1990, and they had meanwhile been joined by six new members.[27] The changes in the outer circles of the oligarchy – the Politburo's non-voting (candidate) members, the Central Committee (CC) Secretariat, and the Government presidium – were even more drastic. Five of the seven Politburo candidates at the beginning of 1990 had been appointed as recently as September 1989. Although even then perhaps only two or three of the full members and three or four of the candidate members were persons totally committed to Gorbachev, the overall political balance had moved constantly in his favour, as several leaders thought to have been conservative critics of his policies had been removed – four of them since September 1988. It is true that the

Table 9.1 POLITBURO CHANGES 1986–1990 (Full Members Only)

Composition March 1986	Date Out	Date In	Composition January 1990
Gorbachev			Gorbachev
Aliev	Oct 1987		
Vorotnikov			Vorotnikov
Gromyko	Sept 1988		
Zaikov			Zaikov
Kunaev	Jan 1987		
Ligachev			Ligachev
Ryzhkov			Ryzhkov
Solomentsev	Sept 1988		
Chebrikov	Sept 1989		
Shevardnadze			Shevardnadze
Shcherbitsky	Sept 1989		
		June 1987	Slyun'kov
		June 1987	Yakovlev
		Sept 1988	Medvedev
		Sept 1989	Kryuchkov
		Sept 1989	Maslyukov
		Dec 1989	Ivashko

eager reformer Boris Yeltsin's removal from the Politburo and the Moscow party secretaryship in 1987 was a victory for the conservatives, but it also helped Gorbachev consolidate his authority for a further advance the following year.

A number of job and role decisions and structural reorganisations also reflected and then boosted the General Secretary's growing ascendancy. These included his own belated assumption of the

Chairmanship of the Supreme Soviet Presidium in October 1988, converted into the more authoritative Presidency of the Supreme Soviet in May 1989, and his appointment at the end of 1989 as Chairman of the new RSFSR Bureau of the Central Committee; the appointment of his adherent A.I. Lukyanov as First Deputy President; of G.P. Razumovsky as CC Secretary for cadres and organisational matters; of V.S. Murakhovsky as First Deputy Premier for Agriculture; of V.A. Kryuchkov as KGB Chairman in place of the Brezhnev hold-over V.M. Chebrikov; of B.K. Pugo as Chairman of the Party Control (that is, disciplinary) Committee; of A.V. Vlasov as the Premier of the Russian Republic; of E.M. Primakov as chairman of the Council of the Union; of economic reform advisor Leonid Abalkin as Deputy Chairman of the Council of Ministers, and of his personal assistant I.T. Frolov as CC secretary and editor of *Pravda*. As the leadership consensus came under strain in 1986–87 and the conservative-leaning Yegor Ligachev emerged as the strongest alternative focus of authority, Gorbachev succeeded first in depriving him of jurisdiction over ideology (including the media), and in late 1988 of the *de facto* role of 'second secretary', relegating him to oversight of agriculture. This coincided with a reorganisation of the Central Committee machinery, in which the Secretariat (whose meetings Ligachev had usually chaired) ceased to operate as an executive body, being replaced by a number of policy commissions each headed by a CC secretary and reporting directly to the Politburo (which Gorbachev usually chaired), and later most of the CC's industrial departments, essential to the operation of the traditional command economy, were abolished.

Gorbachev was undoubtedly helped by the great international authority and popularity he acquired after 1986, and by the generally acknowledged lack of an alternate leader of comparable standing, but no less important was his impressive political resourcefulness and dispatch, and his remarkable capacity to combine symbolic concessions with gains in real power resources. Perhaps the most striking example is the package of major leadership and organisational changes presented to the Central Committee and the USSR and RSFSR Supreme Soviets between 30 September and 3 October 1988, and which some have labelled 'Gorbachev's *coup d'état*'. Another was the April 1989 CC plenum, convened in response to pressure from regional party leaders so they could air their concern at the adverse impact of political and economic changes, and which Gorbachev used as the occasion to bring on an unprecedented collective resignation of older (mostly retired) members and promotion of candidates to voting membership, thus significantly altering the political complexion of the Central Committee in his favour. His extraordinary political talents were further displayed in his nurture, leadership and management of the USSR's infant parliament in 1989.

Nevertheless Gorbachev's authority within the leadership remained far from absolute, his totally committed supporters remained a minority in the core group, and it was necessary for him to seek alliances, and therefore effect compromises and trade-offs, with other leaders, particularly the three most senior 'technocrats', Prime Minister N.N. Ryzhkov and CC secretaries L.N. Zaikov and N.N. Slyun'kov.

There were good reasons why Gorbachev's popularity waned while his political ascendancy grew. Any revolution from above – and this is not too strong a term for the complex of profound changes in train by the late 1980s – is bound to cause disruption and damage many interests before its intended benefits are generally felt. This is why, of course, revolutions from above are usually accompanied by a sharp intensification of state coercion and centralised direction. Gorbachev's revolution, however, was one whose effectiveness was seen as depending on the *abatement* of state coercion and centralised direction. This laid it unusually open to the risk of unintended consequences, which were soon to erupt menacingly, especially in the economy and inter-ethnic relations.

In 1987–88 the first substantial moves were made towards transforming the command economy into one governed primarily by market mechanisms and allowing a significant role for something like private enterprise. However, they came to be seen by many reformers as half-measures whose side effects militated against more decisive reform. On paper the June 1987 Law on State Enterprises[28] gave the latter considerable commercial autonomy, but this was largely negated by a system of obligatory 'state orders'. Operations outside the state order framework often brought enterprises substantial profits, allowing them to buy the cooperation of the workforce with wage rises in excess of productivity increases. Since the artificial, bureaucratically determined price structure rarely directed this additional production to ease shortages in the mass consumer market, the net effect was to aggravate frustrated mass demand. Meanwhile efficiency in the industrial, planning and distribution bureaucracies suffered as a result of administrative changes, severe staff cuts, and low morale due to anxiety about their collective and individual futures (and, some would add, to direct sabotage). Mass dissatisfaction flowing from the resultant general and local shortages in the consumer market had grown to dangerous levels by 1989.[29]

Meanwhile in May 1988 the Supreme Soviet had passed a Law on Cooperatives which was destined to make a far larger impact than the 1986 Law on Individual Economic Activity mentioned above.[30] Within a year over 100,000 cooperatives were in operation, employing over two million members.[31] Nevertheless the hope that the new cooperative enterprises would soon make a major contribution to meeting mass demand for high quality goods and services was to be disappointed. A disproportionate share of their activities was directed towards the luxury end of the market, where large profits were to be made. For this reason, aggravated no doubt by the traditional Russian resentment of those who thrive by striking out on their own, the cooperatives became a further source of mass dissatisfaction, extending even to many individuals who benefited from their services.[32]

A further source of unintended consequences was the worthily motivated campaign against alcohol abuse. For one thing it caused a sharp fall in state revenue, which was the main factor in an enormous blow-out in the budget deficit. The inevitable boom in illicit distilling was not long in coming, with its consequent nationwide sugar shortage and its desperate suicidal fringe. The resentment it evoked among drinkers was intense, especially in blue-collar milieux.

A further paradox is the failure of serious reform to eventuate in the grossly inefficient food production sector, despite its great economic and political costs and the exemplary role played by *de facto* privatisation of agriculture in the earlier economic reform programmes in Hungary and China. One reason is that conservative opposition on this issue found enough support within the leadership to frustrate the efforts of Gorbachev, who made a series of public statements in favour of family farms.[33] Even when legislation allowing family and cooperative leaseholdings was enacted, it made limited impact owing to the non-cooperation of local officials and to the hard-bitten scepticism of the peasantry.[34]

All major élites in the USSR, with the exception of the creative, scholarly and professional intelligentsia, were aggrieved by Gorbachev's reforms. We have noted the concerns of the most powerful and prestigious category of government officials – those staffing the industrial ministries and central economic administration. The party apparatus at all levels was faced with the loss of their key traditional roles. On the one hand the breakthrough to relative freedom of information, expression and association had cost them their right to constantly direct and supervise all public communications and organised public activity. On the other hand, by decision of the Nineteenth Party Conference in June 1988, party committees were also told to stop issuing directives to economic agencies,[35] and three months later Gorbachev announced to the Central Committee a follow-up Politburo decision drastically reorganising and cutting the party apparatus, especially at the higher levels.[36] In the upshot party committees lost the personnel and organisational capacity to perform the dominant role in economic life which had been their first concern, especially at regional and local levels, since the 1930s. This change, of course, was essential if the economy was ever to be governed primarily by market signals rather than by administrative command, but this made it no more congenial to most career party officials. The party's role was henceforth to be a purely *political* one – framing overall policy and convincing people of its correctness – while specific measures were to be decided by the soviets and their executive bodies. This placed a premium on leading party officials gaining election to the soviets, but the elections to the Congress of People's Deputies in 1989, substantially manipulated though they were, showed that local party leaders stood a good chance of being rejected by the voters, and the earlier idea that the top position in the soviet and the corresponding party committee at each level should normally be held by the same person (as in the case of Gorbachev at the centre) was now quietly dropped. Meanwhile, since no alternative to the old system was yet in place, regional and local party leaders were still being expected to sort out major economic and other problems in their areas, despite their loss of the powers and the staff to do it, and were blamed if they failed. Small wonder that many of them were seething with frustration and resentment, which found reflection at the April 1989 CC plenum mentioned above and at a conference of regional first secretaries presided over by Gorbachev three months later.[37]

The thousands of officials of party-directed 'voluntary' organisations, notably the Komsomol and the trade unions, were no less anxious and vulnerable. One consequence of increased freedom of expression and association was to display their almost total irrelevance to the central concerns of their ostensible constituencies, and they realised that a broadening of those freedoms could cost them their jobs.

Under Brezhnev the armed forces had fared better than ever before in peacetime, in terms of material resources, public honour, and salience in the extension of Soviet international influence. Gorbachev's *perestroika* put an end to that. Its foreign policy components, discussed below, sharply lowered the role of the military, heralding a reduction in scale, budgetary support and prestige. Unlike his Brezhnev-era predecessors, the new Defence Minister Marshal D.T. Yazov was not made a voting member of the Politburo, but only a candidate member. The careers of thousands of officers were blighted by early retirement or non-promotion. The Soviet withdrawal from Afghanistan, popular though it was, left a bitter aftertaste with many who had served there.[38] And, finally, ethnic passions released by the run-down of political controls exposed the Soviet Army to what soldiers of all ranks most abhor, namely firing on their fellow citizens in defence of public order.

The impact of *perestroika* on the KGB is more ambiguous. On the one hand, the more benign posture of the Soviet regime both at home and abroad, and especially the new tolerance of a wide range of activities previously treated as state crimes, substantially narrowed the scope of 'traditional' KGB powers and responsibilities. Gorbachev seems to have been behind moves to curb the KGB in 1986–87, and the organisation lost its immunity to public criticism and exposure.[39] On the other hand they were now called upon to play a major part in the campaigns against crime and corruption, at the expense of the discredited Interior Ministry police, and there was some evidence of an enhanced monitoring and 'prophylactic' role in relation to expanded commercial contacts with foreign firms. More speculatively, the conservative Chebrikov's successor as KGB Chairman, V.A. Kryuchkov, appointed direct to voting Politburo membership in September 1989 without the usual probation as a candidate, was generally seen as an ally of Gorbachev's, and the KGB is sometimes credited with having a greater share of enlightened, reform-oriented officers than other major élites. Be this as it may, it seems likely that a great many KGB personnel were out of sympathy with Gorbachev and his reforms because of the diminution of their powers and prestige and the spread of disorder and 'dangerous' ideas.[40]

This picture of widespread and growing disaffection within the country's key power structures calls for some qualification. It rests basically on arguments from group interest, backed by substantial but unsystematic evidence, and one cannot be certain as to the actual balance and intensity of opinion within these élites. Moreover, they all contained a considerable minority of officials who had demonstrated exemplary commitment to Gorbachev's reforms and been rewarded by promotion into the upper echelons. Thus the behavioural implications of this widespread élite disaffection remained unclear, and specific circumstances could perhaps greatly affect how they would act in a crisis.

Disaffection, of course, was by no means confined to the élites. As we have noted, there were good reasons for its salience among the blue-collar workers. They shared the aggravations of consumer-supply shortages with the rest of the population, while suffering disproportionately from the anti-alcohol and workplace discipline campaigns and the new quality control procedures. The first major reflection of this came in July 1989 with largescale miners' strikes in Siberia, the Donbass and other localities. Under Brezhnev, a strategy had been evolved for localising and speedily ending work stoppages by a combination of immediate concessions and judicious repression, under cover of an information black-out. This strategy could not survive the new freedoms. The scale and impact of the miners' strikes were directly due to their unprecedented power to organise, hold mass meetings and gain media publicity. The costs in lost production and the major improvements in pay and conditions constituted a serious blow to the country's beleaguered economy which conservatives could put down to Gorbachev's *glasnost'* and *perestroika*.[41] They also raised the spectre of widespread distress and disorder should similar stoppages in the transport or energy sectors occur in the winter.

It is in the sphere of federal and inter-ethnic relations that the unintended consequences of *glasnost'* and *perestroika* had their most dramatic and fateful impact. History began to exact its revenge. After 1917 it had been primarily through the Red Army and the Cheka that the Bolsheviks extended their sway to most of the Tsar's non-Russian dominions, but it was largely the evolving mono-organisational system, with its comprehensive direction of all economic, social and cultural activity, that then kept them compliant. In these lands pseudo-democracy was blended with pseudo-federalism, complete with a full range of 'autonomous' institutions and a culture which was allowed to be 'national in form', at the price of staying 'socialist in content'. What followed presents the best of all illustrations of the pattern noted earlier, where institutionalised hypocrisy sustains the very values and ideals it traduces.

The insensitivity of Soviet leaders and their theoreticians to the intensity of national sentiment, frankly admitted and regretted by the late 1980s, reflects in part the deception and self-deception built into the traditional system of ideological and organisational control. This insensitivity was manifested in, and perhaps exacerbated by, the substantially increased predominance of ethnic Russians in the ruling oligarchy in the early Gorbachev period.[42] The first sobering warning came in December 1986 with the riots in Alma-Ata following the replacement of the Kazakh Kunaev by the Russian Kolbin as the republic's First Secretary. It was to be followed in 1987–89 by a wide variety of developments, all illustrating the power of submerged national commitments, aspirations, grievances and antipathies to explode into organised mass action. The essential prerequisite, of course, was the sharp curtailment of centralised control and direction of all forms of public expression and association, the more general consequences of which we have discussed above. With this key component of the mono-organisational system gone, a process was set in train which could culminate in the situation prevailing at the outset of Soviet rule, when only the massive deployment of armed force could secure the compliance of non-Russian nations to Moscow's demands. The Soviet leaders then had to decide whether the potential benefits outweighed the domestic and international consequences of such. armed action. The stage was now set for the belated break-up of the Russian Empire, or at least its transformation into a genuine federal or confederal system.

Our task here is not to chronicle these developments republic by republic, but to identify their chief components and underlying dynamic.[43] They operated on three levels:

1. inter-ethnic conflict within republics – for example, Abkhazians and Ossetians versus Georgians over the former's autonomous rights within the Georgian republic, pogroms against the Meskhetian Turks in Uzbekistan, and the opposition by the Russian communities in Estonia, Moldavia and elsewhere against the objectives of the local national movements;

2. inter-republic conflict, of which the only major case was that between Armenia and Azerbaijan over the future of the Nagorno–Karabakh Region; and

3. conflict – particularly in the Baltic and Transcaucasian republics – between republic leaders and Moscow, over the level of local autonomy and the issue of ultimate independence.

There was likewise a range of structures and processes involved. There were the single-issue unofficial associations and movements - for example, on ecological or language issues – which brought pressure to bear, sometimes successfully, both on local and central agencies. There were the popular (or national) fronts, the earliest of which, especially in Estonia, sought legitimacy through their support for *perestroika*, thereby capitalising on their common interest with the Moscow reformers against local conservative leaderships, while the later ones tended to be more blatantly focused on national rights and freedom. Then there were the official 'voluntary' organisations, especially the writers' and other 'creative' unions, which in several cases threw off their 60-year old role as instruments of regime control and began to voice their members' and their nations' concerns. Even the notoriously reactionary Komsomol was not everywhere immune to this tendency. And finally, this process spread to the formal political institutions – the republic party central committees, the councils of ministers, the supreme soviets, and so on, whose leaderships first found themselves mediating between their Moscow masters and their local constituencies, and then when a major centre–republic conflict forced them to choose, tended to opt for their nation's cause. The Baltic and Transcaucasian republics again afford the most graphic examples. In the earlier stages the unofficial national movements operated through petitions, *samizdat* publications, meetings in clubs, and the like, and through moderate-sized open-air demonstrations (which were sometimes brutally dispersed). As the process unfolded they gained access to the official media and, later, with the blessing of the local party and state leaders, were able to convene enormous mass meetings of protest and national celebration. In such ways *glasnost'*, *perestroika* and democratisation exposed the shaky foundations of the Soviet multinational state and evoked a series of critical situations to distract the Gorbachev leadership from the tasks of social and economic renewal.

The impact of Gorbachev's foreign policy on Soviet domestic politics was also ambiguous. The new General Secretary was quick to assume a dominant role in the conduct of Soviet foreign relations, engaging very actively both in personal diplomacy, involving dialogue with a wide range of foreign leaders, and in efforts to influence public opinion in foreign countries, especially the USA and Western Europe. This first major venture in the latter direction was the dissemination of his 1987 book *Perestroika: New Thinking for Our Country and the World*, the title of which also epitomised his stress on the mutual dependence of reform of the Soviet system and reform of the international system. The essence of this 'new thinking' was the proposition – heretical from a traditional Marxist–Leninist standpoint – that the common interests of humanity transcend the conflicting interests not only of nations but also of classes. Hence 'ideological differences should not be transferred to the sphere of interstate relations, nor should foreign policy be subordinate to them, for ideologies may be poles apart, whereas the interests of survival and prevention of war stand universal and supreme'.[44]

There was at first considerable scepticism in Western government and specialist circles. If domestic restructuring was a response to alarm at the decline of the Soviet Union's relative economic power, which if unchecked would threaten its relative military power, was not the shift to a cooperative, non-confrontational international posture not essentially a device to gain time for the benefits of economic recovery to accrue, with a view ultimately to regaining the military capacity to resume an expansionist policy? By 1989 such suspicions were largely dispelled, and Gorbachev was generally credited with believing what he professed to believe, although some still warned that the benefits flowing to the Soviet Union from Gorbachev's 'new thinking' policies might be inherited and exploited by a less benign Soviet leadership.

Meanwhile, within three or four years these policies had produced a radically improved international image of the USSR, one inextricably linked with the image of Gorbachev himself. They had brought a shift from hostility to goodwill in relations with the USA and Western Europe, along with large-scale weapons cuts and the promise of more; to the abjuring of interference in the internal affairs of their Warsaw pact allies; and to the withdrawal of Soviet troops with Afghanistan and the scaling down of Soviet political and military involvement in other Third World countries. As suggested above, Gorbachev's international respect and his reputation as a peacemaker was also a major political asset at home, inhibiting any aspiration to depose him. Moreover, he had proved right what some Soviet strategic theorists had long argued, namely that a more relaxed military posture would actually strengthen rather than diminish the security of the USSR, and the potential security costs of seeming to reject his 'new thinking' were therefore formidable.

There was again, however, a negative side. The Gorbachev-led retreat from empire was viewed as weakness if not betrayal by the imperial-minded within the Soviet élites and population. Others saw the improved relations with the USA and Western Europe, in combination with market-oriented reforms at home, as opening up the country to decadent Western influences inimical to traditional Russian moral and cultural values. Ideological conservatives saw the 'new thinking' as a negation of 'proletarian internationalism', a sell-out to the international bourgeoisie. Such critics could claim irrefutable and the alarming justification for their positions in the collapse of the communist monopoly of power in Eastern Europe during 1989, first in Poland, then in Hungary, and in the final weeks of the year in East Germany, Czechoslavakia, Bulgaria and Romania.

An End to Mono-organisational Socialism?

As late as February 1990 no unqualified answer to this question was yet available. To be sure, after four years of sundry alterations, the traditional structure of Soviet mono-organisational socialism had been partly dismantled and the whole looked rather shaky. Whether, however, it is destined to be restored, modernised, renovated or completely rebuilt remained uncertain. In any case, the lineaments of a new structure were not yet apparent. The same point had been made in less metaphorical terms by Moscow social scientist and parliamentary deputy Leonid Batkin, when he characterised the Soviet socio-political order today as 'crippled totalitarianism'.[45]

Several important components of the mono-organisational system as outlined in Chapter 1 and examined more closely in Chapters 2, 3 and 7, had been discarded or substantially modified between 1987 and 1989. Most important was the police-backed monopoly enjoyed by the party and party-licensed agencies over all public association and public expression. Second there was the transformation of formal representative bodies from docile instruments of the party–state bureaucracy into quasi-democratic institutions exercising a degree of constraint on the latter. Third came the weakening of the *nomenklatura* system, linked with the revival of genuine, contested elections. And, finally, there were the varied moves away from the bureaucratic command economy towards a socialist (or mixed) market economy.

Along with these changes in socio-political structures and processes there came shifts in official and unofficial thinking which undermined the legitimacy of the traditional system. Of central importance here was the pejoratively-used concept of the 'command–administrative system', which by 1988 was taken up by Gorbachev himself and thereby imbued with quasi-official status. Its meaning is very close to that of 'mono-organisational socialism' as used in this book, *viz.* the running of all aspects of social life through official bureaucracies, coordinated by the party apparatus and under the arbitrary direction of a personal dictator or tiny oligarchy.

The command–administrative system has been treated as an aberration from Marxism–Leninism and blamed primarily on Stalin, but there are those who have gone beyond this to point to aspects of Lenin's Bolshevism which facilitated its emergence,[46] and others who have disclosed its roots in Marx's utopianism and in particular his anathematising of commodity–market relations.[47] Many writers have seen the officials who run the command–administrative system as a ruling, exploitative class or class-like stratum.[48]

Meanwhile the goal of 'communism' has progressively disappeared from party slogans and leaders' speeches as the ultimate justification for the existing order, for official measures and the demands being made on the population. The Word, incarnate in the Communist Party and imbuing it with the absolute authority of inexorable history, has in effect been desanctified.

Whatever 'secret agenda' Gorbachev may have harboured at the time of his accession to power, there is no doubt that his understanding of the crisis besetting Soviet society and the objectives of his *perestroika* have been steadily radicalised over the past five years. Any lingering doubts on this score were dispelled by his article 'The Socialist Idea and Revolutionary Restructuring', published in November 1989.[49] The ideal of communism as a utopian end-point of history is replaced here by that of a humane socialism as an evolving order. The 'socialist idea', is seen as owing much to Marx and Engels, and in particular their concept of a 'kingdom of freedom' emptied of exploitation and oppression, but they had no blueprint for its achievement and they underestimated the vitality and adaptability of capitalism; the 'idea' must now be understood as incorporating the experience and thought of subsequent generations both in capitalist and in socialist states. The way forward is Lenin's way of matching each step to a sober analysis of existing conditions and willingness to make use of people's economic instincts and the commercial mechanisms that flow from these. Humane socialism will involve a redirection of resources towards education, health and the service industries; the rule of law; a democracy that draws *inter alia* on the experience of Western parliamentarism; and a variety of forms of productive property. There is no provision here for the party's traditional leading and directing role, but Gorbachev argues that the continuance of the one-party system is 'expedient... in the present difficult conditions'.

This is a vision that clearly heralds the dismantling of what is left of mono-organisational socialism. Small wonder that the Gorbachev-led Soviet Union has shown no interest in shoring up mono-organisational systems in other communist-ruled countries, most notably those closely allied to it in the Warsaw pact and CMEA. But is it a vision that is likely to be realised? Confident prediction would be totally unwarranted in such a complex and volatile situation. But on a question so fateful for humanity we must try to weigh the possibilities, even if our speculations are bound to prove partly irrelevant by the time they appear in print.

In conversations with Soviet social scientists across the full reactionary–radical spectrum during 1989 I encountered widely differing estimates of the likelihood of a conservative coup against Gorbachev and his restructuring, but no-one who dismissed such a coup as a serious possibility. The most popular variant was a conspiracy involving elements within the military and the ruling oligarchy and backed by large segments of the party and state bureaucracies as well a sizable part of the Great Russian proletariat. Many added that such a coup could degenerate into civil war, since substantial elements in all the élites, including the armed forces and the KGB, would be opposed to it, as would much of the intelligentsia and some, at least, of the non-Russian peoples. One alternative which was widely ignored, but which I viewed as a distinct possibility, is a 'constitutional coup'. Gorbachev is hardly more proof against this than was Khrushchev in 1964; of course the same behind-the-scenes soundings and caucusing would be needed and it would be necessary to secure a majority in the federal parliament as well as the Politburo and the Central Committee, but, given the conservative majority both in the Supreme Soviet and the larger Congress of People's Deputies, this might follow without great difficulty.

The potential support for such a 'coup', whether peaceful or otherwise, was powerfully reinforced between October 1989 and January 1990 by the collapse of 'fraternal' regimes in East–Central Europe and the sharpening resistance to Moscow's authority in several republics, especially Lithuania and Azerbaijan. Public calls to 'stop the rot' became increasingly outspoken.[50] Gorbachev reacted, in a number of meetings and encounters, as well as his article 'The Socialist Idea and Revolutionary Restructuring', by distancing himself from some of the most zealous advocates of change and reasserting his socialist credentials, but without giving way on any of his major reform measures. Then, in February, as on previous occasions when his leadership has come under fire, he produced a dramatic counter-stroke which heavily raised the stakes: he confronted a Central Committee plenum with proposals to bring forward the Twenty-eighth CPSU Congress from the Autumn to the Summer of 1990, and to approve for party-wide discussion a draft programme which envisaged giving up the CPSU's constitutional monopoly of power, radically restructuring its leadership echelons, and further liberalising the socio-economic order. Despite the fact that the collective interests of the party and government officials who formed a majority of the Central Committee were gravely endangered by these proposals, they approved them for discussion with only one dissenting vote – that of Boris Yeltsin. However the speeches at the plenum revealed a sharpening polarisation of reformist and conservative forces,[51] and this seemed likely to deepen further, fuelled by the impending elections to the republic supreme soviets, which could bring humiliating defeats for leading party and government officials, and, beyond that the lead-up to the party congress. Gorbachev's remarkable skill in keeping all but the most extreme political forces in harness and moving in the general direction he desires could prove inadequate in this situation. Thus a number of radically different outcomes still seemed possible, and in the next five paragraphs I shall set these out exactly as they appeared to me at the time.

A successful conservative 'coup' against Gorbachev could result in a substantial patching up of the old mono-organisational structure, but a full restoration seems very unlikely. The moves from a command economy towards a socialist (or mixed) market economy could be halted and partially reversed, controls over information, public expression, culture and association could be reapplied, the directing and supervisory role of the party apparatus reactivated, the embattled *nomenklatura* system salvaged and the parliament and other elective bodies deprived of their independence. Nevertheless the system could never be made to operate again as it did in the 'era of stagnation'. The transformation in people's awareness, knowledge, attitudes and values, and therefore in their behavioural orientations, cannot be reversed by fiat. To attempt it would involve a level of coercion whose political costs domestically and internationally would be prohibitive. What you would get, therefore, would still be a variant of 'crippled totalitarianism', but now without the hope of something better. Ethnic resentments and hatreds would intensify. There might be an initial period of relief at the apparent restoration of order and resolution of uncertainties, but the crisis of mono-organisational socialism would deepen and no longer be amenable to peaceful remedies akin to Gorbachev's restructuring.

An alternative to a conservative coup *against* Gorbachev is a conservative coup *by* Gorbachev: in a context perhaps of widespread and intense ethnic and worker interest, the General Secretary–President might find it in him to preside over a political and ideological clampdown and a slowdown in economic reform in order to halt the slide into chaos. Such a gambit could be undertaken in the spirit of *reculer pour mieux sauter*, but the precariousness of the 'order' now 'restored' might inhibit a restart to restructuring indefinitely, and the end result could be the same as in our first alternative.[52]

A third possibility is the assumption of autocratic powers by Gorbachev for the opposite purpose, to preempt a conservative coup and ensure the continuance of his restructuring program. The most interesting political debate among Soviet intellectuals in 1989 was over the proposition that a period of enlightened authoritarian rule will be essential for the Soviet Union if it is to accomplish the transition from totalitarianism to democracy.[53] Whether or not Gorbachev would prove willing or suitable for such a role, one can easily imagine a scenario (for example, a failed conservative coup or the assertion of emergency powers in the context of a widespread breakdown of order) in which he would fall into it. This might indeed facilitate a more resolute dismantling of the economic and organisational supports of the mono-organisational system, although the middle-term gains for democracy might well prove disappointing.

A fourth possibility is that neither Gorbachev nor his conservative critics would emerge victorious from a crisis of power, but the radical reformers would. This looks far-fetched at present, but so soon after the revolutions in East Germany, Czechoslavakia, Bulgaria and Romania we should know better than to discount what is improbable under *current* circumstances. Circumstances are changing rapidly and unpredictably. They could quickly lead to a situation where the other main contenders were discredited and impotent, giving the radical reformers their chance, although they would certainly need a popular leader to have a chance of winning mass support. It is not so absurd to cast Boris Yeltsin for this role, but a relatively unknown leader could well emerge in the heat of the struggle. The outcome might be the quickest demolition of the remnants of mono-organisational socialism, although not necessarily the surest guarantee of democracy and national well-being.

Of the other possibilities I will mention just one: that Gorbachev will ride out the storms of the coming months, that the restructuring will continue, and the emerging pluralistic patterns of economic, political, social and cultural life will take root. This might not lead straight to the 'kingdom of freedom', but it could prove that long-awaited revolution from above to end all further revolutions from above.

That, then, is how I saw the possible futures in mid-February 1990. *Actual* futures, however, rarely accommodate themselves to our neat predictive scenarios, and so it was in this case. Gorbachev continued his counter-offensive, and by February 27th the Supreme Soviet approved, by a vote of 306 to 65, his proposal to recommend to the Congress of People's Deputies the creation of an executive-style presidency carrying extensive personal powers. Although forced to delay the Congress session and to compromise on certain provisions, Gorbachev won Congress approval for his proposal on March 13th, and two days later, overcoming the pressure to hold a popular election, was duly sworn in as the first 'President of the Soviet Union'.

The possibility of a conservative coup or a surge to power by populist radicals, although not totally eliminated, now looked remote, and the emergent situation promised to combine elements of my second, third and last scenarios. The locus of supreme power was now set to shift from the party Politburo to the state Presidency, and decisions on arrangements for the 28th Congress confirmed the collapse of the party's 'leading and directing role' in Soviet society, a collapse graphically underlined by the poor showing of party officials in the March elections to republic and local soviets. Meanwhile Gorbachev made clear his intention to accelerate the move towards a market-oriented economy with a mixture of forms of ownership. Not faced with parliamentary or presidential elections before 1994, he appeared set to effect a demolition of mono-organisational socialism no less radical than that being carried out in the countries of East-Central Europe. Whether or not his presidential rule would prove more authoritarian than democratic would obviously depend as much on possible threats to public order engendered by ethnic and social tensions as to his personal inclinations.

Mono-organisational socialism has proved a false path for humanity, and humanity is everywhere turning away from it. In the land where the fine intentions of Marx and Lenin first carved out and paved this path, and where its hellish by-ways were first traversed, one cannot yet totally exclude its rediscovery as the 'barracks socialism' of a Russia turning its back not just on empire but on the whole 'post-modern' world. At present, however, it seems to have all but abandoned it.

What about the largest nation on earth? A senior Chinese scholar remarked to me sardonically in December 1989, 'we used to be told that only socialism can save China, and now they tell us that only China can save socialism'. But Mao Tsedong led his country off the Soviet path three decades ago and, whatever one might say of China's 'socialism' today, it is not mono-organisational. Until recently a cynic might have suggested that the present contrast between the Soviet Union and China is not one of embourgeoisement versus proletarianisation, as I characterised it in the 1960s, but of competing formulas of embourgeoisement, both with a socialist label. Since the Tiananmen massacre China begins to look more like a blend between oriental despotism and compradore socialism, but perhaps that will soon pass. Where something like traditional mono-organisational socialism persists, it is covered with the bizarre outgrowths of an Albania or North Korea.

The death agonies of mono-organisational socialism should not become the occasion for crowing or self-congratulation, but rather for relief that we are now freer to concentrate on the daunting problems now facing all humanity, problems largely due, moreover, to the dynamics of our own bourgeois market-organisational society. The experiment of mono-organisational socialism, however, should stand as a warning as we seek to master these problems in the coming decades. As new technologies emerge, the prospects of a mono-organisational system that really works may grow ever more tempting, especially if our problems seem unresponsive to other quick solutions. Let us not be seduced again, for the next time the unforeseen consequences of our splendid intentions could prove incorrigible.

Notes and References

1　*Materialy Vneocherednogo plenuma TsK KPSS II marta 1985 goda*, (Politizdat, Moscow), 1985, p.6.

2　See M.S. Gorbachev, *Izbrannye rechi i stat'i*, vol.2, (Politizdat, Moscow), (1987), pp.75–108. For further details and discussion, see Anders Åslund, *Gorbachev's Struggle for Economic Reform. The Soviet Reform Process, 1985–88*, (Pinter Publishers, London), 1989, pp.26–7, and Archie Brown, 'Power and Policy in a Time of Leadership Transition, 1982–1988', in Archie Brown, ed., *Political Leadership in the Soviet Union*, (Macmillan, London), 1989, pp.187–88.

3　For details see Rigby, *Political Elites in the USSR*, Chapter 9.

4　Cf. Åslund, pp.25-35, Brown, op.cit., pp.185–95.

5　Most notably in his speeches in Khabarovsk (*Pravda*, 1 August 1986) and Krasnodar (*Pravda*, 19 September 1986).

6　See *Pravda*, 28 January 1987.

7　See Rigby, *Political Elites in the USSR*, p.278.

8　On this incident see Geoffrey Hosking, 'The Paradox of Gorbachev's Reforms', the sixth 1988 Reith Lecture, *The Listener*, 15 December 1988, p.8.

9　On a visit to Moscow in September 1989 I was told by a leading social scientist that the price of publication could still mean the sacrifice of one's most significant ideas, and shown an issue of a journal with blank sections where passages critical of the KGB had been excised.

10　Of the many books and articles already published on the course and impact of this unshackling of culture, perhaps the best general survey is Alec Nove, *Glasnost' in Action: Cultural Renaissance in Russia*, (Unwin Hyman, Boston etc.), 1989, and the best case study R.W. Davies, *Soviet History in the Gorbachev Revolution*, (Macmillan, London), 1989.

11　See Valerii Chalidze, *Ugolovnaya Rossiia*, (Khronika, New York), 1977.

12　See Rudolf L. Tökes, (ed.), *Dissent in the USSR. Politics, Ideology and People*, (Johns Hopkins University Press, Baltimore/London), 1975 and Ludmila Alexeyeva, *Soviet Dissent. Contemporary*

Movements for National, Religious and Human Rights, (Wesleyan University Press, Middletown, Conn.), 1985.

13 For an instructive analysis of the prehistory of today's youthful 'informals', see M. Malyutin, *'Neformaly v perestroike: opyt i perspektivy'*, in Yu. N. Afanasiev, ed., *Inogo ne dano*, (Progress, Moscow), 1988, pp.216–18.

14 The term *neformaly*, an abbreviation of *neformal'nye obshchestvennye ob'edineniya* (informal social groups) was a neologism of the 1970s applied *inter alia* to school gangs, and had already acquired perjorative overtones. See, for example, V. Kravtsov, 'Ne dovol'no li boltovni?', *Kazakhstanskaya Pravda*, 1 December 1988. The more accurate and neutral terms for unofficial associations, independent (*nezavisimye*) and spontaneous (*samodeyatel'nye*), usually employed by more serious writers, have not passed into general use.

15 'Demokratiya i initsiativa', *Pravda*, 27 December 1987.

16 *Pravda*, 10 February 1989.

17 *Argumenty i fakty*, no.31, 1988.

18 Miroslav Bushkevich, 'Demokraticheskoe polovod'e', *Pravda*, 11 November 1988.

19 Vera Tolz of Radio Liberty has chronicled the development of unofficial political organisations in a series of brief, informative articles. See, in particular, her 'Informal Groups in Soviet Political Life', *The Washington Quarterly*, (Spring 1988), pp.137–55, 'Informal Groups in the USSR in 1988', R.L. 487, (30 October 1988), and 'Informal Groups and Soviet Politics in 1989', *Report on the USSR*, vol.1, no.47 (November 24 1989), pp.4–7.

20 I cite examples in the following: T.H. Rigby – L.G. Churchward, *Policy-making in the USSR 1953-1961*, (Australian Political Studies Association monograph no.4, Lansdowne Press, Melbourne), 1962, pp.17–18, 'Party Elections in the CPSU', *The Political Quarterly*, vol.35, no.4 (1964), pp.435–37, 'The Deconcentration of Power in the USSR – 1953-1964', in J.D.M. Miller and T.H. Rigby, eds., *The Disintegrating Monolith: Pluralist Trends in the Communist Bloc*, (The Australian National University, Canberra), 1965, pp.17–45, and 'Bureaucracy and Democracy in the USSR', *The Australian Quarterly*, vol.42, no.1 (1970), pp.5–14.

21 See T.H. Rigby, *Political Elites in the USSR*, pp. 275–83.

22 Ibid.

23 Of particular interest is the April 1989 CC plenum, at which several regional first secretaries painted a highly unfavourable picture of the impact of Gorbachev's *perestroika* policies. See *Pravda*, 27 April 1989.

24 See *Kommunist*, no.10 (July 1988), pp.67–74.

25 A survey conducted on Thursday 31 May 1989 showed that over three-quarters of viewers watched the Congress transmissions 'constantly' or 'more or less constantly'. See *Izvestiya*, 4 June 1989, p.1.

26 For a detailed account and analysis of leadership changes up to early 1989, see T.H. Rigby, *Political Elites in the USSR*, pp.269–75.

27 Members, such as Boris Yeltsin, who came in and went out in the intervening period, are not shown.

28 *Pravda*, 1 July 1987.

29 For a detailed account of economic changes in this period, see Åslund, op.cit., Chapters 4–6.

30 *Pravda*, 8 June 1988.

31 *Pravda*, 1 July 1989.

32 Measures were adopted by the Supreme Soviet in October 1989 which aimed at curbing speculation and other abuses, and thereby at moderating popular hostility towards the cooperatives. See *Izvestiya*, 21 October 1989.

33 See Åslund, op.cit., pp.179–80.

34 For an illustration of the factors involved, see Ilya Kozik, 'I'm Not Sure', *Moscow News*, no.49 (31 December 1989), p.3.

35 *Pravda*, 29 June 1988.

36 *Pravda*, 25 September 1988.

37 *Pravda*, 19 and 21 July 1989.

38 The bitterness would have been greater, however, had it been followed by a speedy collapse of the Soviet-supported Najibullah regime. See T.H. Rigby, 'The Afghan Conflict and Soviet Domestic Politics', in Amin Saikal and William Maley, (eds), *The Soviet Withdrawal from Afghanistan*, (Cambridge University Press, Cambridge), 1989, pp.68–69, 76–78.

39 See 'Bez privlecheniia k ugolovnoi otvetsvennosti', *Argumenty i fakty*, no.48 (8–12 December 1989), p.6.

40 See Amy W. Knight, *The KGB. Police and Politics in the Soviet Union*, (Unwin Hyman, Boston), 1988, pp.96–104, and the discussion by Alexander Rahr, Alex Alexiev, Amy Knight, Peter Reddaway and Mikhail Tsypkin, *Report on the USSR*, no.51 (22 December), 1989, pp.16–30.

41 See Elizabeth Teague, 'Miners' Strike in Siberia Winds Down, Strikes in Ukraine Spread to Other Areas: A Status Report', *Report on the USSR*, vol.1, no.30 (28 July 1989), pp.15–19, and 'Embryos of People's Power', ibid., vol.1, no.32 (11 August 1989), pp.16–18.

42 See T.H. Rigby, *Political Elites in the USSR*, pp. 258–61.

43 The Radio Liberty and Radio Free Europe Research Bulletins, and (from 1989) Radio Liberty's *Report on the USSR*, provide the best detailed chronicling and current analysis of these developments.

44 Mikhail Gorbachev, *Perestroika. New Thinking for Our Country and the World*, (Collins, London), 1987, p.143.

45 Leonid Batkin, 'Mertvyi khvataet zhivogo', *Literaturnaya gazeta*, no.38 (20 September 1989), p.10.

46 Of particular interest here is the article by V. Gudkov, Yu. Levada, A. Levinson and L. Sedov, 'Byurokratizm i byurokratiya: neobkhodimost' utochnenii ', *Kommunist*, no.12 (August 1988).

47 See especially A. Tsipko's 'sketches' on 'The Sources of Stalinism' in *Nauka i obshchestvo*, 11 (November) and 12 (December) 1988 and 1 (January) and 2 (February) 1989, in particular the first of them, entitled 'O zonakh, zakrytykh dlya mysli', ('On zones closed to thought'), ibid., no.11 (1989), pp.45–55.

48 See T.H. Rigby, *Political Elites in the USSR*, pp.282–83; Andrei Nuikin, 'Idealy i interesy', *Novyi mir*, no.1 (January 1988), pp.191–211.

49 M. Gorbachev, *'Sotsialisticheskaya ideya i revolyutsionnaya perestroika'*, *Pravda*, 26 November 1989. The identification of the author by initial only and without titles emphasised that it was his personal work rather than an official party document.

50 Most notably at a joint meeting of the Leningrad regional and city party committees. See *Leningradskaya Pravda*, 22 November 1989. For comment see I. Sidorov, 'Tret'ya volna', *Argumenty i fakty*, no.48 (2–8 December 1989), p.6. In the sphere of economic policy the

polarisation was graphically expressed in the debate on the Thirteenth Economic Plan presented by Prime Minister Ryzhkov on 15 December and at the somewhat earlier conference on the strategy of economic reform addressed by Deputy Prime Minister Abalkin. See articles by Vladimir Gurevich and Laris Piyasheva in *Moscow News*, no.49 (3 December 1949), p.10, and John Tedstrom, 'The Soviet Economy: Planning for the 1990's, *Report on the USSR*, vol.1, no.51 (22 December 1989), pp.1–7.

51 *Pravda*, 6–9 February 1990.

52 Cf. the speculation by N. Mikhailov in *Moskovskaya Pravda*, 18 August 1989.

53 See A. Migranian, 'Dolgii put' k evropeiskomu domu', *Novyi Mir*, no.7 (July 1989), pp.166–84; I. Klyamkin and A. Migranyan, 'Nuzhna "Zheleznaya ruka"?', *Literaturnaya gazeta*, 16 August 1989; and Leonid Batkin, 'Mërtvyi khvataet zhivogo', ibid., 20 September 1989. This debate echoed a similar one in China in the preceding months. See *Inside China Mainland*, May 1989, pp.8–12; Robert Delfs, 'Little Dragon Model. Intellectuals advocate strongmen before democracy', *Far Eastern Economic Review*, 9 March 1989, p.12; for the context see David Kelly, 'Chinese Intellectuals in the 1989 Democracy Movement', to appear in George Hicks, ed., *'The Broken Mirror: China after Tianenmen'*, Oxford University Press, forthcoming. It is of interest that Klyamkin and Migranyan, the two leading advocates of the Soviet version of the 'new authoritarianism', are both researchers in the Institute of the Economics of the World Socialist System.

Index